The
South Atlantic
Quarterly

SAQ

T0341654

119:2 · April 2020

Getting Back the Land: Anticolonial and Indigenous Strategies of Reclamation

Shiri Pasternak and Dayna Nadine Scott, Special Issue Editors

AGAINST the DAY

The Rise of Precarious Workers
Todd Wolfson, Editor

Shiri Pasternak and Dayna Nadine Scott

Introduction: Getting Back the Land

Who brought law to a new land already dense with legal orders and declared theirs universal? Who claims absolute authority to determine land access and use based on these laws? Whose laws *should* govern the resource economy? In Canada, these questions are essential for understanding why dispossession is ongoing and how it can be reversed.

Canada's claim to exclusive territorial authority across all the lands and waters is a failed project. But that fact has only succeeded in more complex legal and political subterfuge as Canada has sought to mitigate this uncertainty with grander performances of recognition. The essays in this issue offer diagnosis, critique, and radical visions for the future from some of the leading thinkers and experts on the tactics of the settler capitalist state, and on the exercises of Indigenous jurisdiction that counter them. It provides readers with the developments on the ground that are continually moving the gauge towards Indigenous self-determination even in the face of ramped up nationalist rhetoric fueled by a divisive politics of extraction.

Canada has always been treated, internationally, as a repository of resources for other nations. Rupert's Land—a massive region that included the

The South Atlantic Quarterly 119:2, April 2020
DOI 10.1215/00382876-8177723   © 2020 Duke University Press

Hudson Bay and every stream, river, lake, and ocean into which it flowed, covering nearly a third of present-day Canada—was literally regarded as a fur warehouse for the British. The abundance of the land was like a windfall for the English. And despite the fact that only a few isolated forts were operated by these countrymen—and that most of the hunting, trapping, long-distance travel, and survival was done by Indigenous labor—these sovereign claims informed a national, masculine, White settler self-image of adventurers taming a vast and rugged wilderness. But none of that wealth was actually theirs to take, or Canada's to give.

The frontier rhetoric that drives the contemporary slogan of national pride, #WeTheNorth, and that produced the influential "staples theory," continues to infuse our politics, churning with protracted debates about specific fossil infrastructure projects, such as the Trans Mountain Expansion Pipeline. These debates, at their core, are as much about to whom the "We" refers, as they are about whether we want, need, or will be saddled with another "outlet" for our dirty tar sands oil.

The "staples theory" is a domestic economic theory that grew out of the particular historical, ecological, and communicative conditions of life in this northern settler colony, as first theorized by Harold Innis (1956). The Canadian economy is susceptible to the "staple trap" that has defined it—prone to crisis based on an over-reliance on raw commodity exports—and the structures of financial and commercial investment associated with primary resources (Watkins 2007). The natural resource sector is also a historically vulnerable *labor economy* in Canada due to harsh winters and the ongoing crisis of seasonal unemployment (Struthers 1983). When a national economy emerged from the regional organization of staples at the turn of the twentieth century, the demand for massive labor consignment shaped the introduction of a federal welfare policy that divided seasonal workers into the "deserving" and "undeserving" poor. Much of this moral disciplining was driven by the farming industry and colonial imperatives to settle the west, urging workers to go "back to the land" to provide the labor power for the capitalist owning classes.

But the capitalist agenda was deeply and necessarily enmeshed in a colonial one. As Struthers describes it, no recognition was paid to the seasonal nature of unemployment. Rather, this moral rationale justified the deliberate formation of reserve armies of surplus labor, accomplished by moral invectives against citizens and through immigration policies designed to drive down wages by driving up supply (Struthers 1983). A key underlying agenda of these policies on migration, labor, and resource development was driven by the need to secure the land. Without physical occupation, *legal* possession is insecure and land cannot be controlled. So, one way to read the political economy of Canada is by trying to understand how Canadians are disciplined through economic policy in ways that enmesh colonial capitalism. That is, by securing racial antagonism between Indigenous peoples and working-class peoples. For example, to gain social license to drill, Kinder Morgan jobs have been promised and exaggerated by hundreds of thousands by industry and governments, as reported by Robyn Allen in *iPolitics* (2017).

But perhaps undertheorized, as the essays in this issue demonstrate, "legality" is also a crucial resource in the struggle (Smith 2019). The underlying assumptions of settler state legality shape all of the mechanisms through which continuing dispossession and land alienation happens: the granting of pipeline easements, mining stakes, timber licenses. When Indigenous peoples put their bodies on the land in every way to contest these incursions (Elliot 2018), they force an encounter between Indigenous and colonial laws (Pasternak 2014), in the form of blockades, camps, checkpoints. And inevitably, this leads to confrontations in courts, and the application of the violent settler law of injunctions, as Ceric demonstrates in this volume. These are the "sharp ends" of the law, the encounters Indigenous peoples are often involuntarily drawn into, which entail the use of foreign legal tools and logics in legal venues not their own.

The stark divergence between the relational, generative, Indigenous economies of care that are celebrated here (for example, in Pictou, as well as in Curran, Slett, and Kung in this issue), and the cold extractive vision of the state that consumes all life in its path (as theorized in Benton-Connell and Cochrane in this issue), informs the trajectory of the complex relationship between movements for Indigenous sovereignty and environmental justice.

The Legacy of Arthur Manuel (b. September 3, 1951–d. January 11, 2017)

The origins of this volume rest on the work Shiri was doing with Secwepemc leader Arthur Manuel for the decade before he passed away suddenly in January 2017. In particular, two of the interrelated projects they worked on closely were around the meaning of Indigenous economies and identifying ways to antagonize capital, leveraging so-called rights and title "uncertainty" to agitate for full recognition of Indigenous inherent rights. As part of the effort to water the seeds of thought Art, as we called him, planted on these issues, Shiri helped organize a meeting in November 2018 hosted by the Yellowhead Institute—an Indigenous-led think tank at Ryerson University, where she is Research Director. Partially funded through a grant held by Shiri and Dayna, land defenders and allies from across the country were invited to come together to discuss the meanings of Indigenous consent, and the barriers to the exercise of full Indigenous jurisdiction on their lands. All of the authors in this volume, save for Winona LaDuke and D. T. Cochrane, attended the workshop and contributed analysis toward resisting further land alienation and restoring Indigenous economies.

Art was always a big fan of these kinds of "think tanks." He understood the value of bringing together academics, activists, and practitioners who were committed to generating strategies for real land restitution, diagnosing the barriers, and devising ways around whatever stands in the way. This volume contains thinking from some of the most experienced and visionary experts on what this change could look like in Canada; tactics that could also be applied far outside its false borders. For instance, these essays contemplate how financialization can be both a weapon used by and against First Nations to fight for land rights and title, how colonial legal mechanisms can also be asserted strategically to defend homelands under attack, where precedents can be refused and overcome. The essays also unequivocally reject various tools through which the settler state seeks to draw Indigenous peoples into the trappings of settler colonial capitalism, as ways of reacting to the mounting pressure from Indigenous peoples asserting their territorial authority, and their own notions of consent grounded in specific Indigenous legal, political and social orders. Theories of contract law, racial capitalism, flesh-eating cultures, and relational economies figure into these essays that contemplate the future of Indigenous life.

But first, to ground these articles, we want to take you to Secwepemcul'ecw, where the Manuel family and their ancestors have lived since time immemorial, to break down the fight they will never give up to get the land back.

Back to Where It Began

On August 24, 2019, the Manuel family organized a symposium. It was held at the community center in Adams Lake reserve on Secwepemc territory, on the western shores of Little Shushwap Lake as it enters and spills into the South Thompson River, under the dry, shrub land mountains fragrant with wild sage. The symposium was called "Recovering the Land, Rebuilding the Economy," after the subheading of Art's book *Reconciliation Manifesto* (2017). The gathering brought together activists and leaders from across the continent to discuss the revitalization of Indigenous economies through the assertion of territorial authority over their lands.

Art, The inspiration for the event, was an extraordinary leader who rose up through the normal violence experienced by Indigenous people in Canada. He attended residential school where the food was worse than what he ate in jail when arrested for train hopping the summer of his sixteenth year. And he experienced the intense fragmentation of his family and systemic poverty of their struggles, as well as employment discrimination in racist small towns near his Neskonlith reserve in the southcentral interior of British Columbia. But he was also born into a community and a family with a resilience so undefeatable it can hardly be imagined. His father was the late Grand Chief George Manuel who helped to form the first national Indigenous rights organization, the National Indian Brotherhood, but also the first international grassroots movement of its kind, the World Council of Indigenous Peoples. George was also a writer, and he penned *The Fourth World* in 1974 (recently reissued by Minnesota Press), theorizing and documenting the internal colonization of modern settler states (Manuel and Posluns [1974] 2018).

Arthur Manuel's daughter, Kanahus Manuel, is of course the grandchild of George, but also of Wolverine Ignace. As Kanahus describes below, Wolverine served one of the longest political prisoner sentences in Canada for his arrest following a sacred Sundance ceremony at Ts'peten, an area the Secwepemc (Shushwap) people have been using for centuries (now called Gustafsen Lake), that was ambushed by police in 1995. The Royal Canadian Mounted Policy (RCMP), shot seventy-seven thousand rounds of ammunition at the Indigenous warriors in the camp in a standoff that lasted a month. When Wolverine came out finally, it was not a surrender letter in his hand, as some reported, but as Tupac Enrique-Acosta recounted at the symposium, it was an indictment of the illegal settler occupation of his lands.

Kanahus Manuel in Her Own Words

At the symposium, Kanahus spoke on the second panel of the morning:

> We made t-shirts that say, "We have to stop crying on the shoulder of the guy who stole our land." And what my dad, Arthur Manuel, meant, was that we've got to stop going to Ottawa. We got to stop going to the oppressors, the ones that continue to oppress us. We have to go international. One of the things that my slé7e, Wolverine, once said is that we are held *hostage* in Canada.
>
> Even after Gustafsen Lake—it ended up being at the time the lengthiest and costliest trials in Canadian history—they were bringing out these Canadian laws, and one of the things my father said before he passed was, "You need to read that 'OJ' Pitawatikwat case. That's going to show you a lot about

what we talk about." Wolverine always said, too, about third-party adjudication: you have to go out of the country for them to look at our rights, our land rights. During the Gustafsen Lake trial, Wolverine, he said, he was in the prison van with OJ. And OJ said, "If I get a day pass, I'm heading over there," and he pointed to the mountains over stateside, where he was going to head for his freedom. And he did, he got his day pass and he fled. He fled over to the US.

And he was picked up, I'm not sure how much longer it took for him to get picked up, but he got to Oregon. And Canada wanted to extradite OJ back to face his Gustafsen Lake charges. And so he went to trial, an extradition trial in Oregon, with Justice Janice Stewart, who was the one who made the decision on that. And they refused to send OJ back. They really looked at the legal arguments. And what they said was that Canada was really political motivated, how they reacted to the Secwepmec land defenders there at Ts'Peten, at Gustafsen Lake. So, Canada went there thinking there were going to get their guy, they were going to cuff him, they were going to transport him, and that he was going to do his time in Canada. But that day, Justice Janice Stewart refused to send OJ back.

So OJ is still in political exile, a political refugee in the US And he continues to watch everything very closely. Wolverine adopted him as his son. I say all this because I not only learned from my father, but I also learned from Wolverine, and I stood by his side as we fought for our lands together, along with Flo [his widow since Wolverine passed away in 2016]. I see a lot of fighters here, we are fighters here in this community. We have a long line of resistance. And education. It comes not just because we are warriors, but because we've had a lot of education, many educators in our lives, about the land.

When we say we are asserting territorial authority, what I see is us going out onto our lands, us leaving the 2 percent Indian reserves. My father made that 2 percent figure famous. He said if you add up all the Indian reserves in Canada, it will add up 2 percent. Indigenous peoples don't even have 1 percent of the land in Canada. And he would say, you don't have to have a PhD in economics to know who will be rich and who's going to be poor, looking at those figures. And it's easier to fight the poor. It's easier to fight the poor, he would say. But he would say, all of us are wealthy, if you look at our Indigenous economies. Our Indigenous economies are everything that flows from the land, and all of our beautiful reciprocal relationships that flow from the land, it's not just the monetary value of the tree. My father would say, they look at a tree they see a 2x4, we look at a tree, we see our brother, our relation. That's the different between how the economy is viewed. It's a beautiful relationship with that tree. There are stories that go back to the beginning of time, with our relationship to these trees. Some of these trees are the most powerful medicine men in our mountains, as elders have said to me.

So, when you want to challenge the government, my father would say, and challenge corporations, he would say, you have to create that risk and uncertainty. The more risk and uncertainty you create, with the businesses, the more certainty we are creating over our title. The more we stand on our title, the more uncertain their projects are. They know that as the title holders to our land, in our nation, the Secwepemcul'ecw, we have ten thousand plus men, women, and children in our nation—those are all the inheritors of the nation. They're the ones who inherent not just the responsibility but the privilege to be able to live on this land, exclusively live and use and occupy the territory—it's a big responsibility—we have a lot of responsibility for our territories—it means going out onto the land, it means building our homes on the land. We have heard many times in our meeting—you have to go out and build on the land to assert your jurisdiction.

Over the past two years, we have embarked on a huge mission to build tiny houses on wheels. We've built six tiny houses on wheels. And we brought the sixth one out to the memorial for my dad yesterday, and had the Secwepemc radio airing live there, and we're going to be building 4 more tiny houses there on wheels. And the reason we built them on wheels is because we've been faced with injunctions, we've been faced with police oppression and repressions, arrest and criminalization, and we built these homes so we could be mobile out on our land.

We come from one hundred eighty thousand square kilometers. And they want five hundred eighteen kilometers of this pipeline to go through Secwepemcul'ecw, our land. So, our hope is to get houses to all the spots where they're threatening construction. And we have someone here who put a drone in the sky, caught Trans Mountain doing construction, which we believe is illegal construction. Under the Thompson River, which is a big threat to our way of life and our salmon. There are over five hundred streams and rivers from the Alberta tar sands to my brother's home in Tsleil Waututh territory. *It must be stopped.*

Disintegration of Colonial Borders

Kanahus was a key organizer of the symposium and is a spokesperson in her family's struggle. She is on the frontlines of a movement to block the Trans Mountain Expansion Pipeline from being twinned through their territory. As she describes in her talk transcribed above, she is part of the Tiny House

Warrior Society that is building mobile houses along the proposed pipeline route. She and her brother, Ska7cis Manuel, have traveled internationally to the United Nations and to meet with investors and insurance companies in Europe to create economic uncertainty for the pipeline proponents and assert their jurisdiction in the face of state authorization for the pipeline's construction.

Today, Kanahus is a hero to so many, but she is also a lightning rod attracting racist and violent attacks on the frontlines in Clearwater, BC, where the Tiny House Warriors are currently attempting to stop a "man-camp" from being built. It is planned to house a thousand or more men as a mobile labor force for the pipeline. The dangers to women of these man-camps are well known and other communities have gone as far as stocking up on rape kits when such temporary settlements are built nearby.

Kanahus's safety is not secured by anything but the support of her family, community members, and the cross-movement alliances she has built across the world, and perhaps by her high-profile social media accounts. She is very clear, however, that wherever she goes in Secwepemc territory she is on her territory and the RCMP, pipeline workers, man-camp force, etc., have no jurisdiction on her land. She shows no fear in asserting this jurisdiction. Nor does she speak on behalf of only herself, but also, as all Salish people do, she speaks on behalf of the salmon—the critical foodstuff that literally keeps people alive and has been like kin to riverside communities since time immemorial. Kanahus is a fierce leader but she is defending the territory not just for her nation but also for the salmon nation, the critical food that literally keeps people alive and has been kin to both coastal and interior communities since time immemorial. She is deeply grounded in her responsibilities to care for these relations—at heart of the Secwepemc economy—and do what she must do to defend them. She is what stands between capitalist destruction and the future of Indigenous life.

Indigenous resistance is also the face of meaningful and just climate activism, which foregrounds the problem of land in a settler state. The Tiny House Warriors mark one point in a global constellation of Indigenous resistance. As the new Special Report on Climate Change and Land, the Intergovernmental Panel on Climate Change (IPCC) report states, where Indigenous peoples are stewards of their lands and their customary tenure is recognized, their knowledge and conservation economies hold powerful mitigation and adaptation strategies for holding the global temperature rise to 1.5 degrees C. This is the materialism of struggle, survival beyond rhetoric and hyperbole, keeping Indigenous justice in the foreground.

Just as her father had warned Indigenous people not to "cry on the shoulder of the guy who took your land," at our workshop in November, Kanahus did not want to talk about negotiating with the Canadian government to get her land back. She implored the land defenders gathered around the table: "We have to burn down the forts."

References

Allan, Robyn. 2017. "Those Trans Mountain Employment Numbers? They're Bogus." *iPolitics*, August 30. ipolitics.ca/2017/08/30/those-trans-mountain-employment-numbers-theyre-bogus/.

Elliot, Alicia. 2018. "A Memo to Canada: Indigenous People Are Not Your Incompetent Children." *Globe and Mail*. January 5. theglobeandmail.com/opinion/indigenous-memo-to-canada-were-not-your-incompetent-children/article37511319/.

Innis, Harold. 1956. *The Fur Trade in Canada: An Introduction to Canadian Economic History*. Revised Edition. Toronto: University of Toronto Press.

Manuel, Arthur. 2014. *Unsettling Canada: A National Wake-Up Call*. Toronto: Between the Lines.

Manuel, Arthur. 2017. *Reconciliation Manifesto*. Toronto: Lorimer Books.

Manuel, George, and Michael Posluns. (1974) 2018. *The Fourth World: An Indian Reality*. 2nd ed. Minneapolis: University of Minnesota Press.

Pasternak, Shiri. 2014. "Jurisdiction and Settler Colonialism: Where Do Laws Meet?" *Special Issue: Law and Decolonization*, Canadian Journal of Law and Society 29, no. 2: 145–61.

Smith, Adrian A. 2019. "Toward a Critique of Political Economy of 'Sociolegality' in Settler Capitalist Canada." In *Change and Continuity: Canadian Political Economy in the New Millennium*, edited by Mark P. Thomas et al., 167–84. Montreal, CA: McGill Queen's University Press.

Struthers, James. 1983. *No Fault of Their Own: Unemployment and the Canadian Welfare State, 1914–1941*. Toronto: University of Toronto Press.

Watkins, Mel. 2007. "Comment: Staples Redux." *Studies in Political Economy* 79: 213–36.

Deborah Curran, Eugene Kung, and Ǧáǧvi Marilyn Slett

Ǧviḷás and Snəwayəɫ: Indigenous Laws,
Economies, and Relationships with
Place Speaking to State Extractions

> Ǧviḷás has been described as the ethos of our
> people. Ǧviḷás governs not only our relationship
> and responsibilities to land and sea resources,
> but also social relationships and obligations with
> respect to people, stories and all animate beings in
> our territory. Broadly defined, Ǧviḷás means that
> we as Heiltsuk people derive our strength from our
> territory by following specific laws that govern all
> our relationships with the natural and supernatural
> world. It is the basis of Heiltsuk respect and reverence
> for the surrounding eco-system.
> —Heiltsuk Tribal Council 2018: 5

> We stand here together as Tsleil-Waututh people
> and we say "no." We say "no" the risk is too great.
> Our obligation is not to oil. Our obligation is to our
> land, our water, our people, our life, our *snəwayəɫ*.
> According to our *snəwayəɫ*, our law, this project repre-
> sents a risk that we the Tsleil-Waututh people, are not
> willing to take. . . . Tsleil-Waututh law includes both
> 1) the obligation to protect, defend, and steward our
> territory and 2) the responsibility to restore the condi-
> tions that provide the foundation our nation requires
> to thrive. These obligations and responsibilities
> require us to think about more than today. We must
> ensure that future generations have the benefits of our
> territory and access to the wisdom of our ancestors.
> —Tsleil-Waututh Nation 2015: 2, 86

The South Atlantic Quarterly 119:2, April 2020
DOI 10.1215/00382876-8177735 © 2020 Duke University Press

A discussion about Indigenous economies, governance, and laws begins with relationships. These relationships are centered in a place, a traditional territory, and include responsibilities towards that place. As expressed in many Indigenous worldviews, space is imbued with relationships that include responsibilities for nurturing those relationships (Kelly 2017: 195). Indigenous economies are, therefore, enabled and limited by these relationships and responsibilities to place that demand equal attention to caretaking of the environment and treating all beings—human and non-human—with respect. Indigenous economies, therefore, are motivated by "relations of interdependence" inherent in many Indigenous legal and political orders that prioritize reciprocal relations between past, present and future generations, and the earth (Starblanket and Kiiwetinepinesiik Stark 2018: 175–208; Borrows 2018: 49–82).

The traditional territories of most Indigenous communities in Canada are outside of major population centers and are treated by the state as extractive zones, defined as "the colonial paradigm, worldview, and technologies that mark out regions of "high biodiversity" in order to reduce life to capitalist resource conversion" (Gómez-Barris 2017: xvi). While all lands in British Columbia (BC) are Indigenous traditional territory, colonial natural resource laws make virtually all of the province available for extraction (Hemmera 2016) as if traditional territories are still "waste lands of the Crown," meaning unoccupied and unused lands over which the colonial government has jurisdiction to permit extraction (*Gold Fields Act*, 1859: s V; *Gold Mining Ordinance*, 1867: s 22; *Mineral Act* 1936: s 14(1). In contrast, a place- and relationship-based foundation for Indigenous economies is at odds with an extractive economics, which is based on taking the maximum amount possible subject only to mitigating against unacceptable "risks." Responsibility towards a region or territory necessitates a very different approach to risk assessment, and precludes the area being sacrificed for national interests of people and governments outside of the region.

This divergence between relational Indigenous economies and extractive state economies fuels much of the conflict between Indigenous peoples and the state. Many of the longstanding disputes between the provincial and federal governments and Indigenous communities relate to natural resources extraction and management, such as the siting, operation, or historical impacts of mines. For example, the Tsilhqot'in National Government has opposed the proposed Prosperity Mine through three assessment processes, maintaining the position that converting Teztan Biny (Fish Lake) into a tailings pond is contrary to their laws. The proposed mine's location at the headwaters of the Taseko, Chilko, Chilcotin, and Fraser River systems is a "cultural keystone place" for the Tsilhqot'in people. Likewise, the Stk'em-lúpsemc te Secwépemc Nation undertook a community assessment of the proposed Ajax Mine near Kamloops using its own Indigenous decision-making process. In rejecting the project as proposed, the Stk'emlúpsemc te Secwépemc Nation concluded that it had not given its free, prior and informed consent for the project, in particular because its proposed location would cause irreparable harm to Pipsell (Jacko Lake).

Indigenous communities are also challenging cyclical state government decisions about the allocation of different parts of the environment, called natural resources or land and marine resources, with little regard to the impact of those allocations on the wider ecosystem community, both human and non-human. A good example of this is the recurring need for communities to challenge federal authority to permit commercial herring fisheries. After securing a court judgement acknowledging their Aboriginal right to fish all marine species, five Nuu-chah-nulth Nations challenged the federal Minister of Fisheries and Ocean's decision to permit a commercial herring fishery in their territories in 2014. The court granted the application for an injunction to prohibit the fishery from going ahead in part because it had recently acknowledged the First Nations' commercial Aboriginal right to harvest almost all marine species and agreed that the First Nations' would be harmed if they lost the opportunity to negotiate the extent of those rights with the state (*Ahousaht Indian Band v. Canada (Minister of Fisheries and Oceans)*). The court also found that the Minister's explicit disregard for the advice of federal fisheries scientists in permitting the fishery would call into question the integrity of the entire Canadian fisheries management regime. The following year the court denied the same First Nations an injunction, finding that although conservation was still a concern the ongoing negotiations between the parties would be sufficient for accommodating the First Nations' Aboriginal rights. In contrast, in the same year a court granted an injunction to the Haida Nation because the stock assessment science did not support a commercial fishery, and the parties had not completed a marine area management plan as part of their government-to-government agreement. Acknowledging the extensive relationship between the parties, the court noted that such a relationship would fail if one party exercised jurisdiction unilaterally (*Haida Nation v. Canada (Minister of Fisheries and Oceans)*).

These examples underscore the fundamental conflict between Indigenous responsibilities expressed as jurisdiction and the state-sponsored extractive regimes in BC, a conflict rooted in the state's refusal to acknowledge the inherent legal rights of First Nations and regulatory regimes that have continued to allow significant ecological impacts to First Nations' lands and waters (Garvie, Lowe, and Shaw 2014: 45). These impacts disrupt and alter Indigenous economies that are based on relationships with the territory, and preclude Indigenous communities from exercising responsibilities to their territories through long-term land- or ecosystem-based notions of care and consent that are in conflict with the state extractive regime of shallow consultation.

In a landscape where all land is Indigenous traditional territory, most Indigenous peoples in British Columbia have never ceded or surrendered these territories. Their inherent rights to self-government and self-determination are expressed through their laws and customs, and are dictated through oral histories and acts of governance. Since 1982, the Canadian Constitution has acknowledged and affirmed Aboriginal and Treaty rights, and Canadian settler jurisprudence recognizes the continued existence of Indigenous laws and governance as an Aboriginal right. However, this case law has not yet grappled with decisions made under both Indigenous and settler legal traditions that conflict:

> [A]boriginal rights, and in particular a right to self-government akin to a legislative power to make laws, survived as one of the unwritten "underlying values" of the Constitution outside of the powers distributed to Parliament and the legislatures in 1867. The federal-provincial division of powers in 1867 was aimed at a different issue and was a division "internal" to the Crown. (*Campbell v. British Columbia (Attorney General)*: para. 81)

From international law, the United Nations Declaration on the Rights of Indigenous Peoples (UN Declaration) affirms the rights of Indigenous peoples to participate in decision making about their traditional territories, and be entitled to give free, prior and informed consent before development can occur (United Nations General Assembly 2007: Article 19).

In this Indigenous rights landscape now focused on consent (Borrows 2017; Christie 2017; Morales 2017), this article explores Indigenous responses to the disruption in Indigenous laws, governance and economies by state regulatory processes that sanction extraction from traditional territories. We begin with a discussion of the state's recognition of Aboriginal rights, its failure to acknowledge relationships with territories in facilitating the extraction of natural resources, and the danger of channeling Indigenous dissent into state sponsored "consultation" processes. We follow with an exploration of the response from two Indigenous communities—the Heiltsuk Nation in the central coast and the Tsleil-Waututh Nation on the south coast near Vancouver. In particular, the action by these communities highlights their legal and governance responsibilities in light of their relationships to their land and marine territories. These responsibilities and relationships—the foundation for Heiltsuk and Tsleil-Waututh laws and economies that rely on a healthy natural environment—are in direct conflict with state-permitted extractive industries. In a legally pluralistic context where both legal orders apply, and, in some places, where state law must make way for exclusive indigenous juris-diction, increasingly Indigenous law is directing decision-making about extractions and changing the landscape of environmental management in Canada. It is the relations-in-place of Indigenous communities that are lead-ing to these long-term, ecosystem-based approaches to consent that directly challenge the shallow consultation endorsed by state extractive regimes.

Indigenous Economies Conflict with Extractive Economies

Settler courts have interpreted the purpose of section 35 of the *Constitution Act, 1982*, which acknowledges and affirms Aboriginal and Treaty rights, as the "reconciliation of the pre-existence of Aboriginal societies with the sover-eignty of the Crown" (*R. v. Van der Peet* 1996: para. 31 and affirmed in *Del-gamuukw v. British Columbia* 1997: para. 186 ("*Delgamuukw*")). Reconcilia-tion is viewed as the result of "negotiated settlements, with good faith and give and take on all sides, reinforced by judgments of this Court." (*Del-gamuukw* 1997: para. 186). These negotiations are a process not a final legal remedy (*Haida Nation v. BC* 2004: para. 32 ("*Haida Nation*")). The routine framework for reconciliation of Aboriginal rights with the interests of Cana-dian society is the application of the Crown's duty to consult and accommo-date First Nations when it is making decisions about proposed activities in a traditional territory that may have an impact on a First Nation's Aboriginal rights, for example to fish, hunt, or pursue cultural activities (*Haida Nation* 2004: paras. 20, 25, 32, and 35; *Mikisew Cree First Nation v. Canada (Minister of Canadian Heritage)* 2005: paras. 54 and 63 ("*Mikisew Cree*")). According to settler courts, the "best way" to achieve reconciliation is to require provincial and federal governments to justify activities that infringe or deny Aboriginal rights (*R. v. Sparrow* 1990: para. 1109; affirmed in *Tsilhqot'in Nation v. British Columbia* 2014: para. 119 ("*Tsilhqot'in Nation*")).

It is important to note that section 35 does not "protect" Aboriginal rights. Many of the contemporary court cases dealing with section 35 address whether or not the Crown has fulfilled it procedural duty to consult and accom-modate, and largely accept infringement of Aboriginal rights as justified (*Adams Lake Indian Band v. British Columbia* 2012; Ritchie 2013). Court cases that address reconciliation focus more on its process than on substantive principles or ultimate outcomes. The Supreme Court of Canada initially articulated the standard of meaningful consultation as an interim measure pending resolution of Aboriginal title and rights claims (*Haida Nation* 2004: paras. 27, 38).

Significantly, the language the Supreme Court of Canada uses to define the process of reconciliation includes a relational component where consultation and accommodation "preserves the Aboriginal interest pending claims resolution and fosters a relationship between the parties that makes possible negotiations, the preferred process for achieving ultimate reconciliation" (*Haida Nation* 2004: para. 38). To be meaningful this relationship requires governments to uphold the honor of the Crown, which precludes exploiting a resource such that an Indigenous community is deprived of benefit of that resource (*Haida Nation* 2004: para. 28). While virtually all of Canada is subject to settler common law Treaty and Aboriginal rights claims, the Court sees the process of claims resolution and continued Crown governance of extractive activities as a relationship expressed through consultation and accommodation.

In practice, consultation is treated by the Crown as an indefinite norm, with the underlying land title issues largely ignored. Settler courts will rarely direct specific consultation and accommodation procedures, nor will they give substantive direction on reconciliation efforts. They are, however, providing more direction as to the qualities of consultation as Crown governments continue to interpret the consultation relationship and activities as requiring minimal action. For example, settler courts have been clear for decades now that the Crown has a positive obligation to ensure that First Nations have "all necessary information in a timely way," the opportunity to express their interests and concerns, and have their views considered and integrated into project proposals (*Halfway River First Nation v. British Columbia (Ministry of Forests)* 1999: para. 160; *Mikisew Cree* 2005: para. 64; *Chartrand v. British Columbia (Forests, Lands and Natural Resource Operations)* 2015: para. 77 (*"Chartrand"*)). Governments must also conduct consultation in good faith "with the intention of substantially addressing the concerns of the Aboriginal peoples whose lands are at issue" (*Chartrand*: para. 77; *Sambaa K'e Dene First Nation v. Duncan* 2012: para. 89; *Enge v. Canada (Indigenous and Northern Affairs)* 2015: para. 137).

As a largely procedural requirement providing few substantive remedies nor circumscribing Crown approvals in traditional territories, with the most notable exception being the proven Aboriginal title claim of the Tsilhqot'in Nation (*Tsilhqot'in Nation* 2014), the application of section 35 has been criticized as discriminatory in approach: Settler courts have limited its interpretation to historic realities, rather than allowing it to develop organically like other areas of constitutional law (Borrows 2016: 129–131). In traditional territories, overarching provincial jurisdiction for lands and water continues unquestioned—except in a few pockets (*Haida Gwaii Reconciliation Act*)—and the extraction of elements of the environment continues.[1]

A pernicious by-product of the process of consultation and accommodation is the depoliticization of responses to proposed harm to traditional territories, Indigenous economies and the relationships between the two. Processes of consultation—whether they be pursuant to permitting, environmental assessment, or other administrative frameworks—channel assertions of Indigenous rights into state-based administrative and legal processes that purport to unilaterally establish the boundaries or scope of the conversation. These processes define how Indigenous peoples can interact with the proposed threat to their traditional territories and economies, and typically limit the evaluative scope to the specific project apparatus and not cumulative or broader watershed impacts. Problems with the scope and scale of governance are channeled through narrowly defined administrative practices, which validates the process of decision-making while controlling the means by which opposition to a project is expressed (Dunlap 2017). More fundamentally, state-prescribed consultations about environmental and natural resource decision-making do not provide a fora within which Indigenous communities can address the question of jurisdiction itself, and how their own governance processes are expressed. Participation in state consultation processes also creates legitimacy in, and reliance on, those processes that depoliticize the decisions being made (Schilling-Vacaflor 2017; Anshelm, Haikola, Wallsten 2018). In effect, consultation can channel and dissipate dissent, thus depoliticizing these processes and rendering them administrative exercises rather than addressing the underlying issues about who has jurisdiction, is making decisions, and has authority to govern a watershed.

In contrast, the Truth and Reconciliation Commission (TRC) of Canada's interpretation of reconciliation includes developing new relationships between Indigenous peoples and the state because the economic sustainability of Canada depends on accommodating the rights of Indigenous peoples (Truth and Reconciliation Commission of Canada 2015: 202–12). Natural resource development is entwined with reconciliation (206), and "sustainable reconciliation involves realizing the economic potential of Indigenous communities in a fair, just, and equitable manner that respects their right to self-determination" (207). Therefore, economy and use of the environment is, at its foundation, about self-determination. The TRC also calls on governments to reconcile Indigenous and state legal orders (Call to Action 45), and points to the UN Declaration as the appropriate framework for reconciliation for all levels of government (15).

Indigenous communities are initiating Indigenous legal processes based on a responsibility to their traditional territories in the face of state-sponsored extractive economies. These relations-in-place, performed over millennia, interact with colonial governance in the form of assertions of jurisdiction and refusal to give consent to new extractive activities. In the next section, we detail the Heiltsuk Nation's longstanding conflict with the federal Department of Fisheries and Oceans over the commercial herring fishery, and now more recent experience dealing with a marine diesel spill in their territory, highlight the failure of the state to obtain consent to permit risks to Aboriginal rights and relationships.

Ǧviḷás: Balancing the Health of the Land and Waters with the Needs of the People[2]

The Heiltsuk are a maritime society in the central coast of what is called the Province of British Columbia, but we do not distinguish the land, water, and people as separate entities; we are an extension of our territory (Heiltsuk Tribal Council 2018). We have always been wealthy with the resources of the land and sea, and the foundation of our economy is the ocean. We have managed our traditional territories, through fishing and other harvest practices, and sustained ourselves for over fourteen thousand years and seven hundred generations (Heiltsuk Nation 2019; Nair 2017). The potlatch is part of how we govern ourselves through ceremonies, dances, songs, and rituals that are carried out publicly. The potlach is much more than a feast; parts of it can be Indigenous legal processes, such as naming, and expressions of jurisdiction. Our wealth from the ocean supports us to be who we are today with a sophisticated set of laws and practices, particularly as expressed through our language. Our management and governance all reflect back on our relationship with the waters in our territory and the ocean. It is part of our Ǧviḷás (laws) that we will take care of the sea, and the sea will take care of us.

These millennia of management in our territory reflect the reliance that we have on the ocean, and our laws are ones of responsibility to the ocean as "our health as a people and our society are intricately tied to the health of the land and waters" (Brown, Brown, and Biodiversity BC 2009).

Heiltsuk care of the ocean within our territory has ensured a balance between ecosystem and socio-economic health. Our management has always been deliberate and overt (Housty et al. 2014). As renowned ethnobotanist Nancy Turner summarized:

> These ancestors have learned from careful monitoring and knowledge exchange that salmon stocks can be strengthened by selectively and judiciously harvesting the weaker fish and leaving the most robust to continue up the rivers to reproduce. By looking after the salmon streams, and keeping them clear of too much debris, they found, long ago, that the salmon runs would be maintained and the salmon healthier and more numerous. They learned also in ancient times that by harvesting the spawn of the herring from kelp fronds or from hemlock branches anchored out in the quiet ocean bays instead of by killing the herring and removing their eggs, the runs of herring will keep coming back year after year without being depleted. . . . They learned to "transplant" populations of salmon, herring and oulachen, and to prune their blueberry, huckleberry, currant and salmonberry bushes to make them more productive. . . . All of these practices, and many many more, that were developed through careful observation, experimentation, monitoring, and sampling, perhaps at times driven by shortage or necessity, are as important for all of us to know about as knowledge generated through academic learning (Brown, Brown, and Biodiversity BC 2009: foreword).

Within this sustainable management paradigm the Heiltsuk economy also included trade with other Indigenous communities (Harris 2000). Heiltsuk commerce involved herring spawn on kelp but the desire for trade or to extract ocean resources never compromised the herring populations as our responsibility to maintain healthy herring within the larger ocean ecosystem directed our management practices.

Ocean Extractions and Responsibilities to Herring

Herring sustain the Heiltsuk community and economy. The centrality of herring is woven into the social, economic and governance fabric of our community. Herring are one of the major economic drivers for the Heiltsuk, and this relationship makes us proud; it is part of who we are (Gauvreau et al. 2017a; Gauvreau et al. 2017b). Gathering herring spawn-on-kelp kicks off our harvest year (Brown, Brown, and Biodiversity BC 2009), which starts in March. The community gathering and dinner to celebrate the beginning of harvest is a new year celebration. Herring also have broader cultural and diplomatic importance. For example, we went to Prince Rupert for senate committee hearings on April 16, 2018. The night before the hearings representatives from many of the coastal communities—Kitasoo, Nuxaulk, Kitkatla, Metlakatla, Haida, Tsimshian, and Heiltsuk—had a feast together to gather as a broader coastal community. We Heiltsuk brought herring spawn on kelp to share with the other Nations and it was a real treat for everyone. Herring populations have collapsed all over the coast but we were able to share with our neighbors and bring this important food and cultural good to them.

Heiltsuk have always sustainably managed herring by harvesting the roe, not the fish itself, so that the fish continue to live. This is in contrast to the commercial herring fishery licensed by the federal Department of Fisheries and Oceans (DFO) where the fish are harvested and then eggs removed, which kills the fish. We also enhance the herring population by spreading herring spawn to different areas to increase the spawning area (Gauvreau et al. 2017b). The Heiltsuk herring fishery is part of our stewardship of our territory and how we interact sustainably as directed by our Ǧviḷás.

The Heiltsuk have always had conflict with DFO because DFO management of different fisheries has resulted in significant declines in fish populations, and has disenfranchised Heiltsuk from their management and stewardship responsibilities (Harris 2000; Powell 2012). Ever since the federal government asserted jurisdiction over fisheries in the late 1800's state management has systematically squeezed Heiltsuk out of commercial fisheries and undermined our traditional herring spawn on kelp harvest (Harris 2000). A flashpoint for this conflict was the Gladstone case, when Heiltsuk brothers who were charged with illegally selling herring spawn on kelp without a proper license in Vancouver. The Gladstone's defense was that they had a commercial Aboriginal right to sell herring spawn on kelp, a practice that the Heiltsuk people had pursued long before contact with colonial officials. The Supreme Court of Canada ultimately found that the Heiltsuk have a commercial Aboriginal right to herring spawn on kelp, which was the first time a Canadian court acknowledged a commercial (rather than subsistence) Aboriginal right and practice integral to a First Nation's economy (*R. v. Gladstone* 1996):

> [E]xchange of herring spawn on kelp for money or other goods was a central, significant and defining feature of the culture of the Heiltsuk prior to contact. Moreover, those facts support the appellants' further claim that the exchange of herring spawn on kelp on a scale best characterized as commercial was an integral part of the distinctive culture of the Heiltsuk. (para. 26)

For over twnty years the Heiltsuk Nation has negotiated with DFO for mean-ingful expression of our Gladstone rights and recognition of our jurisdiction over herring. However, for many of those years there has not been a com-mercial spawn on kelp fishery due to insufficient herring. Between 1951 and 1960 the average annual catch in the Central Coast, as permitted by DFO, was 22.1 kilotonnes whereas the catch fell to a low of 3.7 kilotonnes in 1996 (Fisheries and Oceans Pacific Region 1998).

This situation reached a crisis when, in 2015, the Minister of Fisheries and Oceans approved a commercial herring fishery in Spiller Channel in front of the Heiltsuk village of Bella Bella after the Heiltsuk Nation had informed DFO that there was no justification for a commercial fishery that year and in the midst of trying to establish no go areas for industry to harvest herring. Heiltsuk members delivered a letter to the DFO office, which is not a decision-making office but an instrument of the state, across the Channel stating that the fishery was closed due to insufficient herring biomass. At the same time, the Heiltsuk Tribal Council and Hemas (hereditary Heiltsuk lead-ership) declared a ban on a commercial sac roe fishery in the area (CBC News 2015a), and agreed to serve an eviction notice to the DFO office (Gill 2018).

Heiltsuk Nation members delivered an eviction notice and then occu-pied the adjacent Coast Guard offices. When Heiltsuk staff and elected leader-ship arrived,[3] we spoke with the approximately fifty Heiltsuk and supporters present, who ranged from grandmothers and mothers with their children, researchers in the community, hereditary leadership and people who have married into our community who were present on behalf of a father-in-law who could not attend (Harper et al. 2018). DFO allowed a few of us into their offices and we declared that we were occupying the building because as Heilt-suk we were no longer going to stand by and watch DFO mismanage a com-mercial fishery (CBC News 2015b). We occupied that office for four days, and our community outside of Bella Bella supported us by protesting in Vancou-ver, until DFO agreed to change the approach to herring management in the Central Coast. While the commercial herring fishery opened in Spiller Chan-nel for one day on March 31, no herring were caught (Gill 2018).

The Heiltsuk Nation signed a memorandum of understanding with DFO in 2016 to negotiate a joint management plan and catch agreement each year. Significant changes are a decrease in the allowable catch from 10 to 7 percent of biomass, area closures, and the ability to have a Heiltsuk observer on some DFO boats. In 2018 DFO agreed to cancel the herring fishery in the Central Coast on the basis of reconciliation commitments (Shore 2018).

The example of the herring protest in 2015 and subsequent collaborative management with DFO demonstrate how Heiltsuk are united as a community in protecting our inherent rights as recognized in the Gladstone decision and exercising those rights in a sustainable manner. Our public activities like the herring protest not only reinforce our commitment to a healthy economy for which herring is central but are also serving to bring our Heiltsuk social fabric together. We are reinforcing our responsibility to reject the extraction of herring from our territory and to uphold sustainable elements of our Indigenous economies, like the spawn on kelp herring fisheries.

Adjudicating the Harms from Extractive Economies Pursuant to Indigenous Laws

Another form of harm related to extractive economies is the long-term damage to our territories, and thus the Heiltsuk economy, resulting from environmental pollution and disasters. On October 13, 2016, the articulated-tug-barge (ATB) which included the Nathan E. Stewart vessel ran aground in Gale Pass, an important village, cultural, and food harvesting site in Heiltsuk territory. The ATB sank and released over one hundred ten thousand liters of diesel fuel and lubricant oils. The lasting impacts of the spill continue to affect our economy and livelihood, including the abundant clam fishery in that area.

The oil spill not only damaged our territory and our environment, it had impacts that reverberated culturally through our community. Heiltsuk people physically felt impacts from the damage of the oil to our territory, which is inseparable from us. It was like we had gone into mourning. What happens here in our territory is also felt by Heiltsuk people who live elsewhere like in Vancouver; they had a deep sense of loss. The spill and pollution had an impact to our very core and we likened it to cultural genocide. Any harm to the environment has a fundamental effect on our economy, government, laws, and culture. As a Heiltsuk elder expressed in the 1970s when giving testimony at Namu about the potential expansion of oil ports, "if we have an oil spill here it will finish us as Heiltsuk."

The spill was devastating to our community. Despite this, we decisively exerted our jurisdiction throughout the spill response process. The spill was a catalyst for the community to assert and exercise our own laws and jurisdiction in furtherance of our responsibility to our territory. A Heiltsuk Tribal Council-elected councilor participated as part of the Unified Command Team for the emergency, and we insisted that spill response be handled from Bella Bella, the residential hub of the Heiltsuk people. Because

Transport Canada and the ATB owners refused to include Heiltsuk in their investigation of the marine accident and spill, even though we have jurisdiction and are the governing body in this territory, we undertook an independent inquiry, from a Heiltsuk legal, jurisdictional, economic and cultural standpoint, of what happened in the first forty-eight hours (Heiltsuk Tribal Council 2017a). The purpose of this report was to ensure there was a public record of our people's firsthand accounts of environmental impacts and the mismanagement of the spill response effort by the Canadian state and the various non-state actors including the company that owned the ATB.

Through that process two things became clear—that such a spill and mismanagement of harm to our territory cannot happen again, and that the Canadian state and vessel owners needed to make reparations to Heiltsuk for the damage caused to our culture and economy. We developed a vision for an Indigenous marine response center for which Heiltsuk would gain the capacity to act as the spill responders in the Central Coast (Heiltsuk Tribal Council 2017b). In addition, we established the Dáduqvḷá Committee to adjudicate the spill according to Heiltsuk laws and render a judgment on what Heiltsuk laws the state and vessel owner violated (Heiltsuk Tribal Council 2018). This Heiltsuk legal process was "an exercise in self-governance and authority over the territory and in response to the failure of the responsible federal and provincial agencies to recognize Heiltsuk jurisdiction during and in the aftermath of the spill" (6). The adjudication report sets out the relevant Ǧviḷás and describes how the activities of non-Heiltsuk actors were negligent, disregarded Heiltsuk knowledge, and were ineffective in containing the spill. The Dáduqvḷá Committee recommendations seek to hold those responsible for the harm accountable, and to change future procedures. As reparation, the judgement requires the owner of the vessel to participate in several ceremonies with us as an apology, and to provide funding for ecological and cultural assessments and restoration. Canada must agree to reconciliation protocols, fund the marine response center, and create space for independent Heiltsuk jurisdiction to bring into effect the Heiltsuk Marine Use Plan.

The governments of Canada and B.C. have still not undertaken a meaningful post-spill environmental impact assessment of the extent of the contamination and spill impacts on marine life. On October 9, 2018, we filed an admiralty action in the British Columbia Supreme Court seeking compensation for the losses from the spill to the Heiltsuk (Supreme Court of British Columbia Vancouver Registry 2018). The claim goes beyond compensation for damages for loss of traditional harvest, associated cultural losses, commercial losses, and costs for Heiltsuk-led oil spill response, impact assessment, and remediation. It challenges the state's unilateral assertion of jurisdiction to the foreshore and marine areas, limits on marine oil spill compensation under federal law, and the duty to consult communities affected by spills.

Heiltsuk identity, economy, and laws are inextricably tied to our land and ocean territory. We continue to live according to our Ǧviḷás that embodies the relationships and responsibilities that we have to the natural world. However, our ability to carry out those responsibilities continues to be undermined by the Canadian state and we do not given consent to the state's facilitation of the extraction of natural resources—our relatives the salmon and herring—at unsustainable rates, and its permitting of the extractive economy to harm our waters without full accountability. Like our Coast Salish neighbors the Tsleil-Waututh Nation, Heiltsuk are relying on both Ǧviḷás and Heiltsuk legal processes as well as colonial law and state legal processes (where necessary) to restore balance in our territory and revitalize the Heiltsuk economy.

Snəwayəɬ: Tsleil-Waututh Stewardship Obligations to Restore Conditions that Provide the Environmental, Cultural, Spiritual, and Economic Foundation for Community to Thrive[4]

The Tsleil-Waututh Nation (TWN), the "People of the Inlet" and formerly known as the Burrard Indian Band, are a distinct Coast Salish nation, whose territory includes Burrard Inlet and the waters that connect to it in the Metro Vancouver region (Tsleil-Waututh Nation 2015). Tsleil-Waututh speak *Hən'q'əmin'əm'* or Downriver Halkomelem, and *snəwayəɬ* (sna-wey-uth) is the word they use for law, or teachings.

Tsleil-Waututh origin stories take place in Burrard Inlet. The sheltered, deep water and abundance of finfish and shellfish are a source of food and sustain cultural practices, with 90 percent of the protein in ancestral diets coming from marine foods (56, 59; Chisholm, Nelson, and Schwarcz 1983: 396–98). Burrard Inlet is the foundation for the Tsleil-Waututh economy. Tsleil-Waututh's population was once several thousand people before it was decimated by small pox introduced by colonizers (Morin 2015: 2). The Tsleil-Waututh have lived in villages in eastern Burrard Inlet for millennia and at least eight villages existed at the time of contact. Today, TWN's population is around five hundred and their primary community on Indian Reserve 3 is located on the north shore of Burrard Inlet in North Vancouver.

The TWN have never signed a treaty with colonial governments and therefore continue to self-govern pursuant to their inherent Indigenous rights under the restrictions of the Canadian state. TWN's exercise of its governance authority has many aspects, but the stewardship and restoration of Burrard Inlet is a key priority. Tsleil-Waututh's 2017 Burrard Inlet Action Plan sets out a vision for a productive, resilient, and diverse Inlet (Lilley et al. 2018), where:

- Healthy, wild marine foods are abundant and can be harvested sustainably and eaten safely
- Water and sediment are clean especially in places where cultural spiritual, ceremonial, or recreational activities take place
- Important habitats are plentiful, productive, and connected; and
- High levels of biodiversity and healthy populations of key species are viable and persistent (at 66).

TWN also has a Stewardship Policy, which governs how the Nation assesses proposed activities projects within their traditional territory, and opens with the TWN declaration:

We are the Tsleil-Waututh First Nation, the People of the Inlet. We have lived in and along our Inlet since time out of mind. We have been here since the Creator transformed the Wolf into that first Tsleil-Wautt, and made the Wolf responsible for this land. We have always been here and we will always be here. Our people are here to care for our land and water. It is our obligation and birthright to be the caretakers and protectors of our Inlet. . . . Therefore, be it known far and wide that our Tsleil-Waututh Nation, the People of the Inlet, are responsible for and belong to our traditional territory. Let it be known that our Tsleil-Waututh Nation is a Nation unto itself, holding traditional territory for its people. (Tsleil-Waututh Nation 2009; emphasis in original)

These two documents are a modern expression of TWN *snəwayəł* or laws, and focus on TWN responsibilities to and relationship with the Inlet and the wider traditional territory. It is within this context that a proponent and the federal government propose to increase the oil tanker traffic traversing the marine waters of the Inlet by 700 percent.

Expressing *Snəwayəł* to Pipeline Extractions: TWN Assessment of the Trans Mountain Expansion Project

This larger vision for a healthier Burrard Inlet, and resulting restoration of TWN's community, health, economy, and culture, informed the

Nation's opposition to the Trans Mountain Expansion Project (TMX), which Kinder Morgan first proposed in 2011. The project vision is to build a second 987 km pipeline to twin the original Trans Mountain pipeline built in the 1950s to supply local oil refineries. It would triple the volume of diluted bitumen (a heavy crude diluted with lighter petroleum products to enable it to flow through a pipeline), triple the oil storage capacity on Burnaby Mountain, triple the size of the Westridge Marine Terminal and increase tanker traffic by seven times, up to four hundred tankers per year. Following a community referendum, in which one hundred percent of TWN members present voted to oppose the project, the TWN government launched the Sacred Trust Initiative, the mandate of which is to stop the proposed pipeline.

As with all of TWN decisions, the opposition to TMX is grounded in Tsleil-Waututh culture, spirituality and law and included water ceremonies, sacred fires, honoring ceremonies, and a spiritual leaders' gathering that resulted in the signing of the Treaty to Protect the Salish Sea.

In May 2015, TWN released the communities' independent *Assessment of the Trans Mountain Expansion Project* (Tsleil-Waututh Nation 2015). The TWN Assessment, "Grounded in truth, backed by science" is one of the most prominent contemporary applications of Indigenous law that included leading-edge scientific studies on oil spill probability and oil spill behavior.

The Assessment sets out TWN legal principles that are grounded in Coast Salish stories and teachings:

> The Tsleil-Waututh Stewardship Policy rests on the foundation of our ances-
> tral laws and is interpreted in accordance with them. The following section
> of the assessment provides an overview of applicable legal principles as laid
> out by Tsleil-Waututh teachings and other traditional and contemporary
> Coast Salish sources.
>
> . . .
>
> Just as Canadian common law consists of a body of case law developed over
> the centuries, Coast Salish stories express the ancestral laws of the Tsleil-
> Waututh. Tsleil-Waututh elders have told us that in light of substantially
> common legal traditions on matters of stewardship throughout the Coast
> Salish world, the principles contained in stories from all Coast Salish peoples
> are also applicable to Tsleil-Waututh. These expressions of Tsleil-Waututh
> law are referred to interchangeably here as *stories, traditional narratives,* or
> *teachings.* (52)

TWN summarizes its legal principles as follows (52–55):

Principle 1: Tsleil-Waututh has a sacred obligation to protect, defend, and steward the water, land, air, and resources of the territory.

Our stewardship obligation is to act with respect for all beings, human and non-human, and for all elements of the natural and spirit worlds. This responsibility is reflected in the principle of ʔaχʷəstəl' (reciprocal giving/reciprocity). If respect is shown, the syəwenəɬ (collectively, the spirits of those who came before us; the ancestors; our brethren—all creatures that live on the earth with us) will also care for and support us in return. However, if respect is not shown, negative or even disastrous consequences for the Tsleil-Waututh may be expected. . . .

Principle 2: Tsleil-Waututh's stewardship obligation includes maintaining and restoring conditions in our territory that provide the environmental, cultural, spiritual, and economic foundation for the following:

2.1 Cultural transmission and training that will allow Tsleil-Waututh individuals to reach their full potential and for Tsleil-Waututh, as a people, to thrive. . . .

2.2. Spiritual preparation and power. . . .

2.3 Harvest and consumption of safe, abundant wild foods from Tsleil-Waututh waters and lands to feed the present community, our ancestors, and other beings. . . .

2.4 Control over and sharing of resources according to Tsleil-Waututh and Coast Salish protocols

Principle 3: Failure to be "highly responsible" in one's actions toward the people, the earth, the ancestors, and all beings has serious consequences, which may include the following:

3.1 Loss of physical sustenance. . . .

3.2 Loss of access to resources or social status. . . .

3.3 Loss of the tools and training that allow Tsleil-Waututh individuals to reach their full potential and the related social and cultural impacts of this loss.

The TWN legal lens, summarized in these principles, was then applied to expert reports by scientists, anthropologists, and archaeologists to determine whether the project met TWN laws. The Assessment concluded that the TMX project had the potential to deprive past, current, and future generations of the Tsleil-Waututh community of control and benefit of the water, land, air, and resources in the territory. On that basis, TWN Chief and Council passed a resolution confirming the ban on the project under TWN law, and withholding their free, prior and informed consent.

TWN filed the Assessment with the National Energy Board—the state administrative body responsible for undertaking the environmental assessment for the project—as evidence of TWN's lack of consent to the project, according to an FPIC standard. The embattled regulator, ill-equipped to navigate questions of Indigenous rights and governance, treated the document as competing evidence on oil spills and failed to acknowledge TWN's jurisdiction (National Energy Board 2016: 134, 276, 390).

TWN also delivered the Assessment to Kinder Morgan directly at their Annual General Meeting of Stockholders and to many of Kinder Morgan's top institutional shareholders. While it is impossible to measure the precise impact of this work, it likely had an impact on Kinder Morgan's ability to finance the project. After Kinder Morgan was unable to find a joint venture partner for the project, it resorted to an initial public offering for a newly formed company to raise funds for construction. The final valuation of that company (Kinder Morgan Canada Limited (KML)) was Can$1.2 billion lower than Kinder Morgan's target valuation (Hayward 2018).

TWN also provided the Assessment to the Canadian federal cabinet tasked with deciding on the project. However, Prime Minister Justin Trudeau announced federal approval on November 29, 2016. TWN and five other First Nations judicially reviewed the approval at the Federal Court of Appeal (FCA). The FCA heard the consolidated legal challenges in October 2017 in the longest hearing in FCA history (Perry 2017).

The TMX story took an exceptional twist in May 2018 when the federal government announced that it would purchase the Trans Mountain system from Kinder Morgan for Can$4.5 billion, after the company decided to abandon the expansion project. At the time of the purchase, the expansion had valid federal approvals that were subject to the legal challenges.

On August 30, 2018, the FCA issued a unanimous decision (*Tsleil-Waututh Nation v. Canada (Attorney General)* 2018), quashing the federal approvals due to the failure to meaningfully consult affected First Nations and illegal exclusion of marine shipping (and its effect on whales) from the Environmental Assessment. The case confirms that consultation is not just a procedural right, but has substantive elements:

> The duty [to consult] is not fulfilled by simply providing a process for exchanging and discussing information. There must be a substantive dimension to the duty. Consultation is talking together for mutual understanding (*Clyde River*, paragraph 49). (para. 500)

The judgement did recognize the TWN Assessment; Tsleil-Waututh had conducted its own assessment of the Project's impact on Burrard Inlet and on Tsleil-Waututh's title, rights and interests and traditional knowledge (para. 649). However, because the approvals failed at the consultation stage, the court did not rule on arguments made by Tsleil-Waututh and other First Nations about the exercise of their governance rights, including through the TWN Assessment. As a result, the FCA did not grapple with free, prior, and informed consent. However, it is difficult to imagine a clearer application of the FPIC standard than TWN's work on the Trans Mountain Expansion Project.

National Economies Trump Place-Based Risk

Following the FCA decision, the Canadian government referred the decision back to the National Energy Board for further review, and began to re-engage in consultation over a six month period. On June 18, 2019, the federal government re-approved the twinning of the pipeline, accepting all 156 conditions imposed by the NEB and the NEB's additional sixteen recommendations within the jurisdiction of the federal government (Prime Minister of Canada 2019). These include a Marine Mammal Protection Program that focuses on mitigating the effects of increased tanker traffic, a marine spill prevention and response plan, and a regional cumulative effects management plan (National Energy Board 2019). Chief Leah George-Wilson of the TWN responded immediately to news of the approval indicating that the TWN will appeal the decision to the Federal Court of Appeal (Tasker 2019), stating: "Our obligation is not to oil. Our obligation is to the land, to the water, to our people, and to the whales" (Ross 2019).

The rationale for the approval of the TMX expansion is a transparent performance of the direct conflict between national state-sponsored extractive economies and local Indigenous economies:

> The environment and the economy go hand-in-hand. When we create prosperity today, we can invest in the clean jobs, technologies, and infrastructure of the future—and help Canadians benefit from opportunities presented by a rapidly changing economy. The key to creating prosperity is finding new markets for our businesses to sell their products and services. Nowhere is the need to diversify greater than for our energy sector, where 99 per cent of our conventional resources are sold to one market—and often at large discounts. Canadians understand that we need to open up new international markets, in order to get a full and fair price, support workers and their families, and foster competitiveness. (Prime Minister of Canada 2019)

The messaging from the Prime Minister's Office is about using the revenue from an extractive industry with specific place-based impacts to fuel the transition to a green economy. Such an approach proceeds without the consent of the TWN whose existing laws prohibit this type of disturbance and risk to the ecosystem of the Burrard Inlet and the TWN economy. The TWN has clearly said no to the project, yet the state continues to exert its jurisdiction to override TWN's decision and laws in the Canadian interest. Tsleil-Waututh Nation's opposition to the TMX project continues to be grounded in their unextinguished Indigenous laws that are inextricably linked to the relationship to and health of the Burrard Inlet. It is these relationships and responsibilities to the Inlet that a state-centered economy cannot reconcile with its emphasis on extraction.

Conclusion: Relationships, Responsibility, and Consent to Extract

Indigenous nations' inherent and ongoing relationship to and responsibility for their territory is often expressed through assertions of jurisdiction to decide whether or not they consent to state-sponsored (extractive) projects. The Heiltsuk's and Tsleil-Waututh's exercise of place-based responsibility and jurisdiction as expressions of their Indigenous laws and in defense of their economies provide two examples of the meaning of consent. It is clear that consent cannot be mediated through state-initiated and -defined "consultation and accommodation" processes. Rather than continuing to conflict with colonial legal processes, state legal systems will need to recognize Indigenous jurisdiction as determined according to Indigenous legal principles and processes that are communicated to the state. This is what a legal expression of free, prior and informed consent can look like in environmental governance. As affirmed in the UN Declaration, Indigenous communities require participation in decision making, and developing relationships that nurture processes for assessing and giving ongoing consent. The Declaration states that Indigenous people have the right to participate in and adjudicate decision-making processes using their own procedures, institutions, laws, and land tenure systems (UN General Assembly 2007: Articles 18, 27; Askew et al. 2017; Szablowski 2011).

Indigenous-defined governance procedures that embody the place-based responsibility held by specific First Nations and Indigenous organizations such as hereditary leaders, and also model ongoing consent, are emerging. For example, following the devastating wildfires in 2017, in 2018 the Tsilhqot'in National Government administered morel mushroom harvesting permits with the support of the Provincial government (Province of British Columbia 2019). The map accompanying the permit designated the wildfire area, and the no-harvest areas such as parks and Tsilhqot'in areas of concern (Tsilhqot'in National Government n.d.). The permits and regulations that pickers were required to adhere to were grounded in Indigenous laws, and Tsilhqot'in Rangers, the Royal Canadian Mounted Police, and conservation officers monitored the harvest (Dickson 2018). Another example is the Northern Secwepemc te Qelmucw Leadership Council's adoption of the Northern Secwepemc te Qelmucw Mining Policy in 2014. The Policy's first guiding principle prohibits mining without the free, prior and informed consent of the Northern Secwepemc te Qelmucw (Section 4.1.1).

In September 2017, the Province of BC made reconciliation a cross-government priority and reviewed policies, programs and legislation with a view to operationalizing the UN Declaration (Province of British Columbia 2017). At a high level, the provincial government drafted principles intended to guide its relationships with Indigenous people, which includes acknowledging "[t]he right of Indigenous peoples to self-determination and self-government, and the responsibility of government to change operating practices and processes to recognize these rights" and FPIC (Province of British Columbia 2018a). Two notable expressions of these commitments emerged in 2018—consent to operate fish farms in traditional territories and a memorandum of understanding (MOU) that acknowledges Indigenous jurisdiction. The provincial government imposed a consent requirement on fish farm operators as a condition of tenure renewal. The operators must negotiate agreements with First Nations in whose territory they propose to continue operating (Laanela 2018; Province of British Columbia 2018b; Province of British Columbia 2018c). The MOU is between five First Nations in the Nicola Valley and the provincial government to address severe water issues. The MOU includes clauses expressing the commitment of all parties to the implementation of the UN Declaration, and acknowledging the distinct perspectives each party brings to the partnership that arise from different legal and governance traditions (Upper Nicola Band of the Okanagan (Syilx) Nation et al. 2018). The First Nations intend the collaborative governance approach contemplated in the MOU to be a "first step toward broader recognition of Nlaka'pamux and Syilx jurisdiction and legal authority" (4).

While these are empowering and essential moves, there are fundamental cultural, temporal, and spatial differences between Indigenous economies and extractive state-supported capitalist economies. State decision-making on a project-by-project basis focused on risk management with benefits accruing to the national interest, no matter how much process occurs, cannot meaningfully reflect a long-term relationship with and responsibility for a territory that is based on ecological health. More radical attention to Indigenous economies would require, for example, the return of a region to 80 percent old growth forest over a 250-year timeframe where upwards of 50 percent of that landscape has permanent protected status where Aboriginal rights can be exercised, as occurred in the Great Bear Rainforest on the BC Central Coast (Curran 2017: 813). As the Heiltsuk and Tsleil-Waututh Nations have emphasized, their economies are entwined with a place, their culture, their laws, and their responsibilities. This worldview requires state authorities to support and be bound by long-term, ecosystem-based processes of consent.

Notes

This article is written pursuant to the Tsleil-Waututh Nation Research Agreement, which is a protocol between researchers and the Tsleil-Waututh Nation establishing how research will be conducted and for what it will be used. In particular, the agreement reads: "The Researcher respects the cultural and political sensitivities around the Research Project and recognizes and acknowledges the negative impacts that academic research has often had upon First Nations. The Researcher is committed to research activities which advance the process of recognition, empowerment and self-determination for TWN."

1 The decision *Grassy Narrows First Nation v. Ontario (Natural Resources)*, 2014 SCC 48 at para. 50 confirmed provincial governments' primary role in managing natural resources in the context of Aboriginal rights.

2 The text in this section is recounted from oral history of the Heiltsuk people and from the lived experience of Chief Councillor Marilyn Slett.

3 Kelly Brown, Director of the Heiltsuk Integrated Resource Management Department and Chief Councillor Ǧáǧvi Marilyn Slett.

4 Written with consent pursuant to the Tsleil-Waututh Nation Research Agreement.

References

Adams Lake Indian Band v. BC, 2012 BCCA 333.

Ahousaht Indian Band v. Canada (Minister of Fisheries and Oceans), 2014 FC 197.

Anshelm, Jonas, Simon Haikola, and Björn Wallsten. 2018. "Politicizing Environmental Governance–a Case Study of Heterogeneous Alliances and Juridical Struggles around the Ojnare Forest, Sweden." *Geoforum* 91: 206–15.

Askew, Hannah et al. 2017. "Between Law and Action: Assessing the State of Knowledge on Indigenous Law, UNDRIP and Free, Prior and Informed Consent with Reference to Fresh Water Resources." West Coast Environmental Law. wcel.org/sites/default/files /publications/betweenlawandaction-undrip-fpic-freshwater-report-wcel-ubc.pdf.

Borrows, John. 2016. *Freedom and Indigenous Constitutionalism*. Toronto: University of Toronto Press.

Borrows, John. 2017. "Revitalizing Canada's Indigenous Constitution: Two Challenges." In *UNDRIP Implementation Braiding International, Domestic and Indigenous Laws*, Centre for International Governance Innovation, 20–28. cigionline.org/sites/default/files/documents/UNDRIP%20Implementation%20Special%20Report%20WEB.pdf.

Borrows, John. 2018. "Earth-Bound: Indigenous Resurgence and Environmental Reconciliation." In *Resurgence and Reconciliation: Indigenous-Settler Relations and Earth Teachings*, edited by Michael Asch, John Borrows, and James Tully, 49–82. Toronto: University of Toronto Press.

Brown, Frank, and Kathy Brown (compilers). 2009. *Staying the Course, Staying Alive. Coastal First Nations Fundamental Truths: Biodiversity, Stewardship and Sustainability*. Victoria, BC: Biodiversity BC.

CBC News. 2015a. "Heiltsuk First Nation Says Commercial Herring Fishery Violated Constitutional Rights." *CBC*, March 23. cbc.ca/news/canada/british-columbia/heiltsuk-first-nation-says-commercial-herring-fishery-violated-constitutional-rights-1.3005000.

CBC News. 2015b. "Heiltsuk First Nation Occupies Federal Office over Herring Fishery." *CBC*, March 30. www.cbc.ca/news/canada/british-columbia/heiltsuk-first-nation-occupies-federal-office-over-herring-fishery-1.3014855.

Campbell v. British Columbia (Attorney General), 2000 BCSC 1123.

Chartrand v. British Columbia (Forests, Lands, and Natural Resource Operations), 2015 BCCA 345.

Chisholm, Brian, D. Erle Nelson, and Henry Schwarcz. 1983. "Marine and Terrestrial Protein in Prehistoric Diets on the British Columbia Coast." *Current Anthropology* 24, no. 3: 396–98.

Christie, Gordon. 2017. "Indigenous Legal Orders, Canadian Law and UNDRIP." In Centre for International Governance Innovation, *UNDRIP Implementation Braiding International, Domestic and Indigenous Laws*, 48–55. cigionline.org/sites/default/files/documents/UNDRIP%20Implementation%20Special%20Report%20WEB.pdf.

Curran, Deborah. 2017. "'Legalizing' the Great Bear Rainforest Agreements: Colonial Adaptations toward Reconciliation and Conservation." *McGill Law Journal* 62, no. 3: 813–60.

Delgamuukw v. British Columbia, [1997] 3 SCR 1010, [1997] SCJ No 108.

Dickson, Courtney. 2018. "Mushroom-Picking Restrictions Hailed a Success by B.C. First Nation." *CBC*, August 9. cbc.ca/news/canada/british-columbia/tsilhqot-in-mushroom-picking-success-1.4779159.

Dunlap, Alexander. 2018. "'A Bureaucratic Trap': Free, Prior and Informed Consent (FPIC) and Wind Energy Development in Juchitán, Mexico." *Capitalism Nature Socialism* 29, no. 4. doi: 10.1080/10455752.2017.1334219.

Enge v. Canada (Indigenous and Northern Affairs), 2017 FC 932.

Fisheries and Oceans Pacific Region. 1998. "Central Coast Herring: DFO Science Stock Status Report B6–02." waves-vagues.dfo-mpo.gc.ca/Library/228285.pdf.

Garvie, Kathryn, Lana Lowe, and Karena Shaw. 2014. "Shale Gas Development in Fort Nelson First Nation Territory: Potential Regional Impacts of the LNG Boom." *BC Studies: The British Columbian Quarterly* 184: 45–72.

Gauvreau, Alisha Marie, Dana Lepofsky, Murray Rutherford, and Mike Reid. 2017. "'Everything Revolves around the Herring': The Heiltsuk-Herring Relationship through Time." *Ecology and Society* 22, no. 2: 10.

Gauvreau, Alisha Marie, Dana Lepofsky, Murray Rutherford, and Mike Reid. 2017. "Response to: 'Everything revolves around the herring': the Heiltsuk-Herring Relationship through Time. 2017. Gauvreau, A. M., D. Lepofsky, M. Rutherford, and M. Reid." *Ecology and Society* 22, no. 3.

Gill, Ian. 2018. "Of Roe, Rights, and Reconciliation." *Hakai Magazine*, August 28. www .hakaimagazine.com/features/of-roe-rights-and-reconciliation/.

Gold Fields Act, 1859.

Gold Mining Ordinance, 1867 (Legislative Council British Columbia).

Gómez-Barris, Macarena. 2017. *The Extractive Zone: Social Ecologies and Decolonial Perspectives*. Durham, NC: Duke University Press.

Grassy Narrows First Nation v Ontario (Natural Resources), 2014 SCC 48.

Haida Gwaii Reconciliation Act, SBC 2010, c 17.

Haida Nation v British Columbia, 2004 SCC 73.

Haida Nation v. Canada (Minister of Fisheries and Oceans), 2015 FC 290.

Halfway River First Nation v. British Columbia (Ministry of Forests), 1999 BCCA 470.

Harper, Sarah, Anne K. Salomon, Dianne Newell, Pauline Hilistis Waterfall, Kelly Brown, Leila M. Harris, and U. Rashid Sumaila. 2018. "Indigenous Women Respond to Fisheries Conflict and Catalyze Change in Governance on Canada's Pacific Coast." *Maritime Studies* 17, no. 2: 189–98.

Harris, Douglas. 2000. "Territoriality, Aboriginal Rights, and the Heiltsuk Spawn-on-Kelp Fishery." *University of British Columbia Law Review* 34: 195.

Hayward, Jonathan. 2018. "Kinder Morgan Canada share target cut as growth hopes fall post pipeline deal." *Financial Post*, May 30. business.financialpost.com/pmn/business-pmn /kinder-morgan-canada-share-target-cut-as-growth-hopes-fall-post-pipeline-deal.

Heiltsuk Nation. 2019. "New Website Brings Together Thousands of Years of Heiltsuk Voices." *Heiltsuk Nation*, January 24. www.heiltsuknation.ca/new-website-brings-together -thousands-of-years-of-heiltsuk-voices/.

Heiltsuk Tribal Council. 2017a. "Investigation Report: The Forty-Eight Hours after the Grounding of the *Nathan E. Stewart* and Its Oil Spill." *Heiltsuk Nation*. www.heiltsuk nation.ca/wp-content/uploads/2017/10/HTC-NES-IRP-2017-03-31.pdf.

Heiltsuk Tribal Council. 2017b. "Indigenous Marine Response Centre (IMRC): Creating a World-Leading Response System." *Heiltsuk Nation*. www.heiltsuknation.ca/wp-content /uploads/2017/11/HTC_IMRC-Report_Nov-15-2017.pdf.

Heiltsuk Tribal Council. 2018. "Dáduqvḷá qn̓txv Ǧviḷásax̌ To Look at Our Traditional Laws: Decision of the Heiltsuk (Haíɫzaqv) Dáduqvḷá Committee Regarding the October 13, 2016, *Nathan E. Stewart* Spill." *Heiltsuk Nation*. www.heiltsuknation.ca/wp-content /uploads/2018/10/Heiltsuk_Adjudication_Report.pdf.

Hemmera. 2016. "Framing the Future of Mineral Exploration in British Columbia: AME BC Mineral Land Access and Use Report." Association for Mineral Exploration. www .amebc.ca/wp-content/uploads/2017/06/AME-BC-Mineral-Land-Access-and-Use -Report-2015-No-AppF-1.pdf.

Housty, William, et al. 2014. "Grizzly Bear Monitoring by the Heiltsuk People as a Crucible for First Nation Conservation Practice." *Ecology and Society* 19:2: 70.

Kelly, Dara. 2017. "Sq'ewlets: A Sto:lo-Coast Salish Community in the Fraser River Valley Virtual Museum." *BC Studies*, no. 194: 195.

Laanela, Mike. 2018. "BC Fish Farms to Require First Nations Approval Starting in 2022." *CBC*, June 20. cbc.ca/news/canada/british-columbia/bc-fish-farms-first-nations -approval-1.4714036.

Lilley, Patrick et al. 2017. "Burrard Inlet Action Plan: A Tsleil-Wauuth Perspective." Tsleil-Wauuth Nation (TWN). twnsacredtrust.ca/burrard-inlet-action-plan/.

Mikisew Cree First Nation v Canada (Minister of Canadian Heritage), 2005 SCC 69.

Mineral Act, RS 1936, c 181.

Morales, Sarah. 2017. "Braiding the Incommensurable: Indigenous Legal Traditions and the Duty to Consult." In Centre for International Governance Innovation, *UNDRIP Implementation Braiding International, Domestic and Indigenous Laws*, 63–80. cigionline .org/sites/default/files/documents/UNDRIP%20Implementation%20Special%20 Report%20WEB.pdf.

Morin, Jesse. 2015. "Tsleil-Wauuth Nation's History, Culture, and Aboriginal Interests in Eastern Burrard Inlet (Redacted Version)." Tsleil-Wauuth Nation Sacred Trust. twnsacredtrust.ca/wp-content/uploads/2015/05/Morin-Expert-Report-PUBLIC -VERSION-sm.pdf.

Nair, Roshini. 2017. "Archaeological Find Affirms Heiltsuk Nation's Oral History." *CBC*, March 30. www.cbc.ca/news/canada/british-columbia/archeological-find-affirms -heiltsuk-nation-s-oral-history-1.4046088.

National Energy Board. 2016. "National Energy Board Report—Trans Mountain Expansion Project." *Government of Canada*, May 2016. apps.neb-one.gc.ca/REGDOCS/Item/Filing /A77045.

National Energy Board. 2019. "Conditions and Recommendations Overview—Trans Mountain Expansion Project Reconsideration Report." *Government of Canada*, February 22. neb-one.gc.ca/pplctnflng/mjrpp/trnsmntnxpnsn/trnsmntnxpnsnrprtcndtn-eng.html.

Northern Secwepemc te Qelmucw Leadership Council. 2014. "Northern Secwepemc te Qelmucw Mining Policy." fairmining.ca/wp-content/uploads/2014/12/NStQ-Mining-Policy _Nov19.20141.pdf.

Perry, Elizabeth. 2017. "Work and Climate Change Report September 28 2017." https://work andclimatechangereport.org/2017/09/28/the-new-british-columbia-government -tackles-climate-change-policy-and-controversies-site-c-kinder-morgan-and-carbon -tax-neutrality/.

Powell, Miles. 2012. "Divided Waters: Heiltsuk Spatial Management of Herring Fisheries and the Politics of Native Sovereignty." *Western Historical Quarterly* 43, no. 4: 463–84.

Province of British Columbia. 2019. "Mushroom Picking—a Guide to Picking Morel Mushrooms in Wildfire Affected Areas." www2.gov.bc.ca/gov/content/industry/crown -land-water/crown-land/crown-land-uses/mushroom-picking (accessed 18 June 2019).

Province of British Columbia. 2017. "Statement of Premier John Horgan on the 10th Anniversary on the UN Declaration on the Rights of Indigenous Peoples." *BC Government News*, September 13. news.gov.bc.ca/releases/2017PREM0083-001562.

Province of British Columbia. 2018a. "Draft Principles Guide B.C. Public Service on Relationships with Indigenous Peoples." *BC Government News*, May 22. news.gov.bc.ca/releases /2018PREM0033-000978.

Province of BC. 2018b. "BC Government Announces New Approach to Salmon Farm Tenures." *BC Government News*, June 20. news.gov.bc.ca/releases/2018AGRI0046-001248.

Province of BC. 2018c. Letter of Understanding Regarding a Government-to-Government Process to Address Finfish Aquaculture in the Broughton Archipelago June 27 2018. www2 .gov.bc.ca/assets/gov/environment/natural-resource-stewardship/consulting-with -first-nations/agreements/lou_broughtonfn_27june2018.pdf.

Prime Minister of Canada. 2019. "Trans Mountain Expansion Will Fund Canada's Future Clean Economy." June 18. pm.gc.ca/eng/news/2019/06/18/trans-mountain-expansion -will-fund-canadas-future-clean-economy.

R. v. Gladstone, [1996] 2 S.C.R. 723.

R. v. Sparrow, [1990] 1 SCR 1075, 70 DLR (4th) 385.

R. v. Van der Peet, [1996] 2 SCR 507, 137 DLR (4th) 289.

Ritchie, Kaitlin. 2013. "Issues Associated with the Implementation of the Duty to Consult and Accommodate Aboriginal Peoples: Threatening the Goals of Reconciliation and Meaningful Consultation." *UBC Law Review* 43: 397.

Ross, Andrea. 2019. "Tsleil-Waututh Nation to Appeal Trans Mountain Expansion Once Again." CBC News, June 18. www.cbc.ca/news/canada/british-columbia/tsleil-waututh -to-appeal-tmx-decision-1.5180743.

Sambaa K'e Dene First Nation v. Duncan, 2012 FC 204.

Schilling-Vacaflor, Almut. 2017. "Who Controls the Territory and the Resources? Free, Prior and Informed Consent (FPIC) as a Contested Human Rights Practice in Bolivia." *Third World Quarterly* 38, no. 5: 1058–74. doi:10.1080/01436597.2016.1238761.

Shore, Randy. 2019. "DFO Shuts Down Fishery, Citing First Nations Reconciliation." *Vancouver Sun*, March 3. vancouversun.com/news/local-news/dfo-shuts-down-fishery-citing -first-nations-reconciliation.

Starblanket, Gina and Heidi Kiiwetinepinesiik Stark. 2018. "Towards a Relational Paradigm-Four Points for Consideration: Knowledge, Gender, Land, and Modernity." In *Resurgence and Reconciliation: Indigenous-Settler Relations and Earth Teachings*, edited by Michael Asch, John Borrows, and James Tully, 175–208. Toronto: University of Toronto Press.

Supreme Court of British Columbia Vancouver Registry. 2018. "Notice of Civil Claim No. S1810902: Heiltsuk Himas and Heiltsuk Tribal Council v Kirby Offshore Marine LLC and the Attorney General (Canada and British Columbia)." www.heiltsuknation .ca/wp-content/uploads/2018/10/Heiltsuk-Notice-of-Civil-Claim.pdf.

Szablowski, David. 2011. "Operationalizing Free, Prior, and Informed Consent in the Extractive Industry Sector? Examining the Challenges of a Negotiated Model of Justice." *Canadian Journal of Development Studies* 30, nos. 1–2: 111–30.

Tasker, John Paul. 2019. "Trudeau Cabinet Approves Trans Mountain Expansion Project." *CBC*, June 18. www.cbc.ca/news/politics/tasker-trans-mountain-trudeau-cabinet-decision -1.5180269.

Truth and Reconciliation Commission of Canada. 2015. *Canada's Residential Schools: Reconciliation*. Volume 6 of *The Final Report of the Truth and Reconciliation Commission of Canada*. Montreal: McGill-Queen's University Press.

Tsilhqot'in Nation v. British Columbia, 2014 SCC 44.

Tsilhqot'in National Government. n.d. "2018 Mushroom Harvesting in Tsilhqot'in Territory." www.tsilhqotin.ca/Portals/0/PDFs/PublicMushroomInformationPamphletDraft2 _SG.pdf.

Tsleil-Waututh Nation. 2009. "Stewardship Policy." http://www.twnation.ca/en/About%20 TWN/~/media/Files/Stewardship%20January%202009.ashx.

Tsleil-Waututh Nation. 2015. "Assessment of the Trans Mountain Pipeline and Tanker Expansion Proposal." twnsacredtrust.ca/wp-content/uploads/TWN_assessment_final_med -res_v2.pdf.

Tsleil-Waututh Nation v. Canada (Attorney General), 2018 FCA 153.

UN General Assembly. 2007. "United Nations Declaration on the Rights of Indigenous Peoples." www.un.org/esa/socdev/unpfii/documents/DRIPS_en.pdf.

Upper Nicola Band of the Okanagan (Syilx) Nation, et al. 2018. "Nicola Watershed Pilot Memorandum of Understanding." www2.gov.bc.ca/assets/gov/environment/natural-resource-stewardship/consulting-with-first-nations/agreements/nicola_watershed_pilot_mou_-_signed_2018.pdf.

Winona LaDuke and Deborah Cowen[1]

Beyond Wiindigo Infrastructure

For the Ojibwe, history and legends are passed
down orally. There are the stories of Wiindigo,
a giant monster, a cannibal, who killed and ate
our people. Colonization was our Wiindigo.
—Bezhigobinesikwe Elaine Fleming,
"Nanaboozhoo and the Wiindigo" (2017)

"why you telling wiindigo stories all the time?"
"maybe because they're about greed and evil and
imbalance, and we're all living surrounded by that."
"well then why you want to be surrounded by more
of that?"
"i dunno. so we see the wiindigo in ourselves?"
"gaa. you young ones forget everything nowadays.
wiindigo more about the inside than the outside."
"so what should we be telling, then?"
"you know."
"i don't think i do, know, that is."
"tell the ones about that strong young nishnaabekwe
who wasn't afraid of those wiindigo. who was smart
and strategic. who was patient, so, so patient. waiting
until just the right time. waiting, watching. tell those
ones, so those young ones will know what to do.
teach those ones. make it so they'll want to listen.
make it so they'll pay attention."
—Leanne Betasamosake Simpson, "gezhizhwazh"
(2016)

The South Atlantic Quarterly 119:2, April 2020
DOI 10.1215/00382876-8177747 © 2020 Duke University Press

These are decisive times. We are now perilously close to planetary ecological collapse. In 2017, the Intergovernmental Panel on Climate Change announced a miniscule twelve–year window for radical global action on climate change, and as we write in summer 2019, the melting Arctic indexes an unfolding failure to steer our collective path away from apocalypse. This year, reports on the extent of species extinction added another incontrovertible measure of the evolving catastrophe. The ecological crisis is a direct result of a broader social and spiritual one. It is lived in dramatically uneven ways, with Indigenous peoples and people of color bearing the brunt of toxicity, habitat destruction, and displacement. Colonial theft and unceasing extraction proceed apace, despite, or even through, talk of reconciliation. The crisis is a direct result of an economic system predicated upon accumulation and dispossession, that denigrates the sacred in all of us. Winona calls this the *Wiindigo economy*, invoking the cannibal monster of Anishinaabe legend that "symbolizes the potentially addictive part of the human condition—when certain desires are indulged," stimulating "more indulgence until all reason and control are lost" (L. Simpson 2011: 70). The Wiindigo economy is produced through routine attacks on the courage and creativity of women and the gender and sexually diverse. It holds striking concentrations of wealth and poverty. It is organized by an extraordinary expansion of military, security, and carceral power that destroys, separates, and contains peoples based on race and nationality. It is like a cancer, a cancer on Mother Earth, a cancer on our bodies; and indeed, in the world we live in today, many of us will succumb to the disease. We are a reflection of our Mother. As our climate heats up, so does the global political scene, with fascist social orders on the rise the world over. "Man's heart away from nature becomes hard," Standing Bear would say; we lose relationship, we isolate, and we become cruel.

And yet, despite the severity of the situation, the future is not foreclosed. We have agency, and life is magical. In Anishinaabe prophecy, this is the moment of choice, when two paths open before us. We are told there is one path that is well worn but scorched, the second green. The question is how to move off the scorched path. In this writing, we suggest that choosing a good path requires the revolutionary but also profoundly practical work of infrastructure. At the center of the Wiindigo's violence and destruction is infrastructure's seemingly banal and technical world. *Wiindigo infrastructure* has worked to carve up Turtle Island, or North America, into preserves of settler jurisdiction, while entrenching and hardening the very means of settler economy and sociality into tangible material structures. We see this in sharp relief today, with pipelines and dams and roads and prisons and toxic water infrastructures. We know it in the struggles at White Earth and on Secwepemc territory, from Flint to Neskantaga, from Goose Bay to Pelican Bay. And we feel it across the whole length of the national border, and at the detention camps assembled in its name. The transformation of ecologies of the many into systems of circulation and accumulation to serve the few is the project of settler colonial infrastructure. Infrastructure is the *how* of settler colonialism, and the settler colony is where the Wiindigo runs free. Yet, infrastructure is not inherently colonial—it is also essential for transformation; a pipe can carry fresh water as well as toxic sludge. We suggest that effective initiatives for justice, decolonization, and planetary survival must center infrastructure in their efforts, and we highlight *alimentary infrastructure*—infrastructure that is life-giving in its design, finance, and effects. Drawing on our distinct work in communities, classrooms, courthouses, and city streets, we insist that our collective futures hinge on remaking socio-technical systems—on *building beyond* Wiindigo infrastructure.

That settler sociality and economy are enabled and reproduced by infrastructure explains our concern for socio-technical systems, but what about the Wiindigo? What can be gained from engaging infrastructure *as Wiindigo*, but also from stories that move beyond? In "Land as Pedagogy," Leanne Simpson (2014) offers that Indigenous stories are the "theoretical anchor" of critical Indigenous studies. Barker (2018: 20) engages Simpson's work on this question, and offers that stories "'generate and regenerate' meaning, made relevant by those who, in the retelling and representation of them, (re)make their relationships and responsibilities to one another, to nonhumans, to the sky, and to the earth." Stories insist on the ethical, embodied, and affective dimensions of knowing, refusing imperial systems of knowledge that divide fact from fiction, mind from body, and the sacred from survival. Rooted in and routed through this territory, Indigenous stories can help us see and know and walk a different path. Despite settler colonial claims of outright replacement of Indigenous people and their sovereign ways of life, Indigenous ways of knowing the world survive and are seeing a powerful resurgence (A. Simpson 2014; Coulthard 2014; Estes 2019). Can stories about the Wiindigo (which for Fleming describe the experience of colonialism) and stories about "the strong young nishnaabekwe who wasn't afraid of those wiindigo" (which Leanne Simpson figures as stories of resistance and survivance) help us reimagine the critical infrastructures of everyday life on Turtle Island?

In what follows, we combine forces to share stories of infrastructures across Turtle Island. Our discussion focuses attention on Canada, but travels to both sides of the "Medicine Line"—a term for the US-Canada border coined by Indigenous peoples during early colonial settlement that speaks to the seemingly "supernatural manifestation" that governed settler mobilities (O'Brien 1984: 315). We begin by offering reflections on how infrastructure has long been critical to settler colonial futurity and to the destruction of Indigenous life. We then shift focus to dwell in a different set of stories, of people and communities who are assembling infrastructure otherwise. Both old and new, these other stories are anchored in creativity and freedom, in courage and in love, and offer practical and affective possibilities for transformation. With Leanne Simpson, we look to those who "[weren't] afraid of those wiindigo," who are "smart and strategic . . . [and] patient. We tell these stories in hopes of encouraging more people to pay attention to infrastructure, and to create technology, systems, and infrastructure for life, rather than for the Wiindigo. Infrastructure is the spine of the Wiindigo, but is also the essential architecture of transition to a decolonized future. Social and ecological transformation is movement and relies on movements, and both require infrastructure.

Apprehending Infrastructure

And while there are infrastructures of Indigenous resistance, they confront
infrastructures of settler colonialism in the form of police, prisons, dams,
and oil pipelines that intend to destroy, replace, and erase.
—Nick Estes, "Freedom Is a Place" (2018)

On February 14, 2019, over a hundred big-rig trucks departed from Red Deer, Alberta, en route to Canada's capital city. The "United We Roll" convoy monopolized national news for the six days it took them to reach Ottawa. The truckers carried messages of anger and enmity; homemade and professionally printed signs affixed to their cabs and containers read, "We Love Oil," "Build Pipelines," "Trudeau: Step Down, Clown," "Liberty, Free Speech, Capitalism!" and "No Dirty Foreign Oil." This white and masculine backlash animated by climate change denial and hyper-extractivism is diagnostic of a politics that has taken hold across the continent. Motivated by deep emotional and material investment in the expansion of oil and gas infrastructures, the truckers charged the prime minister with stunting the sector. Licia Corbella (2019), the *Calgary Herald* / Postmedia opinion columnist, described and performed the convoy's nationalist affect. Corbella described the "Canadian flags flapping and huge signs declaring love for Canadian oil and gas," and suggested that "it was, indeed, a strangely beautiful and, I'll admit, somewhat emotional sight." The 3,500 km journey included pit stops for rallies as well as refueling. Their numbers grew as they journeyed eastward.

In fact, the convoy carried *two* prominent messages that entwined with disturbing ease: a rally for expanded oil and gas infrastructures, and a call for more investment in border infrastructures to curtail immigration. As Justin Brake (2019) reported for the Aboriginal People's Television Network, "What began in Red Deer last week as a pro-pipeline campaign has transformed into a platform for right-wing activists who have promoted white nationalist, anti-immigrant, anti-Indigenous and other racist messages at rallies along the way." Explicitly signaling their alignment with Trumpism south of the Medicine Line, an oft-spotted "Make Canada Great Again" hat was the popular fashion choice for this white men's pro-carbon convoy. Red Deer had already been dealing with a surge of racist attacks on Indigenous people and people of color in the months leading up to the convoy (Michelin 2018), and media reports describe the broader emboldening of local white supremacism since Trump's election. The Canadian Anti-Hate Network (cited in Belewett 2019) asserted that United We Roll was "entirely co-opted by the far-right including the most extreme anti-Muslim groups in Canada." This was, furthermore, not an affair of the fringe. Canadian Conservative leader Andrew Scheer was criticized for speaking at the convoy's rally on Parliament Hill alongside a renowned white nationalist.

The United We Roll convoy's interest in expanding both border and pipeline infrastructures was rife with painful ironies. Unremarked in popular discourse is the fact that Red Deer, like the rest of the settler cities in the west, was founded only a little more than a century ago during the first massive colonial infrastructure invasion in this part of Turtle Island. Then like now, physical infrastructures of circulation were coupled with affective infrastructures of white supremacy as part of the settler movement westward. Red Deer took shape historically through a Canadian version of the "railroad colonialism" that Manu Karuka (2019) has elegantly documented south of the Medicine Line. The birth of Red Deer took place in 1891, when Fort Normandeau was moved to the city's current site in order to access the newly constructed railroad. The town grew rapidly after the arrival of the rail and Red Deer was incorporated in 1913. Fort Normandeau— a key settler colonial infrastructure itself—housed the Fusiliers Mont-Royal while they fought Louis Riel and the Metis and Cree forces in the 1885 uprising.

In addition to the active military combat against Indigenous peoples and the critical military infrastructure that supported it, European settlement in the Red Deer area involved a systematic attack on the bodies and livelihoods of plains people. The survey and sale of lands could not proceed until plains peoples' relationships to the land were severed, and the building of the railroad infrastructure served this goal. Railroads were key in the mass killing of an estimated 50 million buffalo that had roamed Turtle Island's central plains, reaching north to Alaska and the Yukon Territories and south through the state of Georgia. The life of the buffalo was deeply entangled with the life of plains people and remains so—buffalo provided food, clothing, and tools; their movements shaped the geographies and temporalities of the peoples that relied on them. In just a few decades the herds were decimated in the more northern parts of the range and the people that depended on them were suffering badly, according to colonial plan. It is well known that the most senior American military leaders saw elimination of the buffalo as a military strategy to eliminate Indians. James Daschuk (2013) has further documented how "Canadian officials used food, or rather denied food, as a means to ethnically cleanse a vast region from Regina to the Alberta border as the Canadian Pacific Railway took shape." Land was cleared to make way for the railroad but the railroad also enabled mass slaughter.

It was in the wake of this genocidal violence that land speculators, "colonization companies," and the Canadian Pacific Railway's (CPR) own internal Department of Colonization transformed the plains into real estate profits. Speculators from as far away as London, New York City, and Montreal were able to purchase tracts of land that measured millions of acres (Martin-McGuire 1998: 38). Despite the hard drive to fill the new colony, it was only white settlers who were recruited to homestead on the prairies. Entire communities of Black people, attempting to escape racial terror in the newly formed state of Oklahoma, for instance, were actively discouraged from crossing north (Foster 2019; see also Cowen, forthcoming). Anti-Blackness also underpinned the rail, and the nation; the CPR that made the settler state possible was financed in part through wealth extracted from unfree labor, especially plantations in the Caribbean and southern US states. On both sides of the Medicine Line, Chinese migrants worked—often to death—to build the transcontinental track. Hyper-exploited and then discarded—the Canadian state began enacting restrictions on Chinese migration as soon as the infrastructure was complete. Soon after its completion in the late nineteenth century, the CPR was referred to by first Canadian Prime Minister John A. Macdonald as the "spine of the nation," capturing the way the transcontinental rail literally and materially built settler jurisdiction and cemented the constitution of Canada (cf. Cowen 2018). This has its truth, especially if we understand that nation to be a colonial one where the laying of the railroad tracks was also the laying of white supremacy. This rail enacted these racial logics and defined the collective distribution of life and death in ways that we see echoed in the afterlives of infrastructure today.

Settler Colonial Infrastructure

We might say that energy infrastructures constitute the contemporary spine of the settler colonial nation. Federal politicians frequently draw direct comparisons between these two moments of nation building, suggesting we take lessons from the example of the past. Former leader of the federal opposition Preston Manning (2018), for instance, suggests that Canada needs "Corridor Coalitions" to get pipelines built, as the "twenty-first-century political and economic effort equivalent to the nineteenth-century effort to create the Canadian Confederation and build the original Canadian Pacific Railway." Although the United We Roll convoy directed its anger at the prime minister, Justin Trudeau has in fact demonstrated an unfailing—almost flawless—commitment to ensuring the profitability of the fossil fuel industry and expanding the infrastructures that underpin it. The United We Roll convoy departed less than a month after the prime minister sanctioned a violent deployment of the Royal Canadian Mounted Police on the Unist'ot'en Camp, where water and land protectors have been trying to block Coastal GasLink's work on a natural gas pipeline that would carry fracked methane to an export facility on the coast. Just a few months earlier, Prime Minister Trudeau spent $4.5 billion[2] from public funds to purchase the ailing Trans Mountain pipeline from Texas-based Kinder Morgan, the offspring of Enron. He did this despite active opposition from Indigenous people, whose unceded territories surround the pipeline's path. While Trudeau may well sound and look different than the previous neoconservative national leadership, with his claims to feminism and promises of nation-to-nation relations, the current government's economic plans in fact align closely with the previous one's, in particular around energy. Trudeau famously boasted that he has approved more pipelines than his conservative predecessor Stephen Harper ever did (Ibbitson 2017). Justin Trudeau has in many ways intensified some of the most violent dimensions of the previous government's policies regarding energy, mining, and the protection of logistics systems that get those commodities to global markets.

Not surprisingly perhaps, Trudeau has prioritized investment in infrastructure that can support this activity. New infrastructure spending over recent years amounts to at least $180 billion under the New Building Canada Plan. The "centerpiece" of the federal government plan—the Canada Infrastructure Bank (CIB) (Stanley 2019: 2)—now calls Toronto's financial district home. The CIB is a new kind of institutional arrangement with the purpose of facilitating transnational finance capital's profiteering from publicly facilitated infrastructure, taking its cue from the Asian Infrastructure Bank. As the world's entrepôt for extraction, with 75 percent of global mining companies headquartered here, Toronto's Bay Street has become an important site of command and control of the finance-extractive-infrastructure nexus. In fact, following a risk assessment of US-based extractive companies, First Peoples Worldwide estimates that "about 70 percent of the global equity capital financing oil, gas, and mining comes from the Canadian exchange" (Portalewska 2015).

On the one hand, an economic plan built on extraction requires physical infrastructure. This is the context for the expansion of oil pipelines, rail, and road infrastructure. The expansion of border infrastructure is also funded by the New Building Canada Plan—to enhance the transnational circulation of commodities while constraining unwanted human mobility (Cowen 2014). There has, furthermore, been a marked increase in state surveillance of so called critical infrastructures, to protect them from indigenous peoples' contestation (Pasternak and Dafnos 2018). The Canada Infrastructure Bank is marketed to Canadians as a magical means to get desperately needed sustainable infrastructure built to enable a prosperous future. Yet, a more sober analysis sees it as a tool to privatize infrastructure and extend it deeper into Indigenous territories. In a recent analysis of the CIB, Anna Stanley (2019: 2) outlines the federal government's own explanation for the initiative, "in which it is claimed on one hand that Canada faces several medium- to long-term threats[,] including significant decline in economic per capita GDP growth, and on the other, that as a 'massive northern territory' heavily dependent on trade in energy and natural resources Canada faces a considerable 'infrastructure gap'—a gap, they note[,] which would be particularly well filled by large scale 'nation building projects.' . . . The Bank anticipates leveraging at least 140 billion dollars of private capital for new 'nation building,' 'productivity enhancing,' 'national economic development infrastructure,' . . . a significant portion of which is directed toward so-called natural resource infrastructure (NRI) and specifically prioritizes investments that move resources and energy more efficiently." Stanley (2019: 3) notes that, perhaps not surprisingly, "the Mining Association of Canada (MAC) called the 2016 announcement of the CIB 'bold,' 'essential' to the future of the mining economy in Canada, and sure to attract new investment to the sector." In fact, as Stanley notes, the Prospectors and Developers Association of Canada (PDAC) has already determined that a lack of infrastructure is holding the industry back from exploiting the mineral wealth of the north. She explains how, in order "to lower the prohibitive costs of exploration and extraction, and 'capitalize on the economic potential of remote and northern Canada,' PDAC are campaigning for construction of seven 'infrastructure development corridors' . . . linking major geologic structures to markets."

On the other hand, the creation of the "infrastructure bank" is as much about the demands of finance capital as it is about the creation of physical infrastructure. The CIB is a complicated beast that brings international finance capital into often monopoly ownership of "public" infrastructure. In order for institutional investors—private capital as well as the mammoth pension funds that Canada is also expert in—to be interested in infrastructure, there has to be opportunity for immediate and ongoing revenue. Even the large accounting organization KPMG raised cautions about the CIB in an internal report to the federal government, suggesting "that Canadians are unlikely to support some of the priorities of private infrastructure investors, such as new tolls on roads and bridges" (Curry 2017) In essence, the CIB subsidizes profit-driven financiers to take and hold monopolies over essential infrastructures and then rent their use back to the public. This scheme makes more sense when we consider that the CIB was designed by some of the world's largest investment firms, like BlackRock Inc., with their histories of predatory behavior (Grant 2016).

The initial architecture for the CIB was contracted out to an advisory council made up of leaders from the world of international finance, and the model that the government subsequently proposed for the bank "was, in all essentials, identical to this proposal" (Sanger 2017). BlackRock Inc. played a particularly prominent role in the design, even helping to craft "the briefing notes and presentation about the bank that were prepared for delivery by Trudeau and his ministers at a session for foreign investors," according to Toby Sanger (2017), who continues:

> Corporations are sitting on hundreds of billions of excess cash in Canada and trillions worldwide—money they aren't putting into productive investments. . . . So corporations are now turning to the cannibalization of public-sector assets and infrastructure through public-private partnerships or other forms of privatization, including the new infrastructure bank.

All this leads Stanley (2019: 4) to assert that the "unstated aim is to bring the aspirations of corporate capital and the settler state into functional alignment." She diagnoses the CIB as "a fundamentally colonial institution that marshals private capital to produce and extend state jurisdiction through infrastructure development and, relatedly, accelerated resource development." And indeed, critical scholars of finance capital diagnose its operations as predatory, constituting a form of capitalism that is "cannibalistic" (Soederburg 2010: 224).

The Wiindigo's Spine

Given the picture we have painted of a predatory economy rooted in extraction and exploitation, it may not be a surprise that the infrastructures that corporations and settler governments deem "critical" to the provision of life are deeply toxic (Sellers 2016). Describing what she calls "*invasive* infrastructure," Tlingit scholar Anne Spice (2018: 40) asserts that "the characterization of oil and gas pipelines as 'critical infrastructures' constitutes a form of settler colonial invasion." Spice highlights the struggles of water-and-land protectors not only to defend their territories and their sovereignty, but also to challenge mainstream discourse about what counts as vital infrastructure and for whom. Spice quotes Freda Huson, spokesperson for the Wet'suwet'en encampment that was built in the path of the pipeline, who notes that "the pipelines were proposed to run through the clan's best berry patches. By resisting pipeline construction, she explains, "what we're doing here is protecting our critical infrastructure" (40). Indeed, Huson highlights a conception of infrastructure that is essentially alimentary; infrastructure is not simply "matter that moves other matter" (40), but rather, in its anti-colonial conception, life-giving and capable of sustaining not only the body, but the spirit and law as well.

But what might be gained by engaging these toxic and invasive infrastructures not only as colonial, but as Wiindigo? It is revealing that without naming the Wiindigo as infrastructural, Fleming (2017) offers stories of infrastructure projects to illustrate the Wiindigo's ravages. To explain the Wiindigo to readers, Fleming describes the construction of dams on the Mississippi River, the flooding of reservations, the destruction of burial sites, wild rice beds, cranberry bogs, and villages. In earlier writing, Winona (LaDuke 1999) has defined the mainstream settler economy as "Wiindigo," anchoring an engagement with capitalist relations within an Anishinaabe worldview. "Wiindigo Economics" or "Cannibal, or Wasichu economics," is "an economic system that destroys the source of its wealth, Mother Earth" (LaDuke 2018). LaDuke's approach is rooted in a practice of relationality that understands human and more-than-human life as kin, as familial relations. In this way, apprehending the economy as Wiindigo offers an approach distinct from secular and humanist critiques of capitalism. Simpson (2011: 70) describes the Wiindigo as a "large monster-like creature" that embodies "imbalance and unhealthy relationships." The Wiindigo is "an Ojibwe description of the spirit of excess" (LaDuke 2018). The Wiindigo is often described as a cannibal creature—devouring its own. Thus, Winona describes Wiindigo economics as "the practice of extracting every last bit of oil just because you've got the technology to do it, ecosystems be damned" (LaDuke 2019a). Wiindigo economics—organized by an ethos of disposability and accumulation—is profoundly destructive to many people and life-forms in the present, and to planetary survival in the longer term. The Wiindigo is "the beast that's destroying our collective garden" (LaDuke 2019a) and now is its time.

Wiindigo economics creates havoc and destruction—pipeline spills, methylmercury contamination, toxic water, and so forth. But our task here is to think about the Wiindigo not just in the spill, but in the pipeline—not in the system's failure, but in its smooth operation. We consider the Wiindigo in its invasion of Indigenous territory without consent, in its deepening of our collective dependence on fossil fuel extraction, and in its extension of settler political economy. If Wiindigo economics is theft and greed, *Wiindigo infrastructures* are the material systems that engineer and sustain that violence. In other words, Wiindigo infrastructures underpin social organization and its reproduction in logics of capital, property, and accumulation over life. Wiindigo infrastructures are not only built upon the predatory foundations of finance capital, they are cannibalistic—they feed upon their kin, and through them we are "combusting ourselves to oblivion" (LaDuke 2016: 243).

Today, settler governments and corporations are creative in their methods, not only doing violence *to* Indigenous people, but also *through* Indigenous people. "At the end of the fossil fuel era," Winona (LaDuke 2019b) writes, "the plan is to transfer the liability to Native people. . . . Dressed up as 'equity positions,' or 'reconciliation,' across the continent, corporations and governments are trying to pawn off bad projects on Native people." In a strategy we see repeated over and over again, energy and transportation infrastructures are not simply imposed upon First Nations. Rather, in a context of profoundly constrained options forged by dispossession, Indigenous people are "invited' to become project proponents and owners of Wiindigo infrastructure. We have seen this with the Muskrat Falls dam, in Labrador, and are poised to see it repeated with the mining road in Ontario's Ring of Fire, where Indigenous peoples who were compelled to become project proponents not only have to live with the legacy of ecological destruction, but are now also saddled with deep divisions within and between communities. We see this in the recent attempt to offload a fifty-year-old coal-generating plant—Navajo Generating Station—onto the Navajo Nation, after BHP Billiton, the largest mining corporation in the world, dumped a fifty-year-old coal strip mine, with all sorts of environmental and health liabilities, on the tribe (*Red Nation* 2019).

The latest installment in the long-standing struggle over the Canadian tar sands and the government's and energy corporations' efforts to move the toxic product to market is to sell the Trans Mountain pipeline to Indigenous people. The Trans Mountain pipeline struggle, billed by some as the "Standing Rock of the North" (INET 2018), had been simmering for some time. Approved in 2016, Trans Mountain involves a $7.4 billion investment in a new 980 km pipeline parallel to an old, existing one, almost tripling capacity for oil companies, to up to 890,000 barrels of oil per day from the Alberta tar sands to the west coast of British Columbia. Fiercely defending the project, Prime Minister Trudeau asserted his government's jurisdiction by deeming the project "national infrastructure." Based on this logic, as Winona (LaDuke 2019b) has recently written, "It makes perfect sense that a First Nation, or coalition of First [N]ations[,] should assume Canada's debt and liability on a mega project which will wreak environmental and economic havoc."

Three competing bids to buy the pipeline have emerged from Indigenous peoples—some teamed up with energy corporations—and were warmly welcomed by a federal government scrambling to offload the liability. This direction is encouraged by a government that claims sincere commitment to reconciling relations with Indigenous people and to fighting climate change. Indigenous ownership is cultivated despite the fact that Indigenous Nations from across Turtle Island have signed the Treaty Alliance against Tar Sands Expansion, with the goal of protecting lands and waters from all proposed pipeline, tanker, and rail projects (Treaty Alliance 2016). The Secwepemc Nation is a particularly significant force in the resistance, with more than half the length of the pipeline planned to run through their unceded territory. The Secwepemc Women's Warrior Society has pledged to stop any Trans Mountain development on their lands, while the Tiny House Warriors continue to assert jurisdiction through the construction of a network of little homes along the pipeline's path. Rueben George (pers. comm., July 10, 2019), of the Tsleil-Waututh Nation, a leader in the opposition to the pipeline whose territory on the coastal waters is where the tankers will pass, calls this plan to sell the Wiidigo infrastructure to Indigenous people "a new smallpox blanket."

But another future is possible. That's the green path described by the prophets of the Anishinaabe, the path not yet worn. This is a path toward the regenerative economy, or again from Anishinaabe prophecy: the Eighth Fire. This may well be a time of massive investment and expansion of Wiindigo infrastructure, but Turtle Island is also a place with long histories of fighting the Wiindigo and winning. Fleming (2017) writes that there have been many generations of Wiindigo slayers among Anishinaabeg people: "Those old time Wiindigo slayers of the Termination era were wise and resilient. They united with other Indigenous American nations and organizations like the National Congress of American Indians. The American Indian Movement was formed at the end of this era[,] in 1968, and by the 1970s, the self-determination era began with huge numbers of Indigenous Americans enrolling in college, producing crops of Indigenous lawyers, authors, and activists." Killing the Wiindigo today is possible. Like in the past, it relies upon cooperation among people determined to survive, and it relies upon finding the Achilles heel of the current system. Infrastructure is that Achilles heel. There is inspiration in global divestment campaigns, which are moving trillions out of the fossil fuel industry in the effort to defund profiteering off of toxic pipeline infrastructures—the Black Snake of ancient Lakota prophecy, the creature that would slither across the land, poisoning the water before destroying the Earth. Winona (LaDuke 2019a) reminds us to "look to the social movements emerging as water protectors block 'Black Snakes'—that is, oil pipelines. Enbridge's Line 3 pipeline is another year behind schedule while renewable energy moves ahead." Through brutally hard work, these movements have systematically blocked every effort to expand pipeline infrastructure to get tar sands oil to sea. And the fight is ongoing.

Killing the Wiindigo: Building the Eighth Fire

Communities are increasingly and courageously choosing the green path over the well-worn, even as it is often the path of *most* resistance. Although the Navajo Nation was invited to make a deal with the Wiindigo, in the form of an offer to purchase the aging Navajo Generating Station, they rejected it, and instead built the Kayenta Solar Project. This tribally owned solar facility is the first large-scale solar farm on Navajo Nation lands and the largest tribally owned renewable power plant in the United States. It is said to produce enough power to serve 18,000 Navajo homes—many of which did not have electricity previously. This bold path follows almost a century of colonial energy and mining projects on their lands that left the Navajo people with an unemployment rate above 50 percent, and a median income of US$7,500 per year. In the 1920s, on the promise that uranium, oil, gas, and coal leases would bring in millions in royalty revenues and create thousands of jobs for the community, the Navajo Nation's first Tribal Council signed agreements with energy companies. In the 1970s, the Navajo Nation provided enough energy to fuel the state of New Mexico thirty-two times over, yet 85 percent of the Navajo households had no electricity. Today, Navajo people live in the shadows of massive utilities infrastructures that service power companies and settler cities, as most live without power and clean water.

This long history makes the visionary work of the Navajo Nation in economic and infrastructural transition all the more impressive. In 2009, the Navajo Tribal Council passed the first green economy legislation of any tribal government, creating a Green Economy Fund and Commission. Even earlier, in 2001, young people from across Navajo and Hopi communities created the Black Mesa Water Coalition (BMWC) to address environmental justice and health issues within their communities. "It's not only about transitioning our utility," Nicole Alex of BMWC explains, "but also, how are we going to transition this society that has been impacted, and how are we going to transition this economy that has been devastated by energy development?" Indeed, the BMWC espouses an approach to infrastructure rooted in decolonization and environmental justice and captured in the slogan, "power without pollution and energy without injustice" (Chorus Foundation 2016). While the process has not been smooth or simple, and Navajo scholar Andrew Curley (2018) has offered a deeply critical engagement with early initiatives toward the green economy, the transition toward renewable energy is clearly underway. The Navajo Nation has enough energy from solar to power not only their own reservation, but much of the Southwest, and with efficiency and transition, the power lines that used to move coal-generated electricity can move renewable energy onto the grid.

On the White Earth reservation in northern Minnesota, Honor the Earth, a national Native organization, is also building beyond Wiindigo infrastructure. At White Earth, which holds one of the poorest counties in the state, and where a quarter of tribal income is spent on energy, a series of initiatives are underway to address energy justice through remaking infrastructure. The community manufacturing venture Eighth Fire Solar quite literally embodies Anishinaabe prophecy of a possible future beyond colonial destruction, investing not only in renewable energy retrofits but also in the production of infrastructure itself. The facility's name reflects the choice between the well-worn, scorched path of the status quo and one that is green and unworn. The Eighth Fire will be lit when the green path is chosen and a better future is formed. The facility manufactures solar photovoltaic panels that can be mounted on the south side of homes to reduce heating costs by about 20 percent. This work on renewable energy is one part of Honor the Earth's larger vision for the next economy, which involves food sovereignty and a new textiles economy rooted in industrial hemp production.

Fiber hemp farming has become a cornerstone of work on White Earth over the last few years because of its multiple benefits and multiplier effects. Hemp has three times the tensile strength of cotton and uses a fraction of the water and chemicals associated with other textiles. Cannabis cultivation was once common on the continent before being deliberately suppressed by settler governments—this long history of use is captured in the very word "canvas," which derives from "cannabis." Minnesota used to have eleven hemp mills, providing most of the clothing, canvas, and rope needs of the region, as well as combined hemp with flax for linen. A local textile economy is possible; the hemp renaissance is here. Winona's Hemp and the Anishinaabe Agriculture Institute are working regionally on restoring hemp as a part of an integrated sustainable economy. In North America, many First Nations see hemp as a part of an integrated sustainable economy. "We want to be at the table, not on the menu," is a mantra of Winona's Hemp, in the restoration of tribal hemp economies. All of this requires infrastructure; in this case, manufacturing infrastructure and the infrastructure to move these products to market.

North of the Medicine Line, in the heartland of the Wiindigo energy industry, Alberta First Nations are also becoming leaders in solar power, and through that, becoming energy independent. At Lubicon Lake, Beaver Lake Cree Nation, Louis Bull Tribe, Fort McKay, and countless other communities, Indigenous people are making the transition to renewable infrastructure as part of assertions of self-determination. In Manitoba, Fisher River Cree Nation is building a seven-acre solar farm, constructed entirely by Indigenous workers. This massive shift to green infrastructure across Indian country is taking shape in a context where the vast majority of remote Indigenous communities in Canada—more than 80 percent of the three hundred communities—are already reliant on micro-generation of electricity (Lovekin 2017), but with micro-grids that are frequently supplied by costly, dirty, unreliable, and insecure diesel generators that depend on transporting fuel and equipment long distances via semipermanent infrastructure like ice roads (Weis and Illinca 2010). The shift to renewables is not only about the physical toxicity of the diesel generators, but also centrally about the colonial dependencies they sustain.

To be clear, fossil fuel economies shackle First Nations to the vagaries of international markets and politics, an endless source of economic and social stress. Enlightened vision for the future and energy security necessitates the creation of local renewable energy and massive efficiency. As Robert Stefanelli et al. (2019: 95) report, many Indigenous peoples "are developing renewable energy in their Territories to: break free of colonial ties, move towards energy autonomy, establish more reliable energy systems, and reap the long-term financial benefits that clean energy can provide." The motivation for this transition is at once ecological and social—it stems from "political self-determination resulting from a desired independence from colonial institutions such as the Department of Crown Indigenous Relations and Northern Affairs and the Department of Indigenous Services" (101). Adrian A. Smith and Dayna Nadine Scott (forthcoming) raise important questions about the sourcing of rare earth minerals for the manufacture of photovoltaics, and about proprietary legal arrangements surrounding these kinds of large-scale renewable energy projects that can reproduce rather than elide capitalist logics. Nevertheless, they argue that "the involvement of First Nations in the ownership and control of large-scale renewable energy projects, as well as the emergence of community-based energy cooperatives, holds out the promise of 'democratization' of energy generation, distribution and governance." Energy independence is a key means of asserting autonomy from the state and industry so that community priorities can guide decision-making (Stefanelli et al. 2019; Rezaei and Dowlatabadia 2016). Mi'kmaw renewable energy specialist David Isaac has been helping Indigenous communities to transform their power supply for the last twenty years. Isaac worked with Fisher River on their solar farm and sees this kind of infrastructure as a model for First Nations across the country, but also for sustainable community development more broadly. "The community of the future," Isaac suggests, "is going to be like an Indigenous community, in the sense that hyper-localized power will be generated [by] decentralized utilities from a harmonic source of energy instead of extractive" (Monkman 2019).

Indigenous communities are also reassembling infrastructure to address the chronic problems of food security that plague northern and remote communities, and which concentrate myriad health challenges, from hunger and malnutrition to diabetes. A number of communities are investing in agricultural infrastructure to grow vegetables and fruits and raise chickens, in order to expand food sovereignty. Garden Hill First Nation—a fly-in community 600 km north of Winnipeg—has been building a pathbreaking food security project. The Meechim Farm includes a food market, vegetable farm, chicken coops, and agricultural training and education programs for young people. They call their educational initiatives for youth "school-to-farm" in a direct critique and reworking of the notorious "school-to-prison pipeline" that circulates especially Black and Indigenous people between educational and carceral infrastructures. The infrastructure question for the Meechim Farm is not simply metaphorical—it has been a central challenge for cultivating food and food security in remote communities and it has also been key to their innovative approach. In a discussion of the Garden Hill Initiative, Shirley Thompson (n.d.) explains that "the lack of infrastructure for food systems contributes to food insecurity and poverty in many remote areas world-wide." Thompson explains the "farm-in-a-box" approach that Garden Hill has taken to building infrastructure and capacity, where a shipping container "is loaded with materials to start a farm homestead, with the container serving as the building skeleton for the greenhouse and chicken brooder as well as the storage for farm equipment." In Garden Hill, infrastructure underpins the transformation of the food system.

Seven hundred kilometers north of Thunder Bay, in Ontario's far north, the Oji-Cree community of Kitchenuhmaykoosib Inninuwug (KI) is taking charge of the complex logistics systems that bring them outrageously priced food, often past the "best before" date. Food and medical supplies are notoriously expensive and in short supply in the community, as they are often loaded on a series of flights that take days to arrive from the south. The leadership has implemented price caps on the three retailers that service the thousand community members, while also taking charge of distribution systems—collectivizing and reorganizing them. In partnership with Lac Seul First Nation, KI created a regional distribution center at the Sioux Lookout airport—an en route stop for flights to the community. The twenty-thousand-square-foot hangar stores and dispatches food, bulk medical and education supplies, and other basic necessities. The strategy—to put people and kin before profits—is unusual to say the least in an era of globalized, advanced capitalist logistics (Cowen 2014). Saving cost as well as emissions, the initiative will fill unused cargo space on planes destined for KI. As Indigenous peoples restore seeds, more food grows. We restore our genetic ties to our ancestral foods and become stronger. As Elizabeth Hoover and Rowen White (2019: 333–34) write in the *New Farmer's Almanac,*

Across Turtle Island, there is a growing intergenerational movement of Indigenous people proud to carry the message of the grand rematriation of seeds and foods back into our Indigenous communities. Some of these seeds have been missing from our communities for centuries, carried on long journeys in smoky buckskin pouches, on the necks of peoples who were forced to relocate from the land of their births, their ancestral grounds. Generations later, these seeds are now coming back home to communities of origin, from the vaults of public institutions, seed banks, universities, seed keeper collections, and some lying on dusty pantry shelves of foresighted elders, seeds patiently sleeping and dreaming. Seeds waiting for loving hands to patiently place them into welcoming soil once more so that they can continue to fulfill their original agreement to help feed the people. . . . In the seed movement, we have begun to use the word *rematriation,* instead of the more patriarchal *repatriation,* as it relates to bringing these seeds home again. In many communities, including our Mohawk tradition, the responsibility of caring for the seeds over the generations is ultimately within the women's realm. Both men and women farm and plant seeds, but their care and stewardship are part of the women's bundle of responsibility. So the word *rematriation* reflects the restoration of the feminine seeds back into the communities of origin. The Indigenous concept of rematriation can also encompass the reclaiming of ancestral remains, spirituality, culture, knowledge, and resources. It simply means back to Mother Earth, a return to our origins, to life and cocreation, honoring the life-giving force of the Divine Feminine.

Solutionary Rail

Alimentary infrastructure changes the world. The time to deconstruct the fossil fuels rail system is now, and to the extent that the railroads are the emblem and system of widespread destruction of Indigenous lands, buffalo, and a way of life, they can also be transformative. Technology can be appropriated and infrastructure remade. Trains are efficient; metal on metal creates less friction than rubber on the road. Trains move lots of loads and should move safe stuff. We could harness the power and possibilities of rail to transform the economy. Worldwide, electricity serves nearly a quarter of railroad track miles and supplies over one-third of the energy that powers trains. Forty-one percent of China's rail lines are electrified; in Italy it is 68 percent. But in the US and Canada, less than 1 percent of tracks are electrified. There is no time like the present to change that. In terms of diesel engines, 30–35 percent of the energy in the fuel makes it to the wheels. Supplying electricity directly from an overhead power line means 95 percent of the electricity taken from the power grid is employed by the wheels. No more than 5 percent is lost through the engine transformer and overhead wires. That saves money and energy, and that's smart.

A group south of the Medicine Line has developed a plan called "Solutionary Rail," which proposes a new, green, and potentially decolonized "spine" for the USA. Behind this initiative is an organization literally called the *Backbone Campaign* (backbonecampaign.org), and its members see their work as directly addressing environmental justice through infrastructure. They frame their approach to electrifying American rail networks as part of a paradigm shift. For the Backbone Campaign, "One paradigm idolizes capital, gives corporations rights, and considers everything For Sale. It commodifies people, democracy, communities, and the planet itself. The paradigm we fight for is one in which people communities and nature and our obligation to future generations are considered sacred, and clearly NOT for sale."

Railroads are a unifying system, and railroads can lead a transition to a clean economy. "Unlike other heavy, long-haul transportation vehicles such as ships, planes, and semitrucks," the Backbone Campaign report notes, "trains can be easily electrified, and electricity is increasingly coming from clean sources such as sun and wind. Rail is already the most efficient form of ground transportation, and it has an unparalleled capacity to provide clean freight and passenger mobility" (Moyer and Maza 2016). The Solutionary Rail plan includes provisions for track modernization and is particularly committed to urban sustainability. This would be achieved in part through a proposal to put renewable energy transmission access along the same power lines as the electric rail would use for its own power. Renewable energy, coming out of windy prairies, is stranded power right now; we need to get it on the grid. Solutionary Rail would thus also revolutionize other modes of transportation—for instance, making it possible to have zero emission maritime ports. This is again an issue of environmental justice, as it is most often lower-income communities of color that are located adjacent to ports, where dramatically elevated levels of asthma in children have been documented (Perez et al. 2009). The Solutionary Rail plan also includes provisions for what they call "right-of-way justice" for Indigenous people, with a commitment to renegotiate easements where there are outstanding grievances and claims.

Communities and movements are building physical systems for a future beyond Wiindigo infrastructure in the areas of energy, transportation, and food sovereignty, but they are also rebuilding social infrastructures, to help heal people trying to survive racism and colonialism. Initiatives are underway across Turtle Island to remake the intimate and affective infrastructures of everyday life, to cultivate social beings and relations that can usher in the Eighth Fire. Leanne Simpson highlights the necessity of this work on ourselves, and the reorientation of desire away from the violent accumulation and reckless consumption of Wiindigo worlds. Simpson (2016) writes:

> without the weight of large gaping holes in their beings, people would no longer be willing to pay for disconnection. with nothing to feed, the entire system would fall apart. so while that other one was out carousing, protesting, or pontificating to anyone who would listen, gezhizhwazh was at work as a bami ondaadiziike, circling around those birthing women to protect that ceremony. foiling those interventions, protecting the circle. for now, her battle with the wiindigo was in its resurgence stage. gezhizhwazh was building an army—a diffuse, scattered group of souls that could see through the wiindigo illusion, because they were whole.

No doubt, physical and affective infrastructures are often one and the same, and this is part of our point. Renewable Energy, efficiency, and local food systems entail healthy and reaffirming social organization and relations—the material and spiritual worlds cannot be segregated when "the economy" is *how we live*. We need a renaissance. This renaissance of thinking and this society will not be financed like the last one, by slavery, hyper-exploitation, and the pillaging of the western hemisphere and Africa; it will be financed by the divestment from fossil fuels, and by forcing corporations to pay for their mess, before they go bankrupt.

We are inspired by so many initiatives to rebuild social infrastructure—especially within Black, Indigenous, migrant, Two Spirit, queer, and feminist worlds, but one example worth highlighting is the Radical Monarchs. This multiracial initiative aims to "create opportunities for young girls of color to form fierce sisterhood, celebrate their identities, and contribute radically to their communities." The group was founded in Oakland, California, in 2014, by two moms who wanted to create an affirming and empowering space for their daughters and other young girls of color, explicitly welcoming trans girls into the fold. Anayvette Martinez and Marilyn Hollinquest envisioned the group as a radical alternative to the scout movement, itself born directly out of imperialism with the goal of instilling military discipline in young boys (see Cowen 2008). Like Simpson, Martinez and Hollinquest understood the importance of spiritual and mental well-being as a foundation for social transformation and decolonization. In fact, the Radical Monarchs (radicalmonarchs.org) work to create a space for girls, "so that they stay rooted in their collective power, brilliance, and leadership in order to make the world a more radical place." The initiative looks forward to cultivating a future of powerful women's leadership in communities of color, but it also honors courageous leaders and initiatives from the past; for example, incorporating the beret of the Black Panther movement into its uniform. Like in the Girl Scouts, Radical Monarchs can earn badges for completing particular kinds of learning and skills training, but unlike in the Scouts, their badges are awarded for units on topics such as "LBGTQ allyship, environmental activism and disability justice." The monarch butterfly is furthermore an inspiring creature in this meditation on moving beyond Wiindigo infrastructure. The monarch is not only expert in full system transformation, but also builds its own infrastructure for the transition from one life form to another. Like others of their species, monarchs create the chrysalis that holds them as they pupate from caterpillar to butterfly. And the cells that cause that transformation are called the imago cells; they are transformative cells. The word *imago* shares the same root as the word *imagination*. What might we learn from monarchs about metamorphosis through autonomous infrastructure?

Infrastructure Otherwise: Building beyond Wiindigo

As we wrap up our writing in the summer of 2019, an extraordinary coalition of social and labor movements, including Black Lives Matter Oklahoma City, the Women's March OK, and the International Union of Painters and Allied Trades, come together behind the leadership of the Indigenous Environmental Network in fighting Wiindigo infrastructure (Falcon 2019). This time, it is not a pipeline or dam that is at the center of struggle, but a migrant detention camp expansion and the deepening violence of US carceral and border infrastructure. Indigenous protectors who converged on Fort Sill—a planned migrant camp—announced the success of their efforts: "Fort Sill will not be reopened as a concentration camp for our relatives trying to cross the so-called 'border'" (Falcon 2019). Across the United States, Indigenous people's movements are connecting the dots between the long histories of colonial dispossession and containment on Turtle Island, and President Donald Trump's current experimentation with concentration camps and family separations. At another major action in McAllen, Texas, Native Americans traveled from across the country to protest and call for the immediate end to these camps of loss and anguish. Oglala Lakota and Chicano journalist Simon Moya-Smith (2019) highlights "the same racism with a different name in a different century, and many of the descendants of the very same people brutalized by Columbus and those who followed in his footsteps locked in new chains."

Thinking with struggles like these against the carceral border regime, and with others that implicitly or explicitly center socio-technical systems, we have offered a way to diagnose the contemporary crisis as not only colonial and capitalist but as *infrastructural*. We have outlined how the expansion and reproduction of settler colonial systems of value are literally, physically, enabled by infrastructure. We have furthermore tried to suggest that it is not only the technical or physical aspects of coloniality that rely on infrastructure—feelings, ideas, and attitudes that produce racism and white supremacy are also material systems of social reproduction that sanction the extension of the means of life to some, often through their withdrawal from others. "Social infrastructures" like the police protect the operations of coloniality, causing premature death. As Ruthie Wilson Gilmore (2007: 60–66) has elaborated, white supremacy is both an "infrastructure of feeling" that organizes affect and identification, and is itself *infrastructured* through access to clean water, mobility, shelter, and "protection" from those whose premature death is the condition of possibility for settler futurity. Indeed, Gilmore aptly describes the mass infrastructural abandonment of Black and poor people across the US, and we could say the same for remote Indigenous communities.

Finally, we have anchored our engagement with Infrastructure in Indigenous story and prophecy that diagnose the contemporary crisis as spiritual as well as material. More specifically, the Anishinaabe story of the Wiindigo helps us to see a path forward. Despite its ferocity, the Wiindigo can still be killed. The Diné, or Navajo, talk about needing a new generation of monster slayers—that's this generation. The Wiindigo cannot claim a monopoly on infrastructure. Socio-technical systems are not inherently good or evil; pipelines can carry fresh water as well as toxicity. Infrastructure is how sociality extends itself; it is how life is provisioned or curtailed. In its most immediately material and graspable forms, infrastructure underpins and enacts sustenance and reproduction. Building it beyond Wiindigo, building alimentary infrastructure, is the slow, transformative feminist work of social re/production. It is the return of life forces. "They tried to bury us, they didn't know we were seeds."[3]

Notes

For his inspiration, we dedicate this writing to the late Randy Kapeshesit. We remember you . . . and continue the path you outlined for us.

1   Winona LaDuke, Anishinaabe writer and economist, loves and works on the White Earth reservation, and is the executive director for Honor the Earth. Deborah Cowen is a geographer at the University of Toronto, a settler on the lands subject to the Dish with One Spoon Wampum, and deeply committed to the transformative potential of infrastructure.

2   All figures are in Canadian dollars unless otherwise noted.

3   Widely cited as a Mexican proverb because of its frequent use by the Zapatistas and then in response to the loss of the Ayotzinapa 43, this verse has since been traced to the Greek poet Dinos Christianopoulos and the text "ΜΙΚΡΑ ΠΟΙΗΜΑΤΑ—Τὸ Κορμὶ καὶ τὸ Σαράκι."

References

Barker, Joanne. 2018. "Territory as Analytic: The Dispossession of Lenapehoking and the Subprime Crisis." *Social Text*, no. 135: 19–39.

Blewett, Taylor 2019 "United We Roll Protest Convoy Set to Reach Parliament Hill on Tuesday." *Ottawa Citizen*, February 19. ottawacitizen.com/news/local-news/united-we-roll -protest-convoy-set-to-reach-parliament-hill-on-tuesday.

Brake, Justin. 2019. "Indigenous Rights Activists Confront Yellow Vests as Pro-pipeline Convoy Reaches Ottawa." APTN National News, February 19. aptnnews.ca/2019/02/19 /indigenous-rights-activists-confront-yellow-vests-as-pro-pipeline-convoy-reaches -ottawa/.

Chorus Foundation. 2016. "Claiming Power: Stopping Coal and Going Green at Black Mesa." Medium, July 8. medium.com/chorus-foundation/claiming-power-stopping-coal-and- going-green-at-black-mesa-4936a21d6c59.

Corbella, Licia. 2019. "United We Roll Convoy a Beautiful Sight as It Heads to Ottawa." *Calgary Herald*, February 14. calgaryherald.com/news/local-news/corbella-united-we-roll -convoy-a-beautiful-sight-as-it-heads-to-ottawa.

Coulthard, Glen. 2014. *Red Skin, White Masks: Rejecting the Colonial Politics of Recognition*. Minneapolis: University of Minnesota Press.

Cowen, Deborah. 2008. *Military Workfare: The Soldier and Social Citizenship in Canada*. Toronto: University of Toronto Press.

Cowen, Deborah. 2014. *The Deadly Life of Logistics: Mapping Violence in Global Trade*. Minneapolis: University of Minnesota Press.

Cowen, Deborah. 2018. "The Jurisdiction of Infrastructure: Circulation and Canadian Settler Colonialism." *Funambulist*, no. 17: 14–19.

Cowen, Deborah. Forthcoming. "Following the Infrastructures of Empire: Notes on Cities, Settler Colonialism, and Method." *Urban Geography*.

Curley, Andrew. 2018. "A Failed Green Future: Navajo Green Jobs and Energy 'Transition' in the Navajo Nation." *Geoforum* 88: 57–65.

Curry, Bill. 2017. "Infrastructure Bank Risks Slowing Down Projects, Internal Report." *Globe and Mail*, May 11. theglobeandmail.com/news/politics/be-extremely-careful-in-launching -infrastructure-bank-internal-report-warns-ottawa/article34952796/.

Daschuk, James. 2013. "When Canada Used Hunger to Clear the West." *Globe and Mail,* July 19. www.theglobeandmail.com/opinion/when-canada-used-hunger-to-clear-the-west /article13316877/.

Estes, Nick. 2019. "'Freedom Is a Place': Long Traditions of Anti-Colonial Resistance in Turtle Island." *Funambulist,* no. 20. thefunambulist.net/articles/freedom-place-long-traditions -anti-colonial-resistance-turtle-island-nick-estes.

Falcon, Jennifer K. 2019. "Victory." Indigenous Environmental Network. www.mynewsletter builder.com/email/newsletter/1414050934?fbclid=IwAR0FHF4AjAnbrfD377WWK w7hCEZnNegSk9kyxqNeEWyAAXbfToFhHjUBUTI.

Fleming, Bezhigobinesikwe Elaine. 2017. "Nanaboozhoo and the Wiindigo: An Ojibwe History from Colonization to the Present." *Journal of American Indian Higher Education* 28, no. 3. tribalcollegejournal.org/nanaboozhoo-wiindigo-ojibwe-history-colonization -present/.

Foster, Cecil. 2019. *They Call Me George: The Untold Story of Black Train Porters and the Birth of Modern Canada.* Windsor, ON: Biblioasis.

Gilmore, Ruth Wilson. 2007. *Golden Gulag: Prisons, Surplus, Crisis, and Opposition in Globalizing California.* Berkeley: University of California Press.

Grant, Jason. 2016. "BlackRock Accused of 'Predatory Lending' in Suit Over $844K Late Fee." *New York Law Journal,* August 15. www.law.com/newyorklawjournal/almID/1202765090000 /BlackRock-Accused-of-Predatory-Lending-in-Suit-Over-844K-Late-Fee/.

Hoover, Elizabeth, and Rowen White. 2019. "Our Living Relatives: Maintaining Resilience and Seed Diversity in Native American Communities." In *The New Farmer's Almanac,* vol. 4, Greenhorns. White River Junction, VT: Chelsea Green.

Ibbitson, John. 2017. "Trudeau's Foreign Policy vs. Harper's: There Is Little Difference." April 14. theglobeandmail.com/news/politics/trudeau-taking-foreign-policy-cue-from-tory -playbook/article34241539/.

INET (Indigenous Network on Economies and Trade). 2018. "Standing Rock of the North: An Updated Summary Risk Assessment of the Trans Mountain Pipeline Expansion." April 13. docs.wixstatic.com/ugd/934d11_4666c5875ffa4a0daf1281474788109d.pdf.

Karuka, Manu. 2019. *Empire's Tracks: Indigenous Nations, Chinese Workers, and the Transcontinental Railway.* Berkeley: University of California Press.

LaDuke, Winona. 1999. *All Our Relations: Indigenous Struggles for Land and Life.* Cambridge, MA: South End.

LaDuke, Winona. 2016. *Recovering the Sacred: The Power of Naming and Claiming.* Cambridge, MA: South End.

LaDuke, Winona. 2018. "Winona LaDuke Calls for Indigenous-Led 'Green New Deal' as She Fights Minnesota Pipeline Expansion." *Democracy Now!,* December 7. www.democracy now.org/2018/12/7/winona_laduke_calls_for_indigenous_led.

LaDuke, Winona. 2019a. "How to Build the Zero-Carbon Economy." *In These Times,* April 22. inthesetimes.com/features/green-new-deal-zero-carbon-economy-plan.html.

LaDuke, Winona. 2019b. "Reconciliation Pipeline: How to Shackle Native People." *APTN National News,* July 13. aptnnews.ca/2019/07/13/reconciliation-pipeline-how-to-shackle -native-people/.

Lovekin, Dave. 2017. "Unlocking Clean Energy for Indigenous Communities." Pembina Institute blog, February 24. www.pembina.org/blog/unlocking-clean-energy-opportunities -indigenous-communities.

Martin-McGuire, Peggy. 1998. *First Nation Land Surrenders on the Prairies, 1896–1911*. Monograph prepared for the Indian Claims Commission. publications.gc.ca/site/eng/9.833886/publication.html.

Michelin, Lana. 2018. "Is Racism Becoming More Overt Lately in Red Deer?" *Red Deer Advocate*, June 28. www.reddeeradvocate.com/news/is-racism-becoming-more-overt-lately-in-red-deer/.

Monkman, Lenard. 2019. "Manitoba's New 'Utility Scale' Solar Farm Aims to Spark First Nations Interest in Green Energy." CBC News, June 20. www.cbc.ca/news/indigenous/fisher-river-cree-nation-solar-power-1.5180646.

Moya-Smith, Simon. 2019. "Trump's Immigration Policy Is Caging Indigenous Children. This Is the America Native People Know." NBC News, July 28. www.nbcnews.com/think/opinion/trump-s-immigration-policy-caging-indigenous-children-america-native-people-ncna1035451?fbclid=IwAR1cpUHeWbBM5VgfR3WgvK7mIOC6znKOTh-Kk88C9tpWkIUvgxzh6Ybp6Wc.

Manning, Preston. 2018. "To Build Pipelines, We Must Create Coalition Corridors." *Globe and Mail*, December 16. theglobeandmail.com/opinion/article-to-build-pipelines-we-must-create-coalition-corridors/.

Moyer, Bill, and Patrick Mazza. 2016. Solutionary Rail. Backbone Campaign.

O'Brien, Sharon. 1984. "The Medicine Line: A Border Dividing Tribal Sovereignty, Economies, and Families." *Fordham Law Review* 53, no. 2: 315–50.

Pasternak, Shiri, and Tia Dafnos. 2018. "How Does a Settler State Secure the Circuitry of Capital?" *Environment and Planning D: Society and Space* 36, no. 4: 739–57.

Perez, Laura, N. Künzli, E. Avol, A. M. Hricko, F. Lurmann, E. Nicholas, F. Gilliland, J. Peters, and R. McConnell. 2009. "Global Goods Movement and the Local Burden of Childhood Asthma in Southern California." Supplement, *American Journal of Public Health* 99, no. S3: S622–28.

Portalewska, Anna. 2015. "How We Make Progress, How We Have Change: Rebecca Adamson." *Cultural Survival Quarterly* 39, no. 1. www.culturalsurvival.org/publications/cultural-survival-quarterly/how-we-make-progress-how-we-have-change-rebecca-adamson.

Red Nation. 2019. "Unplug Navajo Generating Station, Demand Diné Liberation." January 6. therednation.org/2019/01/06/unplug-navajo-generating-station-demand-dine-liberation/.

Rezaei, Maryam, and Dowlatabadi, Hadi. 2016. "Off-Grid: Community Energy and the Pursuit of Self-Sufficiency in British Columbia's Remote and First Nations Communities." *Local Environments* 21, no. 7: 789–807.

Sanger, Toby. 2017. "The Canada Infrastructure Bank and the Perversities of Predatory Capital." *Canadian Dimension* 51, no. 3. canadiandimension.com/articles/view/the-canada-infrastructure-bank-and-the-perversities-of-predatory-capital.

Sellers, Chris. 2016. "Piping as Poison: The Flint Water Crisis and America's Toxic Infrastructure." *Conversation*, January 25. theconversation.com/piping-as-poison-the-flint-water-crisis-and-americas-toxic-infrastructure-53473.

Simpson, Audra. 2014. *Mohawk Interruptus: Political Life across the Borders of Settler States*. Durham, NC: Duke University Press.

Simpson, Leanne Betasamosake. 2011. *Dancing on Our Turtle's Back: Stories of Nishnaabeg Re-creation, Resurgence, and a New Emergence*. Winnipeg: ARP Books.

Simpson, Leanne Betasamosake. 2014. "Land as Pedagogy: Nishnaabeg Intelligence and Rebellious Transformation." *Decolonization: Indigeneity, Education, and Society* 3, no. 3: 1–25

Simpson, Leanne Betasamosake. 2016. "gezhizhwazh." *Fantasy Magazine,* no. 60. www.fantasy -magazine.com/new/new-fiction/gezhizhwazh/.

Smith, Adrian A., and Dayna Nadine Scott. Forthcoming. "'Energy without Injustice'? Indigenous Ownership of Renewable Energy Generation." In *Environmental Justice, Sustainable Development, and the Social Pillar,* edited by Sumudu Atapattu, Carmen Gonzalez, and Sara Seck. Cambridge: Cambridge University Press.

Soederburg, Susanne. 2010. "Cannibalistic Capitalism: The Paradoxes of Neoliberal Pension Securitization." In *Socialist Register 2011: The Crisis This Time,* edited by Leo Panitch, Greg Albo, and Vivek Chibber, 224–41. London: Merlin.

Spice, Anne. 2018. "Fighting Invasive Infrastructures: Indigenous Relations against Pipelines." *Environment and Society: Advances in Research* 9, no. 1: 40–56.

Stanley, Anna. 2019. "Aligning against Indigenous Jurisdiction: Worker Savings, Colonial Capital, and the Canada Infrastructure Bank." *Environment and Planning D: Society and Space.* doi.org/10.1177/0263775819855404.

Stefanelli, Robert D., et al. 2019. "Renewable Energy and Energy Autonomy: How Indigenous Peoples in Canada Are Shaping an Energy Future." *Environmental Reviews* 27, no. 1: 95–105.

Thompson, Shirley. n.d. "Growing a Farm in a Fly-In First Nation Community Using Shipping Containers for Building Infrastructure and Capacity." umanitoba.ca/faculties /engineering/departments/ce2p2e/alternative_village/media/16th_NOCMAT_2015 _submission_112.pdf.

Treaty Alliance. 2016. Treaty Alliance against Tar Sands Expansion. www.treatyalliance.org.

Dayna Nadine Scott

Extraction Contracting:
The Struggle for Control of Indigenous Lands

What constitutes "consent" to extraction in the contemporary moment? How do we know when it has been freely given? How does it manifest in the world? Prime Minister Justin Trudeau, when defending his government's support of the controversial Trans Mountain Pipeline Expansion project over the past year, has often included reference to the fact that more than forty First Nations along the proposed route have signed "mutual benefit agreements" with the company. In the context of increasingly contested and politicized resource extraction projects, and of reinvigorated and revitalized Indigenous legal orders, what should we make of the negotiation of private contractual agreements now routinely offered up as evidence of consent?

In this essay, I consider the dynamics of "consent by contract," or what others have called "negotiated justice" (Szablowski 2010; Dezalay 1994), in the extractive sector by thinking through what the specific mechanism of contract accomplishes for the parties, and what governing by contract means for the interests of so-called non-parties. The "contractual turn" of the past two decades has been documented extensively in many contexts (see, for example, Affolder 2012; Gaathi

The South Atlantic Quarterly 119:2, April 2020
DOI 10.1215/00382876-8177759   © 2020 Duke University Press

and Odumosu-Ayanu 2015; Zumbansen 2017), but here I focus on the rise of agreement-making between companies in the extractive sector and Indigenous communities in Canada. These agreements now come in the form of not only "mutual benefit agreements," but also commonly "impact benefit agreements" (IBAs) and "relationship agreements." Here, I build on the critical scholarship examining these contracts by investigating whether there is any significance to the specific *form* in which the parties' expectations are expressed. What does it mean to govern extraction through contract?

The primary literature I draw on is contract law scholarship, including writing about contracts by legal scholars going back several decades to the critical legal studies movement, relational contract scholarship, and the more recent writing examining the contractual turn in private transnational governance (see Cutler and Dietz 2017). I hope to advance understandings of IBAs by applying insights from these fields to a debate that has thus far been dominated by critical geographers and political economists. The interventions of critical geographers and political economists have generated crucial questions about representation, power, jurisdiction, and the interpellations between private and public that IBAs bring to the fore. There is also an important body of interdisciplinary scholarship investigating the social, political, and economic contexts in which the contracts are negotiated, and their consequences, with significant contributions by socio-legal scholar David Szablowski (in the Latin American context) and public administration scholar Ciaran O'Faircheallaigh (in the settler colonies of Australia and Canada). Finally, there have been recent interventions by socio-legal scholars and practitioners examining the interplay between IBAs and settler law in relation to environmental protection, Aboriginal rights, and Indigenous law (see, for example, Graben, Cameron, and Morales 2019; Robertson 2016; Kamphuis 2017; McLean, forthcoming).

In terms of methodology, my reading of these literatures has been supplemented by a small number of key informant interviews with leading lawyers and consultants with extensive experience negotiating IBAs on behalf of First Nations in Canada.[1] I also rely on the close reading of a few recent legal cases that have skirted around the margins of the deal-making dynamics, as well as on documents disclosed through litigation or obtained through access to information requests in the context of contested extraction approvals affecting Indigenous lands.[2]

Several points are immediately obvious upon applying the insights of the contract law scholarship. First, and most basically, is that the form in which the parties' expectations and obligations are expressed determines, at least formally, the remedies that will be available upon breach. Using contracts to govern extraction means that the "remedies" the parties can count on when things go awry will be, for the most part, limited to contract remedies as defined by the settler state's common law. It goes without saying that under this regime, non-parties have no remedies. Further, the remedies available upon breach are understood to determine how the parties approach whether they will decide to breach the agreement, or continue to invest in compliance. But in fact, what we observe on the ground is that the formal contract law remedies matter very little to the parties to IBAs, and are almost never invoked. Further, one of the so-called non-parties to these agreements, the settler state, is not only tangentially involved in the negotiations, it basically sets the terms.

Second, the "contract realists" in the critical legal studies movement observed that employing contract as the form of expressing the parties' expectations has benefits for the parties with the most entrenched wealth. In other words, these scholars would have predicted that companies in the extractive sector stand to gain more from this contractual turn than the contracting Indigenous communities do. This makes sense, since the extractive companies tend to be repeat players and as such become the "architects" of the agreements in the sense that they set the rules, draft the prototypes, and shape the precedents, or at least their lawyers do (Affolder 2012: 448). In a contractual regime, where the parties are "free to choose whatever procedural rules and substantive laws they consider most suitable to govern" their relations (Cutler and Dietz 2017: 4), those rules and laws would be expected to favor the companies. On the other hand, the contracting Indigenous communities may be right to judge that their position under the contractual regime is stronger than it is under the current public law regime provided by settler legislative frameworks and associated jurisprudence.

It would be tempting to argue, then, that the turn to contracts is primarily a mode of risk mitigation employed by both parties to further their own economic interests in a context of pervasive uncertainty or inadequacy in the public law framework. This is indeed how the bulk of the scholarship has approached the interpenetration of the public and private in terms of IBAs—that the contracts are "filling the gaps" of an inadequate regulatory regime and constitutional jurisprudence (see, for example, McLean, forthcoming; Fidler and Hitch 2009). On this understanding, while the use of contract benefits the companies more, reliance on the agreements can mitigate the risk of large losses for both parties. The companies avoid a high-profile, reputation-harming dispute that lands them in court facing delays, and the communities avoid being saddled with the adverse impacts of a project from which they derive no benefits whatsoever. The contracts allow a hedging of bets, then, whereby the worst-case scenario is avoided for both parties, on a case-by-case basis. The First Nation parties may also be able to secure "enhanced environmental protection measures," beyond what is required through settler state law (Robertson 2016), but the prospects for Indigenous communities, collectively, to regain meaningful control and jurisdiction over extraction on their territories in the long term are undermined.

I will argue that this conception paints the state into too passive a role, however. Who are the real parties to these contracts? The evidence reviewed here demonstrates clearly that the state is an active participant in shaping the contractual outcomes. The contemporary practices of extraction contracting in fact conceal a multitude of trade-offs that are incurred as interests and values typically considered part of the public law sphere are moved into the private sphere through the deployment of contract (Affolder 2017). In other words, it is not the contractual form itself that entrenches private authority, but the way that state actors are holding space for these relations to do the governing. The contracts are proliferating, with state support, in the settler state's interests.

Specifically, the private contractual regime normalizes and facilitates the state's provision of access to Indigenous lands for extractive capital. Thus, despite the fact that the emergence of IBAs might be considered an artifact of the crisis caused by Indigenous resistance to the settler state's inclination towards accumulation by dispossession to begin with, the significance of the turn to contracts to govern extraction cannot now be understood without coming to view the deals as a part of the larger legal architecture of settler colonial capitalism that they have been absorbed into. With the contracts satisfying the parties—at least to a limited extent in the short term—there is less pressure on the state to resolve the obvious failure of the public law scheme to ensure that Indigenous peoples can exercise their territorial governing authority. Consent by contract, then, is a crucial node in the contemporary contest over jurisdiction between the settler state and the surging Indigenous resistance.

In the first part of this essay, I outline the dynamics of "consent by contract" that produce a market for consent in the contest over control of resource extraction on Indigenous lands, with a focus on Canada, although there are resonances with the dynamics in many other parts of the settler colonial world, if not beyond. *Consent by contract* is a mode of governance that attempts to define the social, political, ecological, and economic relations regarding the use of Indigenous lands solely through confidential bargaining and agreement-making between private extraction companies and First Nations, but in fact affords the state a key role in setting the terms. Documents filed in relation to the recent Treaty case of *Yahey v. British Columbia* (2018) expose the faulty logic inherent in the assumption that the decision of a Band Council of a First nation to conclude an IBA can be equated with the community's consent to a project.

In the second part, I review briefly some insights from contract law theory, reaching back to critical legal studies theorists of the 1980s and 1990s, to relational contract theorists, and to the contemporary theorists of transnational private governance. Documents disclosed in the recent judicial review decision of *Eabametoong First Nation v. Landore* (2017) demonstrate the high degree of penetration of state actors implementing public law processes, such as permitting for early exploration, into the negotiations between a First Nation and a junior mining company. Ultimately, it is not only that the settler state law sets the context for what can be negotiated between the parties, but also that state actors actively facilitate the agreement-making, influence the parameters of the deal, and are invested in the outcomes. Most significantly, the settler state then draws inferences adverse to Indigenous land interests from the very fact of these negotiations.

Finally, in the third part, I argue that the phenomenon of "extraction contracting," even as it masquerades as a mode of private governance, in fact engages crucial public and constitutional governance questions. I conclude that it is not so much that the contracts are filling a gap in the inadequate public regulatory regime and associated jurisprudence (although the inadequacy is real), but that the public law regime is actively holding open the space for extraction contracting to fill, because it insulates the settler law from demands for reform. If we take a clear look, based on these insights, we can see that the status quo flows from more or less deliberate decisions by state actors to rely on extraction contracting to determine the highly political outcomes to conflicts over land that are in the long run detrimental to the Indigenous parties (with whom the state is in a fiduciary relationship). Why? I argue that it is to delay the inevitable breakdown of the state's jurisdictional authority on those lands, which will entail radical wealth redistribution from capital to Indigenous peoples.

The (Rigged) "Market" for Consent

The dynamics of resource extraction in Canada are largely, and increasingly, shaped by the negotiation of a complex web of contractual agreements. These are not solely IBAs: they also include resource revenue sharing agreements between tribal councils and provincial governments, as were recently concluded in Ontario, and "economic benefits agreements," as in British Columbia; early exploration agreements and memorandums of understanding between First Nations and mining companies; and framework agreements between communities and various governments and agencies over infrastructure or environmental assessment funding, among others. Over the past several years, companies in the extractive sector have come to accept that this "dealmaking" with Indigenous governments is a necessary part of the game—and in Canada, it is one that is considerably more predictable than attempting to comply with the Supreme Court of Canada's consultation framework, established by jurisprudence interpreting section 35 of the Constitution Act, 1982, and hoping for the best (St. Laurent and Le Billion 2015). As many examples in this issue demonstrate, approved projects are not being built because of lengthy court proceedings, and even success in courts cannot guarantee that projects will proceed, because of the increasing capacity of Indigenous land defenders to disrupt extractive operations by asserting jurisdiction (see, for example, Curran et al. and Benton and Cochrane in this issue). The public law framework provided by settler law and jurisprudence, we are told, is not capable of achieving the "resource certainty" that industry demands. Thus, negotiating a deal has become the first priority of companies interested in advancing a controversial extractive project, and—as much as they claim otherwise—facilitating those deals has become a key task of state actors attempting to "relegitimize extraction" (McCreary and Turner 2018). Signed contracts have come to stand in for expressions of consent in the contemporary moment.

Even though it is very difficult to understand how the mere fact of a signed agreement could on its own constitute evidence of "free, prior and informed consent" (FPIC), either as it is understood in international law under the UN Declaration on the Rights of Indigenous Peoples ("the Declaration"), or as it is understood in Indigenous legal traditions, we can observe that extraction is de facto authorized by the signing of a contract between industry and affected communities, in Canada as in other settler societies (Papillon and Rodon 2016). That is, political actors in settler governments are putting forward the successful conclusion of deals as crucial legitimation for supporting contested resource projects, and companies are leveraging that "consent" as a valued asset when marketing their projects to potential investors (Olynyk, Bergner, and Shipley 2018).

But how is this "authorization" granted in law? Extraction is clearly governed on the ground by a range of overlapping and potentially conflicting norms and processes at the intersection of the relevant Indigenous, settler state, and international legal orders. As Pasternak (2017) has demonstrated, Canada is aptly characterized as an uneven patchwork of competing and over-lapping claims to jurisdiction. Ways of authorizing extraction are multiple and include the settler state's common law (from its contractual regime, to its Aboriginal rights jurisprudence under section 35, which details a duty to con-sult and accommodate in respect of Aboriginal and Treaty rights); settler state legislation, such as provincial resource laws governing oil and gas develop-ment, mining and land-use planning; international legal norms, such as the FPIC standard in the Declaration; and, most fundamentally, extraction is authorized, altered or rejected according to the Indigenous laws applicable to the territory in question (Scott and Boisselle, forthcoming). Acknowledging this plurality by drawing attention to contemporary enactments of Indigenous territorial authority challenges and complicates the exercise of presumed-to-be-exclusive state jurisdiction over natural resources (McCreary and Turner 2018).

The contractual regime, in the form of IBAs, emerged in the 1990s. The agreements have gone, according to one insider, "from being discretion-ary to being compulsory" over the past decade, to the point that it is "unthink-able not to have one" (Webster 2019: 28, 29). The basic deal is as follows: the Indigenous community receives a "package of measures" that typically includes promises to minimize or monitor environmental impacts, and var-ious economic benefits, such as annual payments and/or local employment targets (O'Faircheallaigh 2003: 2; Expert Panel 2017; Sosa and Keenan, 2001). In exchange, the community provides access to its lands and offers support for, or acquiescence to, the project. Sometimes the First Nations are also expected to agree to a release of past infringements and future claims (Gilmour and Mellett 2013; McLean, forthcoming).

Many scholars have raised concerns about the way the deals are struck. These include complex questions of representation, not only about whether members of affected communities are able to fully understand the proposed terms of a deal before having to register a view (Cameron and Levitan 2014), but also about who has the authority to provide consent on behalf of a com-munity. Typically, the authority to sign an IBA is presumed to lie with the Chief and Council through a Band Council Resolution, but this glosses over the fact that each Indigenous community will have its own political system structured by its unique legal order (Borrows 2010). Recognizing this fact means acknowledging the potential applicability of multiple avenues for securing the community's consent, including not only resolutions passed by Band Councils established under colonial legislation, but also hereditary processes derived from Indigenous legal orders (Graben, Cameron, and Morales 2019)—generating challenging questions about where authority lies, over which lands, and how community deliberation feeds into its exercise.

There is also widespread concern that confidentiality clauses, which typically prohibit the communication of the contents of the contracts to anyone outside the negotiating process, are inhibiting "cross-community comparisons . . . and holistic discussion of benefits and valuable experiences among communities" (Caine and Krogman 2010: 85). O'Faircheallaigh (2016), who has conducted the largest empirical study of the negotiated outcomes from a number of IBAs in Canada and Australia, found that the competitive element—the sense among communities that gains made by one First Nation would reduce the resources available for a neighboring First Nation—was exacerbated by the confidentiality provisions.

Legitimate worries also exist in relation to the "support and cooperation" covenants that seek to prohibit "beneficiary populations" from opposing the company's project in any regulatory proceedings or undertaking actions that could impede or delay the development. The First Nation is commonly expected to agree that it will not object to the issuance of any licenses, permits, authorizations, or approvals in any regulatory proceedings. These provisions have been compared to "gag orders," in the sense that they purport to prevent community members from voicing concerns if new impacts come to light only after the development gets off the ground (Cameron and Levitan 2014). Reported commitments made by First Nation parties range from "non-objection" to "express support," with the IBA usually listing the kinds of "oppositional activities" that the First Nation is prohibited from undertaking (Bielawski 2003; O'Faircheallaigh 2016). Multiple negotiators I interviewed indicated that some companies seek to bind the First Nations to contractual terms that would require the Chief and Council to take positive steps to publicly defend the project against critiques leveled against it—at least in the context of official regulatory proceedings, if not in the general public domain. As O'Faircheallaigh (2016: 166) sees it, the First Nation parties are accepting constraints on their ability to exercise their rights—be they inherent rights, constitutional rights, or rights granted though settler state legislation—in exchange for very modest benefits that may have also been possible without the IBA.

Finally, there are serious concerns about the equitable distribution of both benefits and potential harms. This is as true within communities as it is among them, with gender being a crucial consideration (Graben, Cameron, and Morales 2019; Fidler and Hitch 2007; Wiebe and Konsmo 2014). Jobs, training, and economic benefits of extraction typically benefit men in the communities, while major extractive projects, through the introduction of "man camps" and the opening up of remote areas with new infrastructure, pose profound risks to Indigenous women and girls (Women's Earth Alliance and NYSHN 2016). The recently released "Final Report into Missing and Murdered Indigenous Women and Girls" (National Inquiry into Missing and Murdered Indigenous Women in Canada 2019: 584) in Canada states explicitly that governments must "do a more thorough job of considering the safety of Indigenous women and children when making decisions about resource extraction on or near Indigenous territories."

On one view of IBAs, Indigenous communities are exercising jurisdictional autonomy as self-determining nations when they negotiate directly with industry toward goals of economic self-reliance. Critics, on the other hand, say that the agreements, because they are "one-offs," confidential, and have no minimum requirements (Mining Watch Canada 2011), undermine the practical ability of First Nations to determine desired land uses for themselves and instead leave them to "self-determine" within the very narrow confines of extractive capitalism (Dempsey, Gould, and Sundberg 2011) and a wage economy. But in the end, it is clear that the opportunity to negotiate a deal represents a chance for a community to "not only gain economically . . . but also affect the trajectory and scale of development" (Caine and Krogman 2010: 77)—an outcome that is hard to otherwise come by through the settler state's public law framework.

And there is the rub: the fundamental problem is that the Indigenous communities whose lands are threatened by extractive projects are not recognized as holding the jurisdiction to decide whether or not permits should be granted in the first place. Strictly considering the current state of doctrine in settler law today, notwithstanding the adoption of the Declaration, the idea of FPIC—and conversely, the possibility that "no" could mean "no"—is not yet a feature of the public law regime in Canada (Peerla 2012; Hamilton 2019), or in other jurisdictions (Szablowski 2010). Whereas the Declaration, according to UN Special Rapporteur James Anaya (2014), is rooted in the affirmation of the right of Indigenous peoples, as self-determining peoples, to have control over their lands and their futures, the Canadian state fears that implementing this vision would amount to giving Indigenous peoples a "veto" over resource development (Imai 2017; Papillon and Rodon 2017). That is because the right of Indigenous consent to development on their traditional lands is seen as threatening to the basic foundational notion of "permanent sovereignty over natural resources" for states (Szablowski 2010).

The primary jurisprudential tool that settler courts in Canada use to decide these disputes is the duty to consult and accommodate—a spectrum of consultation and accommodation rights developed by the settler courts to manage areas on which Aboriginal and Treaty rights have been claimed or recognized. And under this jurisprudence, even on the end of that spectrum where title or Treaty rights provide the most scope for First Nations to consent to or refuse projects, those rights remain subject to the Crown's "justifiable infringement" (Scott and Boisselle, forthcoming; Imai 2017). The situation was summed up well by Chief Allan Adam of Athabascan Chipewyan First Nation, whose community is situated near the Alberta tar sands, in September 2018. Having long been a central critic of the devastating impacts of extractive projects in the territory, he finally signed an IBA with mining giant Teck Resources, stating:

> We've been fighting industry for how long? And we've spent well over $1–million in court fees with nothing tangible in return. . . . So what am I supposed to do? . . . I don't want to do this. I didn't want to make this decision but I had no choice. I had to make sure . . . our people are going to benefit from it for the future. (quoted in McCarthy 2017)

As Shin Imai (2017: 385–86) says, "The problem with the *consult* standard is that the community feels powerless, because they *are* powerless. It is difficult for people to trust a process of discussion when they know that no matter what happens, the final decision is not in their hands." In other words, negotiations toward IBAs are always "premised on the assumption that the project will be approved"; it is merely a matter of deciding on the "compensation package [that will be provided] *in exchange* for consent" (Papillon and Rodon 2017: 13; see also Weitzner 2006). We are asked to believe that consent has a price, and that it can be bought and sold in a private market.

Is a Signed IBA Evidence of a Community's Consent?

Yahey v. British Columbia concerns a larger Treaty rights claim by the Blueberry River First Nation; it is part of the wave of cases now coming forward under the banner of a "meaningful right to harvest" (Imai 2017). The Band is arguing that the cumulative impact of state permitting processes for industrial uses has transformed the landscape to such as extent that it is undermining the community members' abilities to use their traditional territory for hunting and fishing as guaranteed in Treaty 8.[3] In this specific ruling, however, the court answers the state request for disclosure of any IBAs that Blueberry River had signed with project proponents. British Columbia argued that the IBAs would demonstrate the Band's consent to the projects, and that the Band had already been compensated for any violation of their Treaty rights. In documents filed in the ongoing litigation, Blueberry River objects, arguing that "since the matter was out of their hands, signing an impact benefits agreement or otherwise participating in industrial development cannot be viewed as acquiescing in the diminution of their Treaty rights and thus is not relevant to the Province's defence" (Aelene Guingcango, affidavit of April 11, 2018: 4). In fact, the Band stated, it had formally objected at the approvals stage to two gas transmission projects, and only entered into agreements with the companies "after the Province had approved those projects over the plaintiffs' objections" (Merli de Guzman, affidavit of December 9, 2017: 2–3).

In the case of one of the projects, Blueberry River details how it wrote to the ministers responsible for the project requesting that they deny the approval, and asking the Crown to engage the Band to discuss threats to their Treaty rights, but the request was not responded to. The Band offers evidence to show that the approval was granted shortly after, and almost eleven months passed before the IBA was entered into. The Band argues that these approvals demonstrate that the environmental assessment process is flawed and that the Crown failed to fulfill its duty to consult and accommodate the Band's concerns about negative effects on Treaty rights and the environment (Merli de Guzman, affidavit of December 9, 2017: 2–3).

These negotiations occurring as part of the Blueberry River litigation demonstrate explicit state attempts to relegitimize extractive developments, even when they have been approved over the explicit objections of affected Indigenous peoples. One lawyer I interviewed stated in respect of IBAs like these that, "at best, you are negotiating over minor environmental mitigation measures . . . on a territory that really cannot bear any more projects" (pers. comm. August 19, 2019). Until communities actually have the power to say yes—or no—to extractive activities on their ancestral homelands, it is impossible to conclude that an IBA can constitute evidence of meaningful "consent" to a project. There is a structural power imbalance in place, stemming from "the ability of companies to decide which communities they will negotiate with, to end negotiations, and more generally to get projects approved and proceed without IBAs" (St-Laurent and Le Billon 2015: 8).

Contract as Risk Management

From this we could conclude that an IBA is simply extra insurance for companies—"IBAs have proven to be a useful tool for industrial proponents to manage risk," according to three corporate lawyers writing recently in *Lexpert* magazine (Olynyk, Bergner, and Shipley 2018). Patricia Hania (2019: 539) states that an IBA is a "mechanism that stabilizes the risk inherent in [an extractive] project." Similarly, a negotiator that I interviewed agreed that "political risk is a major motivator" for companies in terms of bringing them to the table (pers. comm. April 30, 2019). And risk management is an aim of communities as well. Because settler law does not put First Nations in a position to envision their own projects for the territory, IBAs are often perceived as the "best (and often last) option for influencing the flow of resources back to the community" (Caine and Krogman 2010: 85), meaning that other parties' development priorities are inevitably thrust on First Nations to consider. But communities do have their own priorities, often with built-in notions of environmental sustainability, intergenerational justice, and visions for land-based economies and livelihoods not compatible with a wage economy (L. Simpson 2016).

Unfortunately, as the literature shows, IBAs cannot be relied on for generating "future benefit streams" (Caine and Krogman 2010: 78; O'Faircheallaigh 2016) nor for enacting alternative visions of sustainable economic development (Cameron and Levitan 2014). This failure derives, at least in part, from the fact that IBAs make First Nations more dependent on revenues generated through extractivism in order to meet community members' basic fiscal needs. Extractivism is a mode of accumulation that is nonreciprocal and oriented to the short term, generating profits for distant owners and very little in the way of benefits for local people (Veltmeyer 2012; Acuña 2015). This creates a situation where communities who have signed IBAs, once all the resources are extracted, are left with no trace of the promised wealth and prosperity, but with the lasting legacy of a comprised homeland. As political ecologists have demonstrated, even new forms of "progressive extractivism" that incorporate benefit sharing with Indigenous communities—a function of the contractual turn—tend to push communities toward standard forms of economic development and a wage economy (Gudynas 2016). This is because they depend on growth, an ongoing and linear process of material "progress," forcing communities to accept a redefinition of relations with land into capitalist terms of revenues, assets, and individual gain (Gudynas 2016; Veltmeyer and Bowles 2014).

To conclude this part, I argue that we cannot simply see the turn to contracts as an expression of autonomy or self-determination without investigating the background context for the negotiations, including the underlying power relations. And here it is clear that the backdrop set by the settler jurisprudence takes all of the leverage away from the First Nations. As Szablowski (2010) says, the formal regulatory regime forms the "skeleton" that supports and structures the engagement process, providing valuable resources and bargaining entitlements to the parties. In this way, the settler law's allocation of legal rights and duties comes to shape the private ordering. The most crucial of these allocations is that the Crown claims underlying title to, and jurisdiction over, all of the lands within the settler state's borders.

Contracts clearly include and embed not only private law norms, but state law norms as well. The parties are "bargaining in the shadow" of the public law. As Wai (2008) says, while contractual relations are assumed to be private consensual relations, state law is always ordering the interactions of the parties. But, it is not only that private agreements incorporate and embed regulatory standards and assumptions derived from public law, as I have shown in this part, but that those agreements implicate a broad range of public interests and interests of so-called non-parties, and that the state is actively engaged in shaping the contractual outcomes, as I will demonstrate next.

Relational Contracts, and their Remedies

Much of contract theory depends on a picture of consensual, uncoerced transactions.
—Stewart Macaulay and William C. Whitford, "The Development of Contracts: Law in Action," 2015

American legal scholar Stewart Macaulay spent a career breaking down the formal assumptions of contract doctrine to demonstrate how the real-world conditions of contracting differed sharply from the assumptions in the jurisprudence. Among the assumptions he drew into question: that parties carefully draft contracts on equal terms, which they fully understand and agree to (Macaulay 2003). More often, Macaulay argued, the written contract is incongruent with the actual expectations of the parties. As Treaty people, we should by now be familiar with this idea. One of the key reasons for the disparity, according to Macaulay, is that those who negotiate the deal are not the ones who draft it, and not the ones who have to perform it. But as he demonstrates, "proving what the real deal was can be very costly . . . [as] experts are not free" (44) (also an apt remark in the context of both IBAs and Treaty rights litigation in general).

Macaulay was writing alongside Ian Macneil, another American legal scholar, whose work launched the field of "relational contract theory" with the observation that how parties behave in their contractual relations is less about contract terms and more about how they hope and expect to relate to each other in the future (Macneil 2001). This scholarship takes for granted that there are many factors operating outside of the "four corners of the contract" that shape the relations between the parties, and the decisions they make in relation to its breach (Macaulay and Whitford 2015).

In fact, a point made in early contract law scholarship is that the remedies available for breach of contract essentially determine the "risk sharing" as between the parties (Polinski 1981). The remedy available against a breaching party will influence a party's decision as to whether they will breach, or invest in compliance. In fact, the purpose of providing sanctions for promises broken, according to the classical liberal contract law theory Macneil (1962) critiqued, is to protect the reliance on promises and to prevent unjust enrichment. Unjust enrichment, or the law of restitution, is based on the "moral principle" that the status quo should be restored between the parties where one's loss has unjustifiably become the other's gain (Burrows 2011).

What is "unjust enrichment" in the context of extraction contracting? The company would be unjustly enriched, according to contract law doctrine, if the company receives the social license, permits, or the "acquiescence" of the community, and yet the First Nation does not receive the promised benefits. And the reverse: the First Nation would be unjustly enriched if it received benefits under the agreement (payments, as an example) but withheld or withdrew its support or took other measures to undermine the company's social license, asset value, and so forth. The order in which the parties deliver their "goods," then, clearly matters in the real world of extraction contracting. In the context of most IBA negotiations, the company benefits first and performs later; that is, the First Nation agrees to acquiesce or stay silent through regulatory proceedings (if not stand on a stage and shake hands in front of cameras), and the payments begin rolling in later. On the flip side, the First Nation performs/delivers first and benefits later. In fact, payments are easily interrupted, but regulatory approvals tend to be much more difficult to reverse or rescind. So, the stock response that lawyers give when asked about a community's remedies under IBAs in the case of a company's breach of obligations—that a community can always withdraw its support—seems out of touch with the reality of when and how leverage can be used on the ground. Several of the negotiators I interviewed agreed that the First Nation's points of leverage depend heavily on the timing of the regulatory approvals. In fact, one negotiator acknowledged that a reason why the "expressions of support" provisions of an IBA are typically considered more "enforceable" than most, is that those expressions are expected prior in time to the performance of the companies' obligations (pers. comm. August 20, 2019).

Knowing something about contract remedies—the recourse that is available to parties under the law in the case of breach—and how they can access it, then, is part of understanding the implications of the turn to contract to govern these relationships. The most important thing to know is that the general rule is money damages. "Contract law is generally understood to require no more of a person who breaches a contract than to give the injured party the 'benefit of the bargain'" (Thel and Siegelman 2011: 1181). As long as the company can compensate for the breach (in monetary terms), it is, according to the settler law of contract, free to break its promises. This rule has obvious deficiencies for the Indigenous parties, for whom many of the values whose protection might be sought through the IBA, such as a sacred river system, ecological integrity, or culturally significant sites, are not compensable with money damages.

The other general rule is that the parties may determine and set out in the agreement how they wish to handle disputes. Typically, this includes mediation provisions, and where mediation fails to resolve the issue, the disputes are referred to an arbitrator under the settler state's commercial arbitration legislation. The arbitrator's decision is binding on the parties, and the relevant provisions typically also stipulate that the arbitration process, and any proceedings in connection with it, will remain confidential. There is some indication that IBAs may also contain provisions that contemplate recourse to settler courts for "interim judicial relief in the nature of an injunction or other equitable relief," pending arbitration (Pinehouse Agreement 2012: art. 7). However, the lack of transparency around the agreements means that scholarly understanding of the extent to which IBAs might reach arbitral tribunals, or mediation, is lacking (McLean, forthcoming; Robertson 2015). "The arbitration universe is . . . a closed world; it gives no voice to those parties who are external to the contractual order" (Perez 2016: 105).

Scholarship predicts that private parties may make use of formal contracts to structure their relationships even when they have no intention of using formal contract enforcement mechanisms (Hadfield and Bozovic 2016). That is, parties in relational contracts may be content to rely on other tools, like "reputation," to induce compliance. Here, the central purpose of formal contracting, then, is "to coordinate beliefs about what constitutes a breach of a highly ambiguous set of obligations" (Hadfield and Bozovic 2016: 982). Speaking of a "highly ambiguous set of obligations," consider how negotiators are said to approach the question of the "no-protest" clauses.

As one interviewee stated, "lawyers fight at length about this point," as they try to shape the precise contract language that will put into words exactly "how . . . consent [is] rendered, and how can it be taken away" (pers. comm. April 23, 2019). The negotiators I interviewed confirmed that companies will seek "life-of-the-project consent," "irrevocable consent," and "blank check consent," as well as "no-protest clauses," in which they attempt to "bind everyone" [in the community], and try to get the Band "to promise there will be no trouble." (pers. comm. August 19, 2019). More than one negotiator I interviewed stated that they advise Bands not to concede to these demands, with one explaining that "you can never bind the members, the youth, the hereditary leaders. . . . If they decide to blockade the road, the leadership is at a loss—all they can do is not sanction it" (pers. comm. August 19, 2019). Another interviewee admitted, however, that the First Nation is often forced to agree to terms that obligate the Chief and Council to take "positive steps to deter protestors or to make public statements denouncing their actions" (pers. comm. July 24, 2019).

Beginning with the critical legal studies movement and continuing to this day, scholars have demonstrated how the terms of contracts are almost always imposed by the stronger, better-resourced repeat players (Galanter 1981; Macaulay 2003; and see, recently, Cutler and Dietz 2017). O'Faircheallaigh's (2016) research confirms that this dynamic is present with respect to IBAs as well: companies use their substantial experience negotiating with Indigenous peoples to gain advantageous contract terms. But while size, power, and experience matter in negotiations, as Natasha Affolder (2010: 216) makes clear, there is also a "less visible and pernicious privileging that occurs through contractual norm-setting."

A contract is supposed to be the "quintessential expression of a liberal theory of society" and "a binding basis for a reciprocal commitment" (Zumbansen 2017: xiii). That is, contract law's role has always been one of *facilitating* rather than putting conditions around what may be "autonomously" agreed to (Affolder 2017: 217). But as O'Faircheallaigh (2016: 168) demonstrates by pointing to the widespread use of "boilerplate," or template, agreements, indications are that there really is very little bargaining going on: "The company determine[s] exactly what it [i]s prepared to agree to, enshrine[s] this in the template agreement, and move[s] from that position only when absolutely necessary." Further as Affolder (2017: 215) has argued, "Contract lawyers are well aware that it is in the boilerplate, in the creation of contractual norms, forms and defaults, that power gets divided and that winners and losers are made." Even more crucial in this context is the degree to which non-parties—state actors—seem to set the terms for the "negotiation." Consider the following case study based on a recent judicial review application challenging the issuance of an early exploration permit in Ontario's far north.[4]

Eabametoong v. Landore . . . (and Ontario)

Eabametoong First Nation (EFN) is a remote Anishinaabe community situated in Treaty 9 territory, the far northern reaches of Ontario. A junior mining company, Landore Resources, applied for an exploratory drilling permit in the area of two lakes that are used year-round by several Eabametoong families for sustenance, cultural, and spiritual purposes according to the applicable Indigenous stewardship laws governing family clans (Atlookan 2016). Over a period of several years, the community leaders and company officials engaged in back and forth communications about EFN's wish to strike a memorandum of understanding (MOU) to formalize the parties' expectations on the basis of good faith and respect, and about their desire to meet in person with the company leadership to discuss affected clans' concerns. Officials in Ontario's Ministry of Northern Development and Mines (MNDM) were involved at various stages, attempting to facilitate meetings, taking notes of community concerns, and discussing them with the company. At one point, Ministry officials urged Landore to get in touch with EFN leaders, saying that the permit would not be issued until the community's concerns were met through the negotiation of an MOU (Applicant's factum, p. 7, para. 18). The company presented EFN with a boilerplate agreement, but the community continued to press for various measures specific to their concerns. This exasperated the company, which stated that it had "successfully used this MOU template with [another Band] . . . and suggested to EFN to contact [their Chief]" if they needed further convincing (Landore's factum, p. 10, para. 30).

Later the issue took on a new urgency for Landore, when they were negotiating to sell their assets to Barrick Gold, and MNDM and Landore had a private face-to-face meeting without informing Eabametoong leaders. Landore advised the ministry officials that it needed the permit to be approved quickly. There is some evidence that MNDM pressed the company to address some of the community's key demands at this meeting—including the decommissioning of the company's previous camp in the territory (Applicant's factum: 7). Very soon after, MNDM wrote to EFN informing the leaders that a decision would be made about the permit in a matter of days, and requesting any information the community wished to provide about adverse impacts. Eabametoong requested a meeting with Landore, who refused. EFN leaders subsequently wrote to MNDM expressing concerns about both the project and the process. MNDM responded with possible terms and conditions for permit approval and requested a swift response. EFN provided a letter from the community's lawyer setting out their objections in more detail, but MNDM went ahead and issued the permit without replying to EFN.

On judicial review, the Ontario Superior Court of Justice overturned the approval. It held that since the Crown had "delegated" parts of its duty to Landore, the company's actions and the reasonable expectations they created by making promises to EFN were relevant to whether the duty to consult and accommodate was met. The Court stressed that the duty to consult does not give Eabametoong the right to unilaterally insist that a MOU be in place before the permit can be granted, or that any other process take place, but that because Landore had agreed to both the MOU and the community meeting, there was a responsibility to follow through, or at least offer Eabametoong an explanation. What the Court took issue with in this case was the sense that the purpose of the process had switched from mutual understanding to facilitating approval in response to commercial timelines, holding that the Crown may not conclude a consultation process in consideration of external timing pressures when there are outstanding issues to be discussed.

What is most interesting in examining this case is that MNDM took the position that EFN's insistence on an MOU was "contrary to legal requirements and Ministry policy," but MNDM did not communicate this to Eabametoong during the negotiations, instead seeming to attempt to facilitate negotiation toward an MOU itself (*Eabametoong First Nation v. Minister of Northern Development and Mines*, 2018 ONSC 4316, para. 118). The policy in question is MNDM's operational policy on "Consultation and arrangements with Aboriginal communities at early exploration." It states:

> Early exploration proponents and Aboriginal communities should not underestimate the importance of their role in the process. While MNDM's specific expectations are outlined in Part II of this Policy, early efforts to engage with one another, beyond the minimum processes required pursuant to the Mining Act and this Policy, will lead to more effective and timely results later. Building relationships and goodwill *may lead to mutual commitments and arrangements and provide the certainty and stability for a project that permitting processes alone cannot achieve.* Aboriginal communities and industry proponents must be willing to work constructively to understand one

another's interests and perspectives and to find practical ways of addressing concerns and realizing opportunities that mineral exploration may have to offer. (MNDM 2012: 2; emphasis mine)

This amounts to not only a state endorsement of the "opportunities" that mining presents for communities, but also an admission that contracting can lead to outcomes that permitting cannot provide. Later, the policy reiterates that "proponents are strongly encouraged to make efforts to reach arrangements with communities in advance of submitting an application," and states that "arrangements that address concerns of Aboriginal communities related to consultation and mitigation will enable more timely decision-making by MNDM" (8). MNDM further encourages proponents to support First Nations' capacity to engage in negotiations by directly reimbursing their expenses or paying for technical services, and promises that "MNDM will support these contributions by ensuring they are eligible expenses for assessment credit under the Mining Act" (9). The MNDM states that proponents should strive to include various commitments in their "arrangements" with communities, such as seasonal modifications to work schedules or environmental monitoring, and states that should no agreement be possible, MNDM may include such measures as conditions on the permit (9).

The MNDM even articulates specific content suggestions for the contracts, stating that the arrangements "should, ideally, reflect the following principles: be proportional to the nature, scale and duration of the project and its potential impacts; not place an excessive burden on the proponent or undermine the feasibility of the project; and be sufficiently transparent to satisfy MNDM's reporting requirements while also helping to manage expectations and bring a level of certainty and consistency to the field" (11). Finally, the province also funds a "Community Consultation Liaison Officer," a member of the community's Band office whose job description is to support the community's capacity to engage with MNDM and industry regarding mineral exploration.

As A. Claire Cutler (2018) argues, private capital will always seek to embed risks in the public domain—here, we can see that it is not so much the contract remedies themselves that determine the risk-sharing among the parties, but the structure of the public law regime. Because the duty to consult and accommodate lies formally with the state, companies are free to engage as they wish, exploring whether there are any gains to be made from contracting, but never with a downside risk that it could affect their entitlements to the permit. It is the state that is ultimately on the hook when the

First Nation and company parties fail to come to terms. And, of course, the community, as in this case: if they had not launched the litigation, they would have been saddled with the negative effects of the new drilling as well as the still-not-decommissioned work camp.

What this case demonstrates is the pervasiveness of state actors implementing public law processes, such as permitting for early exploration, into the negotiations toward ostensibly private agreements. State actors delegate certain aspects of the consultation to the company, but they do not completely "check out," as one negotiator put it (pers. comm. August 21, 2019). The result is that First Nations find themselves engaging in discussions with the Crown in which they take hard-line positions so as to raise the bar of what might be expected of the company in their separate, "private" negotiations toward an IBA. Ultimately, it is not only that the settler state law shapes the context and contours of what can be negotiated between the parties; it is almost to the point that the state actors effectively determine the terms, and then—as we saw in the *Yahey* case—the settler state seeks to draw inferences adverse to Indigenous land interests from the very fact of the deals. As relational contract theory would predict, the agreements themselves are embedded in a web of relations, with the structure of the web determined by the settler state's public law. The legal architecture into which any arrangements may fit is systematically structured by the settler state to favor the companies' access to Indigenous lands for extraction.

Extraction Contracting: How "Private" Agreements Serve the Settler State

What is the precise role of the state in the negotiation of IBAs? There is by no means agreement in the literature as to how to characterize the role state governments are playing. Hall (2012) argues that governments are "not neutral arbitrators" in these circumstances; others have observed that industry and government seem to be aligning themselves; or that "government is relegated to an external observational role" (Caine and Krogman 2010: 77). Fidler and Hitch (2009: 6) say that the Crown "underpins" the agreements. A Library of Parliament publication on IBAs from 2014 states that "with a few exceptions, governments are not directly involved in the development or negotiation of these bilateral arrangements" (Kielland 2015: 1). Similarly, Cameron and Levitan (2014) characterize the striking of the deals as a "privatization of the federal duty to consult Indigenous peoples about resource development" (25) and posit that "the longstanding interest of the state in promoting northern resource development is better achieved by not being directly and formally involved . . . except, importantly, at the level of upholding contract law" (27). The more recent evidence, I suggest, tends toward a much more active role for state actors in the contractual regime.

Although the use of IBAs remains formally elective (however necessary it is on the ground), extraction contracting is woven into various public processes, not the least of which is permitting and approvals. To use the most obvious example, that of environmental assessment, IBAs often purport to bind parties to certain predetermined positions on the precise issues that are being adjudicated by public regulators. Further, if "private law" is meant to denote arrangements between two private contracting parties, it is important to remember that IBAs are actually negotiated with Indigenous *governing authorities*, lending the agreements a public character in addition to their backing by the state enforcement of settler contract law and its specific remedies, or so we often assume. The state's regulatory proceedings also layer deadlines into the negotiating process, as do commercial imperatives (as was observed with Landore and EFN), which add pressure to already high-stakes situations. The formal legal authority of public officials contrasts starkly to the actual power and authority exercised by private actors in relation to, say, permitting, to take a classic example. Finally, there is continuing application of the settler law of injunctions, which further structures, in the state's interests, the "remedies" available to the parties to an IBA (Ceric, this issue). The settler law of injunctions mobilizes the threat of state violence through police or military force to bolster the state's claims to exclusive territorial authority. It is clear that there is no way to conceive of these agreements as wholly private. The state is intimately involved—arguably a party to the deal.

In this section, I argue that the phenomenon of extraction contracting, even as it masquerades as a mode of private governance, in fact engages crucial public and constitutional governance questions. I conclude that it is not so much that the contracts are filling a gap in the inadequate public regulatory regime and associated jurisprudence (although the inadequacy is real), but that the public law regime is actively holding open the space for extraction contracting to fill because it insulates the settler law from demands for reform. If we take a clear look, based on these insights, we can see that the status quo flows from more or less deliberate decisions by state actors to rely on extraction contracting to determine the highly political outcomes to conflicts over land that are in the long run detrimental to the Indigenous parties. This is a struggle for the control of lands and resources, and the settler state is invested in delaying the inevitable breakdown of its jurisdictional authority on those lands.

Lex Extractionis

Many of the questions driving my inquiries here are common to the contemporary scholarly literature on transnational private governance, such as: What are the mechanisms through which private authority gains legitimacy? And "How have specific private modes of governance gained standing as (de facto) public authority?" (Szablowski 2007). Extraction in Canada is obviously shaped by dynamics beyond state borders, and the literature on transnational law—attentive as it is to legal pluralism and non-state actors— is instructive even as I believe there is a sui generis character to the way that consent by contract has emerged in Canada.

Perhaps IBAs are doing just what they are intended to do: a contract is a "device . . . for the separation of social relations from state law" (Collins 1999: 123). But who does it benefit? IBAs are certainly not unique in terms of their semipolitical or constitutional character, which can be observed in other types of major contractual regimes as well (Perez 2016). A central preoccupation of scholars of transnational private governance is the question of what justifies the exemption of these transactions, essentially constitutional in character, from public law's grasp? The roots of a "sharp distinction between the private and public orders," according to Oren Perez (2016), lies within the *lex mercatoria*, a body of accepted trading principles used by merchants across early trading routes. "The purpose of the *lex mercatoria* was understood, historically, as protecting business expectations; the primary task of the *lex mercatoria* was to render business relations more calculable" (96). Here, in extraction contracting, we can discern a similar business purpose, but we also observe the way that *"lex extractionis"* (if I may) imposes the costs of contested projects onto what these scholars might call the "extra-contractual community." Extraction encroaches deeply into the social and ecological relations of the territories on which it takes place: "This embeddedness is highly incongruent with the image of an isolated 'business relation'" (Perez 2016: 98).

Cutler (2018: 70), describing the public/private distinction, argues that it is fundamental to liberal theory to ensure that the public realm "constitutes a contested political space subject to regulation by legitimate political authorities," in contrast to the private sphere, which is "understood to be an apolitical realm of individual freedom and autonomy, outside the scope of legitimate political regulation" and primarily dealing with economic activity between rational actors of equal bargaining power. The task of separating public from private, she argues, rests on differentiating economics from politics, which is an analytical distinction that has little empirical validity. The separation of the political and the economic is an analytical and ideological separation engendered by the capitalist mode of production that functions to depoliticize the fundamentally distributional and political nature of economic activity. This separation masks the underlying structural connection between the two spheres and the power imbalances that inhere in capitalist economic and social relations. (71)

Further, and most pertinent here, is Cutler's assertion that "the assumption of the apolitical nature of private/economic exchanges ignores the more generalized and public implications of these exchanges. In essence, the analytical distinction does not bear out in the lived experiences of people who are impacted by private agreements" (71). In the case of IBAs, it is plainly obvious that many interests are engaged in the periphery of these contracts that are conspicuously left out of the deal. These include the interests of a broader public in environmental sustainability, climate stability, biodiversity protection, conservation of intact ecosystems; the pressing questions of Indigenous governing authority, inherent jurisdiction, and the overall impact of projects on Treaty rights, not just those of the contracting parties but also those of neighboring nations. Something else traded away seems to be the leverage of the communities when they instead bargain collectively, including the ability to secure strategic, regional, and long-term interests and visions emerging from their own Indigenous social, political, and legal orders. Thus, while the dynamics around IBAs may share features with those surrounding other types of commercial contracts, the substance of what is being traded here is crucial. As Affolder (2017) demonstrates in another context, the legal form may resemble a commercial contract, but the "subject-matter implicates issues that commercial contract law cannot resolve" (221): rights to land, inherent jurisdiction, sovereignty, the authority to decide.

Norms are shifted through struggle. How can this regime be transformed? Because IBAs are confidential and their contents closely guarded, even considered proprietary by the firms that negotiate them (O'Faircheallaigh 2016), it is not possible to easily advocate turning the agreements into public policy instruments applicable more broadly throughout a region, although the case has been made that this is required (McLean, forthcoming). It is true that it is not only the companies that want confidentiality; First Nations are said to seek and value the confidentiality clauses as well—mostly out of concern about state clawback of what is called "own-source-revenue," again drawing into the picture the larger structural conditions of settler colonial capitalism. But the secrecy leads to distrust and "toxicity within the communities," according to one interviewee (pers. comm. August 21, 2019), while the benefits of confidentiality largely accrue to companies. The lack of transparency also prevents comparison between the magnitude of funds paid to First Nations versus the amounts received in state subsidies to the extractive industry, another area that could benefit from less secrecy.

While it may be true that, as Brad Gilmour and Bruce Mellett (2013) argue, "the regulator cannot offer to a First Nation the kinds of benefits that can be achieved in an IBA," neither can the regulatory process, as it is currently structured under settler law, provide an avenue for a First Nation to offer a definitive no to a project that the community does not ultimately consent to. That is, the contractual regime offers no path toward self-determination in terms of territorial governing authority or proprietary rights to lands and resources. Indigenous peoples need space to envision and pursue development that "responds to the depth of Indigenous territorial responsibilities" (McCreary and Turner 2018: 26).

Consent by contract is a regime that erodes, over time, the territorial rights and sovereignty of Indigenous peoples, and IBAs in particular contribute to the undermining of resistance, criminalization of protest, and division within and between Indigenous communities (Veltmeyer and Bowles 2014). Without recourse to this weak justification that Indigenous peoples are participating, benefitting, or "sharing in the wealth that comes from their territories," we would much more quickly demand the breakdown of the entire edifice. But as Cutler (2018: 16) argues, the mix of public versus private authorities in complex governance questions is "not fixed, but mutable, and open in places to resistance." While the contractual regime may, for now, be insulating the state from more radical and fundamental challenges to its territorial authority, because IBAs provide a thin cover of consent for the contested projects, this is also vulnerable to changing norms and practices.

Conclusions

I have argued here, drawing on Cutler and Dietz's (2017) framing in the context of private transnational governance, that "consent by contract" is a mode of governance that attempts to define the social, political, ecological, and economic relations regarding the use of Indigenous lands solely through confidential bargaining and agreement-making between private extraction companies and First Nations, but in fact affords the state a key role in setting the terms. But consent must require something more than this. As Szablowski (2010: 119) says, "consent processes are clearly political events that mobilize affected community members in a collective experience of active decision making about the future. They take place in public spaces. As a result, they are more likely to galvanize attention, and generate discussion and deliberation within a group." What Indigenous peoples are seeking is not a better contractual regime; it is "a new constitutional order" (114).

Scholars have begun to explore whether the "triumphant rise of contract" (Zumbansen 2017: 1) can be harnessed for creative, transformational change, or what some of them term "radical transactionalism" (Morgan and Kuch 2015; Crowder 2016). Ibironke Odumosu-Ayanu (2014) has proposed a move to tripartite contractual agreements, or "multi-actor contracts," among investors (mining companies), local communities, and "host states," as a way of addressing many of the dilemmas explored here. Gaathi and Odumosu-Ayanu (2015: 69) argue that new contractual regimes demonstrate "real potential to address or mitigate the absence of remedial and responsibility regimes for the adverse impacts of extractive industry activities on individuals and communities." While reforms such as these could certainly mitigate some of the worst aspects of the contractual turn, specifically the lack of remedies for affected non-parties, this analysis has shown that it is in fact the public law regime—the settler law and jurisprudence—that presents the biggest barriers to restoring Indigenous control of lands.

Contract law itself changes slowly, through a dynamic process of mutual adjustment of expectations. The public law framework, it is hoped, could change more quickly. Some scholars believe that the settler courts may (and must) provide openings and new interpretations that could shift the balance of power (see, for example, Kamphuis 2017). Others believe political tides may be shifting in favor of Indigenous peoples, which could usher in a new legislative framework for extraction. But in Canada, these hopes have been repeatedly dashed. This is because, as Julie Tomiak (2016: 222) has argued, the settler state "is no less committed to the elimination and displacement of Indigenous peoples and sovereignty than more overtly genocidal colonial state practices of the past," but simply employs new strategies, centrally among them "an increased reliance on . . . contractual relations."

The settler state continues to be heavily invested in the profitability of the extractive sector. And yet, it is clear that the environmental and social costs of extractivism for the communities and territories in question far exceed the benefits that can be gained through extraction contracting. Further, since the "extractive zone," as Macarena Gomez-Barris (2017) terms it, encompasses the resource-rich regions of high biodiversity and critical ecological functions, there are broader, diffuse costs borne by a wide range of interests—effects on water and air quality, climate instability, biodiversity loss, fragmentation of intact ecosystems, among others, that are completely uncompensated. Meanwhile the "benefits" from the extraction are highly concentrated, accruing to a small number of companies and their investors; even governments do not derive much in the way of revenues from mining (Veltmeyer and Bowles 2014), especially for remote mines (Kuyek 2019).

As Edward Cohen (2017: 156) contends, contractual regimes are "centers of contestation over the boundaries between public and private power and authority"; they constitute "crucial arenas in which patterns of power and purpose are constructed." But as I have argued here, while the contractual form, construed as a matter of private law, is a critical "vector of power" (Cutler and Dietz 2017), the settler state must be considered a party to the deal-making. Consent by contract is a technique of the contemporary settler state to normalize its own tenuous authority over lands and resources in the face of increasingly convincing counterclaims. There are always spaces for resistance, however, and the contractual regime, with its bare veneer of "consent," is coming under increasing pressure from Indigenous land defenders: "The perpetual threat of Indigenous nations is that they are a reminder of the settler's own precarious claims to land and belonging" (Estes 2018: 248).

Notes

1   The interviewees were granted anonymity in order to protect client relations, and the interview protocol was crafted to avoid discussion of specific negotiations or outcomes and to focus instead on broad trends and dynamics. Individuals interviewed were associates or partners with major firms including the Firelight Group, Mandell Pinder, OKT Law, Ratcliff and Co., and Willms and Shier.

2   *EFN v. Landore*, and associated affidavits; *Yahey v. British Columbia 2019 BCSC 972* and associated affidavits; "freedom of information" requests filed with the Ontario Ministry of Energy, Northern Development and Mines, in 2018 and 2019. Records requested included "agreements and arrangements" reported by mining companies in "Aboriginal Consultation Reports" filed under the Exploration Plans and Exploration Permits regulation of the Mining Act, O. Reg. 308/12, section 14, since 2012, and "records of decision" and associated early exploration permits granted under the Mining Act in Ontario since 2012.

3   *Yahey v. British Columbia*, 2015 BCSC 1302 (CanLII) at para 2.

4   *Eabametoong First Nation v. Minister of Northern Development and Mines, Director of Exploration for the Ministry of Northern Development and Mines, and Landore Resources Canada Inc.*, 2018 ONSC 4316 (CanLII).

References

Acuña, Roger M. 2015. "The Politics of Extractive Governance: Indigenous Peoples and Socio-environmental Conflicts." *Extractive Industries and Society* 2, no. 1: 85–92.

Affolder, Natasha. 2010. "Rethinking Environmental Contracting." *Journal of Environmental Law and Practice* 21: 155–92.

Affolder, Natasha. 2012. "Transnational Conservation Contracts." *Leiden Journal of International Law* 25: 443–60.

Affolder, Natasha. 2017. "Transnational Carbon Contracting: Why Law's Invisibility Matters." In *The Politics of Private Transnational Governance by Contract*, 1st ed., edited by A. Claire Cutler and Thomas Dietz, 215–36. London: Routledge.

Anaya, James. 2014. Twenty-Seventh Session, Agenda Item 3. Promotion and Protection of All Human Rights, Civil, Political, Economic, Social and Cultural Rights, Including the Right to Development. Report of the Special Rapporteur on the Rights of Indigenous Peoples. Addendum: The Situation of Indigenous Peoples in Canada. Human Rights Council.

Atlookan, Elizabeth. 2016. Affidavit of Chief Elizabeth Atlookan, December 14, 2016, filed in *Eabametoong First Nation v. Minister of Northern Development and Mines*, 2018 ONSC 4316.

Bielawski, E. 2003. *Rogue Diamonds: Rush for Northern Riches on Dene Land*. Toronto: Douglas and McIntyre.

Borrows, John. 2010. *Canada's Indigenous Constitution*. Toronto: University of Toronto Press.

Burrows, Andrew. 2011. *The Law of Restitution*, 3rd ed. Oxford: Oxford University Press.

Caine, Ken J., and Naomi Krogman. 2010. "Powerful or Just Plain Power-Full? A Power Analysis of Impact and Benefit Agreements in Canada's North." *Organization and Environment* 23, no. 1: 76–98. doi:10.1177/1086026609358969.

Cameron, Emilie, and Tyler Levitan. 2014. "Impact and Benefit Agreements and the Neoliberalization of Resource Governance and Indigenous-State Relations in Northern Canada." *Studies in Political Economy* 93, no. 1: 25–52. doi:10.1080/19187033.2014.11674963.

Cohen, Edward. 2017. "Private Arbitration as a Mechanism for the Construction of the contractual Norms in Private-Public Relationships: The Case of Investor-State Arbitration." In *The Politics of Private Transnational Governance by Contract*, 1st ed., edited by A. Claire Cutler and Thomas Dietz, 151–68. London: Routledge.

Collins, Hugh. 1999. *Regulating Contracts*. Oxford: Oxford University Press.

Crowder, Patience A. 2016. "Impact Transaction: Lawyering for the Public Good through Collective Impact Agreements." *Indiana Law Review* 49: 621.

Cutler, A. Claire, and Thomas Dietz. 2017. *The Politics of Private Transnational Governance by Contract*. 1st ed. London: Routledge.

Cutler, Claire. 2018. "The Judicialization of Private Transnational Power and Authority." *Indiana Journal of Global Legal Studies* 25, no. 1: 61–95.

Dempsey, Jessica, Kevin Gould, and Juanita Sundberg. 2011. "Changing Land Tenure, Defining Subjects: Neo-liberalism and Property Regimes on Native Reserves." In *Re-thinking the Great White North: Race, Nature, and the Historical Geographies of Whiteness in Canada*, edited by Andrew Baldwin, Laura Cameron, and Audrey Kobayashi. Vancouver: University of British Columbia Press.

Dezalay, Yves. 1994. "The Forum Should Fit the Fuss: The Economics and Politics of Negotiated Justice." In *Lawyers in a Postmodern World: Translation and Transgression*, edited by Maureen Cain and Christine B. Harrington, 124–54. Buckingham, UK: Open University Press.

Estes, Nick. 2019. *Our History Is the Future: Standing Rock versus the Dakota Access Pipeline, and the Long Tradition of Indigenous Resistance* London: Verso.

Expert Panel. 2017. "Building Common Ground: A New Vision for Impact Assessment in Canada." Final Report of the Expert Panel for the Review of Environmental Assessment Processes.

Fidler, Courtney, and Michael Hitch. 2007. "Impact and Benefit Agreements: A Contentious Issue for Environmental and Aboriginal Justice." *Environments: A Journal of Interdisciplinary Studies* 35, no. 2: 45–69.

Fidler, Courtney, and Michael Hitch. 2009. "Used and Abused: Negotiated Agreements." Submission to Rethinking Extractive Industry: Regulation, Dispossession, and Emerging Claims Conference, York University, Toronto.

Galanter, Marc. 1981. "Justice in Many Rooms: Courts, Private Orderings and Indigenous Law." *Journal of Legal Pluralism* 19, no. 1: 1–48.

Gathii, James, and Ibironke Odumosu-Ayanu. 2015. "The Turn to Contractual Responsibility in the Global Extractive Industry." *Business and Human Rights Journal* 1: 69–94.

Gilmour, Brad, and Bruce Mellett. 2013. "The Role of Impact and Benefits Agreements in the Resolution of Project Issues with First Nations." *Alberta Law Review* 51, no. 2: 385–400. doi:10.29173/alr71.

Graben, Sari, Angela Cameron, and Sarah Morales. 2019. "Gender Impact Analysis of Impact Benefit Agreements: Representation Clauses and UNDRIP." SSRN, February 21. dx. doi.org/10.2139/ssrn.3339404.

Gudynas, Eduardo. 2016. "Beyond Varieties of Development: Disputes and Alternatives." *Third World Quarterly* 37, no. 4: 721–32.

Hadfield, Gillian, and Iva Bozovic, 2016. "Scaffolding: Using Formal Contracts to Build Informal Relations to Support Innovation." *Wisconsin Law Review* Winter 2016: 981–1032.

Hall, Rebecca. 2012. "Diamond Mining in Canada's Northwest Territories: A Colonial Continuity." *Antipode* 45, no. 2: 376–93.

Hamilton, Robert. 2018. "Uncertainty and Indigenous Consent: What the Trans-mountain Decision Tells Us about the Current State of the Duty to Consult." *Ablawg*, September 10. ablawg.ca/2018/09/10/uncertainty-and-indigenous-consent-what-the-trans-mountain-decision-tells-us-about-the-current-state-of-the-duty-to-consult/.

Hania, Patricia. 2019. "Revitalizing Indigenous Women's Water Governance Roles in Impact and Benefit Agreement Processes through Indigenous Legal Orders and Water Stories." érudit 60(2): 519–56.

Imai, Shin. 2017. "Consult, Consent, and Veto: International Norms and Canadian Treaties." In *The Right Relationship: Reimagining the Implementation of Historical Treaties*, edited by John Borrows and Michael Coyle, 370–408. Toronto: University of Toronto Press.

Kamphuis, Charis. 2017. "Litigating Indigenous Dispossession in the Global Economy: Law's Promises and Pitfalls." *Brazilian Journal of International Law* 14, no. 1: 165–225.

Kielland, Norah. 2015. "Supporting Aboriginal Participation in Resource Development: The Role of Impact and Benefit Agreements." Library of Parliament, Canada, May 5. publications .gc.ca/collections/collection_2016/bdp-lop/eb/YM32-5-2015-29-eng.pdf.

Kuyek, Joan. 2019. *Unearthing Justice: How to Protect Your Community from the Mining Industry.* Toronto: Between the Lines.

Macaulay, Stewart. 2003. "The Real and the Paper Deal: Empirical Pictures of Relationships, Complexity, and the Urge for Transparent Simple Rules." *Modern Law Review* 66, no. 1: 44–79. doi.org/10.1111/1468-2230.6601003.

Macaulay, Stewart, and William C Whitford. 2015. "The Development of Contracts: Law in Action." *Temple Law Review* 87, no. 4: 793–806.

MacLean, Jason. Forthcoming. "Industry-Indigenous IBAs, Confidentiality, and Sustainability." In *Law and Politics of Indigenous-Industry Agreements*, edited by Dwight Newman and Ibironke Odumosu-Ayanu. Routledge.

Macneil, Ian R. 1962. "Power of Contract and Agreed Remedies." *Cornell Law Review* 47, no. 4: 495–528. scholarship.law.cornell.edu/clr/vol47/iss4/1.

Macneil, Ian R. 2001. *The Relational Theory of Contract: Selected Works of Ian Macneil*. Edited by David Campbell. London: Sweet and Maxwell.

McCarthy, Shawn. 2018. "First Nation Chief Who Opposed Oil Sands Signs Deal with Teck Sharing Benefits of Bitumen Expansion." *Globe and Mail*, Sept 23. theglobeandmail .com/business/article-first-nation-chief-signs-deal-with-teck-to-participate-in -frontier-oil/.

McCreary, Tyler, and Jerome Turner. 2018. "The Contested Scales of Indigenous and Settler Jurisdiction: Unist'ot'en Struggles with Canadian Pipeline Governance." *Studies in Political Economy* 99, no. 3: 223–45.

MiningWatch Canada. 2011. "Diamonds and Development: Attawapiskat and the Victor Diamond Mine." *MiningWatch Canada*, December 15. www.miningwatch.ca/fr/node/6857.

MNDM (Ministry of Norther Development and Mines) 2012. Version 1.01 September. MNDM Policy: Consultation and Arrangements with Aboriginal Communities at Early Exploration.

Morgan, Bronwen, and Declan Kuch. 2015. "Radical Transactionalism: Legal Consciousness, Diverse Economies, and the Sharing Economy." *Journal of Law and Society* 42, no. 4: 556–87. doi.org/10.1111/j.1467-6478.2015.00725.x.

National Inquiry into Missing and Murdered Indigenous Women in Canada. 2019. "Reclaiming Power and Place: The Final Report of the National Inquiry into Missing and Murdered Indigenous Women and Girls." www.mmiwg-ffada.ca/final-report/.

Odumosu-Ayanu, Ibironke. 2014. "Multi-actor Contracts, Competing Goals, and Regulation of Foreign Investment." *University of New Brunswick Law Journal* 65: 269.

O'Faircheallaigh, Ciaran. 2003. "Implementing Agreements between Indigenous Peoples and Resource Developers in Australia and Canada." Aboriginal Politics and Public Sector Management Research Paper No. 13.

O'Faircheallaigh, Ciaran. 2016. *Negotiations in the Indigenous World: Aboriginal Peoples and the Extractive Industry in Australia and Canada*. New York: Routledge.

Olynyk, John M., Keith B. Bergner, and Lana Shipley. 2018. "The Impact of Disclosure of Private Impact Benefit Agreements." *Lexpert*, September 21. www.lexpert.ca/article/the -impact-of-disclosure-of-private-impact-benefit-agreements/.

Papillon, Martin, and Thierry Rodon. 2016. "Environmental Assessment Processes and the Implementation of Indigenous Peoples Free, Prior and Informed Consent." Report to the Expert Panel Reviewing Federal Environmental Assessment Processes, December. www.chairedeveloppementnord.ulaval.ca/sites/chairedeveloppementnord.ulaval.ca /files/environmental_assessment_processes_and_the_implementation_of_indigenous _peoples_fpic.pdf.

Papillon, Martin, and Thierry Rodon. 2017. "Proponent-Indigenous Agreements and the Implementation of the Right to Free, Prior and Informed Consent in Canada." *Environmental Impact Assessment Review* 62: 216–24.

Pasternak, Shiri. 2017. *Grounded Authority: The Algonquins of Barriere Lake against the State*. Minneapolis: University of Minnesota Press.

Peerla, D. 2012. *No Means No: The Kitchenuhmaykoosib Inninuwug and the Fight for Indigenous Sovereignty*. Thunder Bay, ON: Cognitariat.

Perez, Oren. 2002. "Using Private–Public Linkages to Regulate Environmental Conflicts: The Case of International Construction Contracts." *Journal of Law and Society* 29, no. 1: 77–110.

Pinehouse Agreement. 2012. The Northern Village of Pinehouse and Kineepik Metis Local Inc. and Cameco Corporation and Areva Resources Canada Inc Collaboration Agreement. December 12. opencommunitycontracts.org/contract/northern-village-of-pinehouse-kineepik-metis-local-inc-cameco-corporation-areva-resources-canada-inc-2012-collaboration-agreement/.

Robertson, Krista. 2016. "A New Deal." *BarTalk*. www.cbabc.org/BarTalk/Articles/2016/August/Features/A-New-Deal.

Scott, Dayna Nadine, and Andrée Boisselle. Forthcoming. "If There Can Only Be 'One Law,' It Must Be Treaty Law: Learning from *Kanawayandan D'aaki*." *University of New Brunswick Law Review*.

Simpson, Leanne Betasamosake. 2017. *As We Have Always Done: Indigenous Freedom through Radical Resistance*. Minneapolis: University of Minnesota Press.

Sosa, Irene, and Karyn Keenan. 2001. "Impact Benefit Agreements between Aboriginal Communities and Mining Companies: Their Use in Canada." October. www.cela.ca/sites/cela.ca/files/uploads/IBAeng.pdf.

St-Laurent, Guillaume Peterson, and Philippe Le Billon. 2015. "Staking Claims and Shaking Hands: Impact and Benefit Agreements as a Technology of Government in the Mining Sector." *Extractive Industries and Society* 2, no. 3: 590–602. doi:10.1016/j.exis.2015.06.001.

Szablowski, David. 2007. *Transnational Law and Local Struggles: Mining, Communities, and the World Bank*. Oxford: Hart.

Szablowski, David. 2010. "Operationalizing Free, Prior, and Informed Consent in the Extractive Industry Sector? Examining the Challenges of a Negotiated Model of Justice." *Canadian Journal of Development Studies / Revue canadienne d'*études *du dévelop-pement* 30, no. 1: 111–30. doi:10.1080/02255189.2010.9669284.

Thel, Steven, and Peter Siegelman. 2011. "You *Do* Have to Keep Your Promises: A Disgorgement Theory of Contract Remedies." *William and Mary Law Review* 52, no. 4: 1181–1245.

Tomiak, Julie. 2016. "Navigating the Contradictions of the Shadow State: The Assembly of First Nations, State Funding, and Scales of Indigenous Resistance." *Studies in Political Economy* 97, no. 3: 217–33.

Veltmeyer, Henry. 2012. "The Natural Resource Dynamics of Post Neoliberalism in Latin America: New Developmentalism or Extractivist Imperialism?" *Studies in Political Economy* 90, no. 1: 57–86.

Veltmeyer, Henry, and Paul Bowles. 2014. "Extractivist Resistance: The Case of the Enbridge Oil Pipeline Project in Northern British Columbia" *Extractive Industries and Society* 1, no. 1: 59–68.

Wai, Robert. 2002. "Transnational Liftoff and Juridical Touchdown: The Regulatory Function of Private International Law in an Era of Globalization." *Columbia Journal of Transnational Law* 40, no. 2: 209–74.

Webster, Paul Christopher. 2019. "Canadian Mines Have Wreaked Havoc in Developing Countries for Decades. Finally, There's Hope for a Solution." *Globe and Mail*, February 19. www.theglobeandmail.com/business/rob-magazine/article-canadian-mines-have-wreaked-havoc-in-developing-countries-for-decades/.

Weitzner, Viviane. 2006. "'Dealing Full Force': Lutsel K'e Dene First Nation's Experience Negotiating with Mining Companies." Case study, North-South Institute and Lutsel K'e Dene First Nation, January.

Wiebe, S., and E. Konsmo. 2014. "Indigenous Body as Contaminated Site? Examining Reproductive Justice in Aamjiwnaang." In *Fertile Ground: Exploring Reproduction in Canada,* edited by F. Scala, S. Paterson, and M. Sokolon, 325–58. Montreal: McGill-Queen's University Press.

Women's Earth Alliance and the Native Youth Sexual Health Network. 2016. "Violence on the Land, Violence on Our Bodies." landbodydefense.org/.

Zumbansen, Peer. 2017. "Liberalism's Global Mirror: Worldwide Contracting and 'No Alternative'?" In *The Politics of Private Transnational Governance by Contract*, 1st ed., edited by A. Claire Cutler and Thomas Dietz, xiii–xvii. London: Routledge.

Shiri Pasternak

Assimilation and Partition:
How Settler Colonialism and Racial
Capitalism Co-produce the Borders
of Indigenous Economies

The history of colonialism in Canada has meant both the partition of Indigenous peoples from participating (physically, politically, legally) in the economy and a relentless demand to become assimilated as liberal capitalist citizens. Assimilation and segregation are both tendencies of colonization that protect the interests of white capital. But their respective prevalence seems to depend on the regime of racial capitalism at play.

This essay attempts to understand this contingency, focusing on how state jurisdiction is maintained as paramount to Indigenous territorial authority through racial constructions of "indigeneity." As Jodi Melamed (2011: 183) writes, "the knowledge apparatuses sustaining economic globalization have had to bring indigenous peoples into representation in a matter that explains their exploitation as inevitable, natural, or fair." In Canada today, each branch of government is beset with two irreconcilables: it must protect colonization, organized through heavy investment in the natural resource sector, *and* commit to decolonization in response to growing recognition of histories of state violence.[1] As a way out of this paradox, depending on circumstance, I argue that the economic rights of Indigenous peoples can be seen as both an obstacle and a new access point to capital.

The South Atlantic Quarterly 119:2, April 2020
DOI 10.1215/00382876-8177771 © 2020 Duke University Press

This paper examines the intersection of settler colonization and racial capitalism to shed light on the status of Indigenous economic rights in Canada. I ask, to what extent are Indigenous peoples understood to have economic rights²—defined here as the governing authority to manage their lands and resources—and, how we can we analyze these rights to better understand the conjoined meanings of colonialism and capitalism as systems of power today?

One way to approach this problem is to contemplate a theoretical frame that can encompass both the enormous *barriers* to Indigenous participation as workers or owners in the capitalist system, and tremendous *pressures* (through increasing incentives) to assimilate.³ In this paper, I look at two sites to address this problem: first, I examine how the Supreme Court of Canada has defined the "Aboriginal right" to commercial economies since the patriation of Aboriginal rights into the *Constitution* in 1982; and, second, I examine how these rights are configured through state resource revenue-sharing schemes with First Nations, in particular from extractive projects, over the past few years. Each case study provides critical material for analyzing the economic opportunities available to First Nations through democratic channels of state "recognition,"⁴ as well as *when* and *why* tensions between state policies of segregation and assimilation emerge.

In the first case, Indigenous peoples are partitioned from participation in the market economy by virtue of how their jurisdiction is circumscribed by the court through a racist cultural anthropology of "indigeneity"; one that denies their proprietary interest, therefore governing authority, in lands and resources. Here, their jurisdiction as Indigenous nations is denied, and the governments' authority to control economic matters is ensured. In the second case, Indigenous peoples are encouraged to participate in the market economy through sharing the spoils of resource extraction in the form of financial re-distribution, but they retain no authority to determine whether the permits, leases, or licenses for development are granted. In this way, the governments' authority to control economic matters is also ensured. In both cases, through partition and assimilation, white capital is secured.

I chose these particular case studies because they offer insight and access into key moments and places of knowledge production around Indigenous economic rights. On the question of Indigenous peoples' economic rights in Canada, I want to contribute to a broader theorization of colonialism by examining how terms of recognition for Indigenous peoples' economic rights in Canada are produced through constructions of racial difference *or* sameness, depending on what the circumstances demand.

Colonialism, Race, Capitalism

In earlier writing (2014) I have argued that jurisdiction is a key means of organizing authority in settler states. In my book on the Algonquins of Barriere Lake (2017a), I look at a slate of policies aimed at transforming inherent forms of jurisdiction, such as Indigenous customary governance systems, into delegated forms of authority that draw down their power from federal and provincial governments. I examine the myriad, quotidian ways that jurisdiction, as a legal mechanism of authorizing law, organizes sovereignty on the ground.

In this essay, I try to understand how jurisdiction works to organize economic power. Economic power is a component of political power; without the authority to control the leasing, permitting, and licensing on their lands, Indigenous peoples face increasing land alienation and loss of meaningful possibility for self-determination and independence. Nations need a land base to survive, but also the governing authority to manage it without constant obstruction. The problem of Indigenous assertions and exercised of jurisdiction for capital is a particularly revealing site of settler colonial power, as witnessed at the massive NODAPL camps at Standing Rock. The insecurities born of an unperfected sovereignty render visible the ongoing wars over land that began with white settlement and continue today. These challenges to state jurisdiction can be resolved in two ways: denial or mitigation, as we will see.

This research builds on critical scholarship linking systems of race and colonialism in the history of Canada, drawing from Indigenous Studies and theories of racial capitalism grounded in the black radical tradition. Racial capitalism is a theory of the inseparability of race and capitalism that was developed by black intellectuals in South Africa (Hudson 2017) and brought to bear in full force on Western civilization by Cedric Robinson in *Black Marxism* (1983). Unlike what Marx predicted—that the rise of capitalism would homogenize workers through the blunt force of exploitation—Robinson found that capitalism requires difference to grind into its gears as fuel for accumulation. As Melamed (2015) puts it, "[c]apital can only be capital when it is accumulating" and it does so by producing, exacerbating, and organizing extreme inequality between people and naturalizing it through fictions of "differing human capacities, historically race" (77). Therefore, theories of racial capitalism understand "the state and concomitant rights and freedoms to be fully saturated by racialized violence" (77). This is true for the origins of the state, founded in colonization and slavery, but also in the ongoing reproduction of this violence through political-economic governance today.

Two fields of research within Indigenous studies are particularly insightful on the relationship between race and colonization: Métis studies and Indigenous feminism. For the former, Chris Andersen's book (2014:6) exemplifies the deeply troubling idea of the Métis nation—the only Indigenous nation to form post-contact through intermarriage between Cree, Anishinaabe, and Scottish and English settlers—to be one of "mixed" blood or race, asking simply and poignantly, *why* this has been the case, and *how* the reproduction of racialization has been central to Canadian colonialism. Though mixedness and Métis are often interlaced in public and academic discourse, Andersen insists that a hyper-emphasis on the racialization of Indigenous identity is not only a misguided understanding of indigeneity and Métis territorial authority, but also broader problem with understandings of indigeneity that are exclusive to his nation. He writes that racialization "has been part of a larger set of colonial projects through which administrators have attempted to usurp all the Indigenous territories upon which colonial nation-states such as Canada have been produced and legitimated and Indigenous peoples displaced and dispossessed" (2014:11). Germain to this history of racialization, he shows, are various links construed by the state connecting "real" Indigenous peoples to land entitlement.[5] The loss of Métis land that was justified by racial logics helped open the west to settlement, energy development, transportation construction, agricultural production, and other commodity markets that supported the industrialization of central Canada (Panitch 1981).

Indigenous feminists have traced a long history linking the ways gender oppression is seared with racialization in the history of colonization. For example, the loss of Indian status for women who married non-Indigenous men caused massive disruption to Indigenous families and governance systems. Indigenous women who "married out" suddenly gave birth to "White" children according to the legal alchemy of the *Indian Act*, and for many years (at times, forever), has meant the loss of formal access to their homelands.[6] As Mohawk scholar Audra Simpson writes (2016:4), the reification of this law through the *Indian Act* in 1876, revealed "a white, heteropatriarchal and white settler sovereignty ascend and show us its face." The expulsion of native women from their communities undermined the self-determination of Indigenous nations and led to a cultural genocide of displacement, dispossession, and disconnection (Gabriel 2011).

Bringing capitalism into sharper focus as an intersecting logic with race and colonization, I also build here on anti-capitalist critiques by Indigenous intellectuals, especially their accounts of the co-constitution of colonialism and capitalism. Leaders in the Red Power movement published critical work in this area. Thinkers like Métis theorist Howard Adams (1975) chronicled how westward expansion throughout the nineteenth century was driven at base by the clash of two economic systems competing to survive. He theorized that capitalism replaced the fur trade economy through industrialization and rendered the Indigenous prairie communities largely surplus to production. Moreover, Adams theorized that the social institutions that developed to control Indigenous peoples, like Residential Schools, promoted "[f]ear, conformity, hierarchy, authority: all indoctrinations to white capitalist settler society."

During this same period, Lee Maracle (1975) also articulated discrepancies between how radical left political theorists understood capitalism compared to how Indigenous peoples saw the necessity of its co-articulation with the institutions of colonization. In *Bobbi Lee, Indian Rebel,* Maracle writes in response to the confident Marxist platitudes prescribing anti-capitalist revolution, that,

> My experience just wouldn't let me accept these wooden arguments about proletarian unity and revolution. "Look, do you want me to believe that those guys I had so much trouble with, who went over to the Reserve looking for Indian women—raping and plundering—are going to make a revolution to free us all from oppression? You gotta be kidding!" (146)

A critique of capitalism that did not account for the reality of colonization, and its particular investments in racism and patriarchy, was literally a joke to the Sto:lo activist. Adams and Maracle demonstrate the importance of understanding the institutions of capitalism from an Indigenous perspective and many other critical Indigenous scholars take up this work (Coulthard 2014; Estes 2019; LaDuke 1992; Simpson 2017; Yazzie 2018).

These anti-capitalist Indigenous articulations are more substantive, historical, and global in nature than represented here. But in this essay, I want to emphasize some of the relationships between colonialism and capitalism already noted, and to articulate an extension of this thinking—in particular, to open the space for discussion of the contingencies of socio-economic geographies, or local regimes of accumulation to these intersections.

The "Income-Bearing Value of Race Prejudice": A Spatial Theory

Insights of the black radical tradition focused on socio-spatial constructions of racial difference are extremely helpful to understanding the economic rights of Indigenous peoples in Canada today. In his paper on W. E. B. Du Bois and Richard Wright, Bobby Wilson (2002) reflects on both thinkers' gradual realization that much of the "race-connected-practices" of segregation fell outside of the scope of the civil rights movement.[7] Du Bois in particular came to see how racial inequality would persist beyond the movement because of uneven development in urban centers. He had undertaken an intensive study of redlining in Philadelphia and saw how pervasively racial fear and hatred could structure economic inequality through real estate markets in ways that would impact for generations. Du Bois called this the "income-bearing value of race prejudice [that] was the cause and not the result of theories of race inferiority" (1986:649). In other words, the inferiority of black people was the necessary construct for the accumulation of white wealth (see also Barker 2018, Karuka 2017).

In Canada, there has also been a long *spatial* history of colonial policy, law, and practices that have structured the enrichment and class advantage of white settlers. Despite advances in legal rights to Indigenous peoples as a result of their own civil rights movement (in particular, one that culminated in the 1980s, which will be discussed below), poverty levels remain exceedingly high compared to the general Canadian population (StatsCan 2016). The state's systemic disinvestment in Indigenous communities is the primary source of disparity coupled with widespread dispossession (AGC 2011; Metallic 2018; Blackstock, 2015; Pasternak 2017b), but the ways in which Indigenous peoples are integrated into or excluded from the market economy has also played a significant role in producing structural inequalities (see especially Altamirano-Jiménez 2004, 2014).

The "income-bearing value of race prejudice" against Indigenous peoples, however, often fails to register, even in well-meaning studies like the infamous "Harvard project" on Native American economic development (Cornell and Kalt 1998). As Sami scholar Rauna Kuokkanen (2011: 284) writes, "the Harvard project is plagued by the same problem as many other current considerations of Indigenous economies: the narrow focus on fairly standard economic development—that is, entrepreneurship and creation of businesses—while 'traditional' economic activities and their continued significance are rarely discussed." She points out that a pervasive weakness in work that promotes participation in neoliberal markets as key to poverty alleviation is that it naturalizes poverty as an outcome of *lack* of participation in markets, rather than seeing poverty as a function of "systemic socio-economic, gender and other inequalities" (284), like land dispossession, that are further exacerbated by capitalist economies.

The dispossession of land from Indigenous peoples enabled development and industrialization in Canada. Happening concurrently with the emergence of industrial capitalism was both ardent assimilation and segregation policies aimed at Indigenous peoples. For example, segregationist policies were introduced restricting Indigenous peoples from starting businesses, selling commodities, and joining wage labour forces. The race-based prejudice legislated in the *Indian Act*, 1876, which reified apartheid law in Canada, is shaped throughout history by space-based practices and local needs of settlers for land-based accumulation. The colonial government also simultaneously took an integrationist approach, for example, encouraging incorporation into the same wage labor market, conversion to Christianity, and transiting Indian Reserves into models of municipal governance. Some of these tensions can be attributed to strategic differences between liberal and Tory paternalism (Brownlie 2009). But while these approaches appear significantly different, examining them from the perspective of jurisdiction shows how they were each aimed at replacing Indigenous jurisdiction with the paramountcy of the state.

Let's take the example of farming. In the prairies, assimilation policies incentivized Indigenous participation in the farming industry, as did Indigenous desire to adapt to new economic opportunities with the decimation of the bison. When Cree farmers became successful competitors to white farmers, however, new statutory restrictions in the *Indian Act*, 1880, were introduced to prohibit the sale of agricultural products by "Indians" to "non-Indians" (Carter 1993).[8] In Ontario, the *Indian Act* amendments, along with further regulations introduced the following year, also deterred the sale of Ojibway agricultural produce to non-Indigenous customers, collapsing a growing, powerful agricultural industry in its prime (Waisberg, and Holzkamm 1993:186). So, despite state fears of Indigenous economic dependency and therefore a drain on public resources that motivated Indigenous assimilation policies, policies designed to support Indigenous participation in the agricultural sector were undermined by the white power base of Canadian politics and white supremacy in its legal order.

Indigenous peoples have been subject to these policies of dispossession and partition but have also powerfully shaped the limits of capitalism and colonialism in Canada. That is because, as many scholars have noted, settler colonialism is not just a form of racialized violence, but a form of domination that is itself constituted by the materiality of land theft and genocide (Byrd, 2011). As Jodi Byrd writes, to conflate these systems, "masks the territoriality of conquest" and the ways land underwrites accumulation (xxiv).

Melamed concurs, arguing that as auxiliary to this claim, identifying the relationships between racial capitalism and settler colonialism provides not only critique but also tools for resistance. Compelled by Ruth Wilson Gilmore's definition of racial capitalism—defined as "a technology for reducing collective life to the relations that sustain neoliberal democratic capitalism" (2015, 78)—Melamed narrows in on its central feature of *antirelationality*. Racial capitalism is a structure that is built through social relations that individuate and isolate communities from deeper webs of reciprocity. While liberal societies are increasingly structured by such instrumental rationalities, Melamed argues that Indigenous movements for decolonization—such as the massive Idle No More movement by Indigenous peoples that exploded in Canada in 2013–2014—embody alternative forms of sociality, or *countersovereignty* principles of deep relationality, not just with other humans, but with water, land, and other-than-human beings within a kinship network (2002: 261). She believes it is these grounds of authority that can undo racial capitalism.

Echoing here the work of Anishinaabe theorists like Deborah McGregor, who understands water as relation (2005; 2014; 2015–16), or Sylvia Plain, who understands her work with canoes to be governed by the water (2019), or Métis scholar Zoe Todd's work on fish kinship (2014), Melamed concludes that *countersovereignties* provide "a principle completely antagonistic to, and capable of superseding, the differentiations racial capitalism requires between people, of territories, and in value" (84). Indigenous forms of life are "valences of reproduction"—of life itself, in its deep relationality—and when "analyzing the co-constitutive dynamics of racial capitalism and settler colonialism, it is important to note that although both forms of power and dominion imagine themselves to be in some sense total, inevitable, and in perpetuity, both in fact remain partial, incomplete, and vulnerable to fundamental undoing" (Goldstein 2017: 48). One site of this undoing takes place through the counter-assertions of jurisdictional authority to the state's rendering of Indigenous economic rights.

Be "Indian" or Prosper

In this section, I examine how the courts have carved out and defended the exclusivity of the state to control Indigenous economies, in particular, the regulation of commercial activities by Indigenous people. In the first court cases following the patriation of the *Constitution Act*, 1982, that "recognized and affirmed" Aboriginal and Treaty rights in section 35, the courts in *Sparrow* and *Van Der Peet* set out to define the nature of these new rights. In *Sparrow*, the case centered around the size of Ronald Sparrow's drift net in relation to the regulations of the *Fisheries Act*, 1985. Sparrow was a Musqueam man who had been fishing in the Fraser River delta and who made his living in the commercial fishery of British Columbia (BC). The Supreme Court of Canada (SCC) refused to speak on the matter of whether Sparrow had a commercial right to fish, but rather deliberated on the limit of the state's legislative authority in relation to section 35 rights. The court concluded that to elicit protection, these Aboriginal rights must derive from "the culture and existence of that group" (1078). So, the commercial rights of Aboriginal people would need to derive from an evaluation of the community's culture, which was then left to the court to define.

The "integral to the distinctive culture" test was established six years later in *Van Der Peet*. The test established that when First Nations people asserted Aboriginal rights, they must prove these rights are connected to customs, traditions, and practices that *preceded* contact. The *Van Der Peet* case itself concerned the alleged criminality of Dorothy Marie Van der Peet, a member of the Sto:lo nation in BC, who was charged with selling salmon without a license. The court determined that she had to prove that fishing—which sustained the nation for thousands of years, but more importantly was sustaining her that day—was "integral to the distinctive culture" of her people. Referred to by Borrows (1998) as the "frozen rights" approach, Indigenous culture is constrained from being understood as inherently adaptive and dynamic; "Aboriginal is retrospective" and "not necessarily about what is central, significant and distinctive to the survival of these communities today" (43). It is constrained by expectations that "real" Indigenous practices preceded European contact, restricting social adaptation in a radically changing environment.

Another aspect of the *Van Der* Peet test is the *continuity* requirement, which ensures Indigenous peoples cannot claim rights that do not conform to the court's understanding of their indigeneity.[9] As such, it also constructs Indigenous economies as essentially survivalist. In her dissent in *Van der Peet*, L'Heureux-Dubé (1996: 515) actually recognizes this problem and argues for an interpretation of Aboriginal rights as "dynamic," that permits their evolution over time. She stated that, among other reservations, the entrenchment of frozen rights "embodies inappropriate and unprovable assumptions about aboriginal culture and society." L'Heureux-Dubé J. also allowed for nuance between livelihood and commercial uses of a resource.

But Chief Justice McLachlin, also dissenting, countered that *all sale* is commercial. McLachlin contrasts commercial use with sustainable use, the latter of which she identifies as an integral aspect of Aboriginal culture. As such, the Indigenous right should not extend "beyond what is required to provide the people with reasonable substitutes for what they traditionally obtained from the resource"—which she defines as "basic housing, transportation, clothing and amenities," and "what was required for food and ceremonial purposes" (518). Indigenous culture is here enmeshed in assumptions about Indigenous economies as discouraging surplus, and defines sustainability as a basic *need* that forms a constitutive cultural practice. Indigenous governance and social orders are evacuated here of any sense of organization or planning, *as well* as being "frozen" in time.

These commercial rights have been tested across the country and nowhere is the competition between Indigenous and white commercial traders clearer than in "*Marshall 1* and *2*," heard in 1999. In Mik'maqi territory in the Maritime provinces, these two cases (respectively) at first awarded, then almost immediately qualified commercial fishing rights for Indigenous harvesters. The Mik'maq argued that the Peace and Friendship treaties of 1760 and 1761 conducted with the British were the source of their commercial rights to fish (*R v. Marshall (No 1)* [1999] 3 S.C.R. 456). In particular, they referred to the "truckhouse" clause in the treaty that gave the British exclusive trading rights with their nation. The *Marshall* decision recognized these commercial rights, which it noted, however, were limited to securing "necessaries" to "achieve a moderate livelihood" (3). In addition, in a subsequent application for a rehearing by the West Nova Fishermen's Coalition, the Supreme Court issued an unprecedented clarification ("*Marshall 2*") emphasizing that *the Crown* has regulatory authority respecting the Mi'kmaq limited commercial "right to fish." However, these infringements on Indigenous rights must be "justified on conservation or other grounds" (*R v Marshall (No 2)* [1999] 3 S.C.R. 533, page 2). Following *Marshall 1*, an immediate and violent backlash erupted against Mik'maq fishers who rushed to lawfully exercise their Treaty rights, throwing lines for eel and dropping lobster traps into the water.[10]

Legal theorist Gordon Christie concludes that while the courts have granted rights to hunt and fish, they "have traditionally been reluctant to extend the validity of Aboriginal claims to cover rights to resources in the pursuit of commercial ends" (245) because of a real fear of interfering with non-Aboriginal access to land and rights. In rare cases, though, the centrality of surplus production and trade in a particular resource has been proven unequivocally to be an integral part of the nation's culture prior to contact, such as in *R. v. Gladstone,* where the Heiltsuk proved the commercial role the herring fishery played in their society, pre-contact. They successfully argued that federal fishery regulations infringed on this Aboriginal right (see also: *Ahousaht Indian Band and Nation v. Canada (Attorney General)* 2018 BCSC 633). But where Indigenous peoples have asserted commercial rights as a general component of the right to self-government, these arguments have been dismissed. A key precedent-setting case in this regard is *R. v. Pamajewon*, where the Shawanaga First Nation and Eagle Lake First Nations authorized gambling on their lands and fared badly. When charged for violating federal legislation regarding gambling, they challenged section 206 of the *Criminal Code* by asserting their section 35 rights. The Supreme Court found that since there was insufficient evidence of pre-contact gambling in these Indigenous societies to pass *Van Der Peet*'s "integral to the distinctive culture" test, it did not constitute an Aboriginal right.[11]

The importance of this bingo and lottery income to maintain these First Nations' vitality as societies today was considered irrelevant in the case by the court. With the money Eagle Lake First Nation was generating through the lotteries, they were able to build a community arena, resort, lodge, conference center and a local school with gymnasium, as well as subsidize construction for Band member homes (Morse 1997). Without this income, most communities are dependent on the federal government to build infrastructure, for which there is a massive deficit across the country (Senate 2015).

The Supreme Court of Canada has reserved conditions for governments to infringe on Aboriginal rights for "valid legislative purpose" (*Sparrow* at 1113). But determining this validity has meant *explicitly* weighing Indigenous economic rights versus liberal capitalist rights, as the landmark *Delgamuukw v. British Columbia*, 1997, held—permitting infringement of Aboriginal rights for "the development of agriculture, forestry, mining, and hydroelectric power, the general economic development of the interior of British Columbia, protection of the environment or endangered species, the building of infrastructure and the settlement of foreign populations to support those aims" (at para 165). While the *Delgamuukw* decision was the first declaration of Aboriginal title in Canada—that is, the first legal decision that recognized that provincial legislation cannot arbitrarily extinguish First Nations' proprietary interest in the land—the Gitskan and Wet'suwet'en plaintiffs had to contend with these racist brackets of infringement. While the SCC claims "the recognition of the prior occupation of North America by aboriginal peoples," as its purpose, regulations that infringe Aboriginal constitutional rights in favor of non-Indigenous commercial rights remain the norm (McNeil 1997: 35).

This competition is particularly salient in Canada in the tobacco wars. In Audra Simpson's work (2008) on the cross-border tobacco business in Haudenosaunee territory, she describes the "problem" of Indigenous commerce as blatantly about "lost revenue" to state and industry. She writes, "when the political subject is indigenous, citizenship takes on a temporal and economic form due to the societal expectation that Indians belong in a certain relationship to capital accumulation, that they be in another time (while simultaneously being within this world), and that they be poor" (194). While oil-rich First Nations are held up as model citizens and subjects by right-leaning think tanks for their *participation* in the resource economy (Bains 2013), the independent Mohawk tobacco industry poses a *threat* to the Canadian economy, rather than a useful crutch. In other words, the limits of liberal tolerance for Indigenous difference can be expressed in two interrelated temporal and economic forms: so long as they are *primitive* and *poor*.

In addition, without Indigenous commercial rights, the consequence of participating in *unrecognized* Indigenous commercial trade has serious legal repercussions. The criminalization of the Mohawk tobacco trade is emblematic of self-government policies that exclude commercial rights out of consideration. Bill *C-10* passed to amend the Criminal Code in 2014, for example, introduced harsher penalties for "trafficking in contraband tobacco," explicitly mentioning First Nations' trade. Pamela Palmater (2018) points out the irony of these restrictions, given that, "Part of the traditional practice of trading in tobacco was trading with Europeans—which is in fact how Europeans came to enjoy tobacco today." Mohawks, who are heavily invested in this production and trade, have insistently linked this economic issue to their *jurisdiction* as inherent rights and Treaty holders (Pratt and Templeman 2018). Here their difference is framed as "threat"—not just to the economic order, but to the national social and legal order—as securitization is justified through association of Indigenous tobacco trade with smuggling, fraud, counterfeit, black markets, terrorism, and illicit gun and drug trade (Pratt and Templeman 2018: 346).

Perceptions of economic rights and political rights are clearly intertwined; often wrapping around ideas of culture. When people learn that Jessica Cattelino's research (2005) concerns a lucrative bingo hall established by the Florida Seminole, it almost always prompts the question of whether gambling makes Native Americans "lose" their culture. She reflects that, "These concerns rest on the assumption that money, more than poverty, erodes culture and difference" (194). Here we could ask: if the courts' objectives in *Sparrow* and *Van der Peet* concern Crown obligations to ensure the *continuity* of Aboriginal culture, could poverty not be considered a primary target for elimination? Conversely, could commercial rights not be considered fundamental to the continuity of culture? Cattelino theorizes that, "[i]f indigenous non-ownership of property was the founding myth of settler colonialism, then indigenous poverty and its imaginings may be one of neo-colonialism's most potent contemporary forms" (195). The *continuity* of culture that courts seek to protect, in effect, entrenches and reproduces Indigenous poverty. It forces Indigenous peoples to perform an *essence* of Indigenous identity that breathes from the air of racist mythology.

Indigenous peoples can, of course, be both grounded in their culture, and participants in a modern market society. But from Canada's perspective, Indigenous difference must be carefully managed to secure access to land. In *The Cunning of Recognition* (2002), Elizabeth Povinelli notes that only what came through the fire of colonial atrocities in Australia is latched upon by settler society as authentic Aboriginal identity. This culture, extracted painfully from post-contact realities, acts to soothe the national conscience of settler violence by creating objects of Aboriginal resilience in their cultural difference. But it also forces Indigenous peoples to attach their subjectivity to a series of "lost indeterminable" objects. The state integrates a *pre-contact story of existence* in order to purify and redeem the nation. Defending Indigenous culture, then, (much like in Canada) becomes an exercise of public reason defending an immobile ancient culture that cannot compete with capital. It can, however, join: on the right terms.

Sharing the Taxes of Capitalist Profits

There is always more to parse doctrinally to make the argument that Indigenous economic rights are stunted by their interpretation in the courts. But I have cited many key precedents that roughly lay out the legal context of these rights for Indigenous peoples in Canada. Interpretation of Indigenous economic rights by the courts has been based to a considerable extent on a discursive construction of Indigenous culture as "frozen" and subsistent. Now I want to turn to an auxiliary model of Indigenous economic rights recognition—provincial resource revenue sharing—and examine the way Indigenous economic rights are rendered through these institutional arrangements, posing the question again of what this says about state configurations of Indigenous jurisdiction.

There is a growing emphasis in Canada on the need for Indigenous peoples to "share" in the resource wealth of the country as an element of reconciliation (Coates and Crozier 2018). While there are various mechanisms for this—private contracts between companies and First Nations (see Scott in this issue), equity ownership (see Cowen and LaDuke in this issue)—I want to focus here on the emerging agreements between Indigenous peoples and provincial governments known as government resource revenue sharing (GRRS).

There are hundreds of millions of dollars to be made in benefit sharing deals for First Nations when companies want access to their territories. Impact and Benefit Agreements (IBAs) are private commercial contracts that are increasingly being negotiated between Indigenous peoples and industry in the consultation phase of a project. These agreements were rare before Indigenous peoples gained constitutional rights; they also point to the power of Indigenous peoples to shape the resource economy of Canada. There are four provinces in Canada that have GRRS policies for First Nations and they all differ in formulas and application. In addition, though we do not have space here to cover these here, Quebec, Newfoundland and Labrador, Northwest Territories, Nunavut, and Yukon all have GRRS policies that were negotiated through land claims agreements with Indigenous governments.

GRRS agreements typically take the form of legal contracts between provincial Crowns and Indigenous people to share revenue from oil, gas, mining, hydro, or forestry can take many forms and may be negotiated in endless configurations, such as with individual Bands, tribal councils, Treaty groups, or clusters of regionally-affected Bands. The Conference Board of Canada (Pendakur and Fiser 2017:3) defines their scope as:

> Any formal agreement between a Crown-representative national or subnational government and an indigenous community for the purposes of sharing government revenues generated from natural resource extraction or use. The revenues in question, that said governments may receive from various natural resource sector activities, differ across jurisdictions and may include royalties, taxes, fees, and so forth.

For mining, in particular, government-allocated RRS always takes its percentage point of First Nation sharing from provincial or territorial tax payments, never from the value of the commodities or company profits. The dollar value of corporate mining profits is inaccessible to Ministries that manage GRRR because company earnings are proprietary information held by Finance departments. Therefore, so much depends on taxation rates and royalties across jurisdictions, as well as federal income taxes and incentive programs. In other words, the rent is paid to the state and then divided further among First Nations. Provinces are under no legal obligation to devise these schemes and some, like Ontario, explicitly refrain from describing them as a legal right, compensation, or reparations (McLean and Karwacki 2019). Rather, they are framed in broad or nebulous "reconciliation" language that critics commonly refer to as "social license" (Browne and Robertson 2009).

The way these revenues are calculated and allocated also differs greatly between jurisdictions. For example, in Ontario there is a fixed standard for GRRS, and beginning in fall 2019, partner First Nations will receive 45 percent of government revenues from forestry stumpage and 40 percent of the annual mining tax and royalties from active mines at the time the agreements were signed, and 45 percent from future mines in the areas covered by the agreements (MEMD, 2019). There are currently thirty-one First Nation communities, represented by the Grand Council Treaty #3, Mushkegowuk Council, and the Wabun Tribal Council who have signed agreements with the Province. With the monies received through these agreements, First Nations cannot spend these funds for per capita distribution to community members, redistribute them to other First Nation communities, use them to cover any costs of litigation, or invest the money to accrue returns without first advancing five key areas: economic development, community development, cultural development, education, and health (Fasken 2018).

On the matter of financial allocation, though: what is being shared? The Narwhal calculated that in 2017 Barrick Gold extracted gold valued at almost $250 million from its Helmo mine in northwest Ontario and paid $14.4 million in taxes, amounting to a mere 5.8 percent of the gold's market value (Wilt 2018). Partner First Nations will receive 40 percent of the annual mining tax and royalties from the mine, which seems significantly less when compared to net profits. Seventeen out of Ontario's thirty-eight operating mines are located in the areas now covered by revenue-sharing deals (MEMD, 2019). But as Scott and Boisselle (forthcoming) argue

> If Ontario recognized Indigenous governing authority and the communities exercised jurisdiction to approve or reject industry permits, then RRS—with the proportions to be "shared" negotiated in this renewed treaty context, and the tax rate increased to ensure that appropriate revenues could be generated—could be a viable long-term mechanism for ensuring mutual benefit from the territory, as long as the development was consistent with the affected communities' visions for their homelands.

In Ontario, the share is generous, but the net benefits low, and the cost high—accepting its basis on Crown jurisdiction and rental authority.

Provinces keep very little of the revenues extractive industries generate to attract business because provinces and the federal government are willing to create an extremely low tax barrier for companies. There are multiple mechanisms for companies to underreport earnings, as well, and Joan Kuyek outlines many of these in her book, *Unearthing Justice* (2019). If provinces promise fair sharing it is important for First Nations to see how much of this revenue they are actually accessing, at what percentage of total company profits. *Base erosion* and *profit sharing* (BEPS) as two central practices that reduce taxable profits and shifts profit between subsidiaries to hide earnings and it is a global problem.[12] The mining tax and royalties collected by provinces represent a fraction percentage of net profit (see Barrick Gold example above). Companies then convert losses in credit against future mining taxes, called "tax assets."

But more than just raising questions of fair redistribution, a deeper matter of jurisdiction is also at stake, which we can examine by focusing here on BC. The first jurisdiction in Canada to introduce a program to share the revenues from extraction with First Nations was the province of BC in 2008. BC first introduced a GRRS policy in October 2008 in a brief news release that remains to this day the only official written document the province has presented on the policy. In part, the policy emerged through request by First Nations and was discussed with First Nations Leadership Council (Clark 2009). But the provincial rationale for the new policy is provided in the brief, linking it to the New Relationship announced in 2005 a few months after the *Haida* decision came down. This is important because in 2004, the "duty to consult" legal precedent was established in both the *Haida First Nation v. British Columbia (Minister of Forests),*2004, and *Taku River Tlingit First Nation v. British Columbia (Project Assessment Director),* 2004, SCC decisions. These cases found that the federal and provincial governments have a duty to consult with First Nations that are asserting their constitutional rights—even in the pre-proof stage of rights and title. Established rights are subject to the federal government's *fiduciary* obligations and trigger a range of other legal protections (Luk 2003; McNeil 2015).

BC is ground zero for resource extraction in Canada, with much of its regional economy dependent on forestry, and mining to a lesser extent. The text of the New Relationship document (2005) states that BC is "building a new relationship with First Nations founded on mutual respect, recognition and reconciliation, which will support Aboriginal people's participation in the province's economic and social progress" (3).[13] In a presentation in 2009, the Government added additional guidance to the policy, including an instructive statement that BC wishes to "minimize litigation," and to "de-emphasize the legalistic aspects" of Indigenous land interests.

These incentives are particularly salient in BC, where a court case changed the resource economy in that province when the *Delgamuukw* decision came down in 1997. *Delgamuukw* is one of five foundational title cases heard in the Supreme Court of Canada that includes: *Calder v. Attorney General of British Columbia; Delgamuukw v. British Columbia; R. v. Marshall; R. v. Bernard*; and *Tsilhqot'in Nation v. British Columbia*. Taken together, the courts have found Aboriginal title to be "held by Aboriginal nations or polities that are the descendants or successors of the Aboriginal people that were in exclusive occupation of their traditional territories at the time of Crown assertion of sovereignty" (McNeil 2016: 17). Aboriginal title encompasses the right to exclusive use and occupation of the land for a range of purposes not limited by traditional use, for example including mineral rights (*Delgamuukw* at para 122). The *Delgamuukw* case, mentioned earlier, also raised the bar of Indigenous jurisdiction from a requirement of consultation to consent, as the court stated: "Some cases may even require *the full consent of an aboriginal nation*, particularly when provinces enact hunting and fishing regulations in relation to aboriginal lands" (*Delgamuukw* at para 168, emphasis added). Though the burden of proof for Aboriginal title, and the cost of bringing a case to court, remain substantial barriers, Indigenous peoples' governing authority over their land potentially opened the door for participation in the resource economy in new ways.

Rather than engage Indigenous peoples as property owners and title holders, the New Relationship re-defined "partnership" in such a way as to maintain the state's exclusive authority over resource regulation and approvals in forestry and mining. One of the ways it accomplishes this is to structure GRRS such that Indigenous parties would share from the profits only once a project approval moved forward from the Ministry of Environment and Climate Change for new or expanding mines. The details of the policy include negotiation on a case-by-case basis. There are in fact very few mining projects in the province—either new and expanding mines—but almost two hundred fifty Forest Consultation and Revenue Sharing Agreements have been signed (BC 2019). The Conference Board of Canada (2017) reports that these payments constitute approximately ten per cent of First Nations' total annual revenues (3).

If we take a closer look at the formulas, we can see that what the large print gives, the small print takes away. The openness of governments to include Indigenous peoples in the market economy through GRRS shows how *erasing the presence of Indigenous peoples on the landscape and denying their governing authority,* as in the jurisprudence cited above, starts to take a backseat to the *urge to maintain access for capital.* GRRS also denies governing authority—through the de facto decision-making power to authorize extraction remaining with the province—but the new efforts at inclusion hold hands with previous colonial histories of enfranchisement into the body of Canada, and the entrance price is concession to the authority of the state (Milloy 1991). Whereas in the first case study of SCC decisions, Indigenous peoples' governing authority over their participation in the commercial economy was denied, in the second case, it is readily accepted. But in both cases, Indigenous jurisdiction is an extremely attenuated thing. The courts and provinces ensure that only a delegated form of authority is recognized, never an inherent right of self-determination.

Conclusion: Racial Capitalism, Frozen Rights, and Sharing Extractive Profits

On the relationship between colonialism, capitalism, racism, I examined how courts and state policy makers allocated value to land along a spectrum of difference called "indigeneity." What at first look like contradictory tendencies in colonial policy to both assimilate and exclude Indigenous peoples from participating in market society upon closer examination reveal a colonial political economy of racial differentiation that is configured according to spatio-specific regimes of accumulation.

In a sense it is assimilation writ large across both these scenarios. GRRS is a way of answering a basic liberal urge for "inclusion" without allowing any questioning of the underlying proprietary interests—just as the denial of commercial rights to Indigenous peoples through the courts is a way of managing the limits of Indigenous jurisdiction and authority, even in light of legal admissions and recognition of underlying Aboriginal title and proprietary interest. As Brenna Bhandar writes, "Being an owner and having the capacity to appropriate have long been considered prerequisites for attaining the status of the proper subject of modern law, a fully individuated citizen-subject" (2019: 5). By being denied this status, Indigenous peoples maintain their quasi-sovereign collective rights (as understood by settler courts) but they also experience the liminal gray zone of never being fully considered proper subjects or or independent nations.

Indigenous peoples are caught in the bind of larger, stickier circuits of capital that require their participation, acquiescence, and surplus status all at once (Pasternak and Dafnos 2017). Racial differentiation is essential to these flows, as Bhandar notes, "The transatlantic slave trade, and the appropriation of indigenous lands that characterized the emergence of colonial capitalism on a worldwide scale, produced and relied upon economic and juridical forms for which property law and a racial concept of the human were central tenets" (6). Therefore, we return to the "valences of reproduction" and counter-sovereignties described above to see outside these containers.

Theorizing Indigenous economies, Dara Kelly pushes back against precisely the ways liberal capitalist discourse attempts to integrate Indigenous economies into Western epistemes. She writes, "The challenge ahead for Indigenous people contesting the foundations of capitalism lies in questioning who benefits from economic success, and who pays the cost of exploited land and resources" (107). While the state shows ambivalence on whether alliances between Indigenous peoples and industry are critical to the perfection of sovereignty or threatening, the deeper questions involve the underpinning questions about who has the authority to authorize land and water use on these lands.

Notes

1   https://www.oecd.org/tax/beps/.

2   See, for example, the recent report on Missing and Murdered Indigenous Women and Girls that names state policies as genocidal and demands redress (www.mmiwg-ffada.ca/final-report/).

3   There is also a small but interesting literature on Indigenous people's participation in wage labor markets, but it is not the central focus here. See, for example, High 1996; Jamieson 1962; Knight 1996; Laliberte and Satzewich 1999; and Lutz 1992.

4   There is another paper to write on the class politics of Canada and its intersection with colonization. In particular, federal policies of austerity provoke racial antagonism by the middle and lower classes against Indigenous peoples. This form of scapegoating masks massive state divestment in social welfare programs, but this analysis will have to wait for another day.

5   Here I refer to Glen Coulthard's critique (2014) of state paradigms of recognition that represent a continuation of colonization through the asymmetrical field of power upon which the state defines and determines the limits of Indigenous authority.

6   Other scholars have focused closely on Treaty history and the exclusion of the Métis as signatories to agreements premised on their racial identity (Adam 1975; Adese 2011; Augustus 2005; Macdougal 2016).

7   For more on Indigenous women's re-enfranchisement efforts over the years, see McIvor, Day, and Palmater 2018; and Gehl 2000.

8   Wilson defines "race-connected practices" as "practices resulting from racism — negative attitudes groups of people or individuals belonging to one race hold about individuals or groups of people belonging to a different race" (31).

9   Though it was deeply flawed, one such assimilationist policy was the Home Farm program, which subsidized agricultural training and provisions for prairie First Nations reeling from the extermination of the bison (Daschuk 2013; Waisberg and Holzkamm 1993). Where successful, it was thwarted by racism, when fear of uprising created a pass system to control Indigenous political movement but was applied to restrict participation in agricultural markets.

10   Proof of "continuity" of practices, customs, and traditions pre- and post-European contact are essential when claiming post-contact practices, customs, and traditions as Aboriginal rights, or post-contact occupation of lands (McNeil, 2004). Therefore, while continuity does not require an *unbroken* chain of use, the integral aspect of this practice to culture in pre- or post-contact times can be an essential aspect of proving Aboriginal rights.

11   For more on the aftermath of the *Marshall* decisions in terms of the First Nation commercial fishery, see Wiber and Milley 2007.

12   In response to the First Nations' self-government claims, the court relied on *Sparrow's* limit-making declaration on Aboriginal rights to conclude that this right was extinguished prior to 1982. The authority by which this disappearance was legalized is apparently the doctrines of discovery: "there was from the outset never any doubt that sovereignty and legislative power, and indeed the underlying title, to such lands vested in the Crown," *Sparrow*, at 1103.

13   "The Transformative Change Accord" also seems to have had an influence – signed in 2005, explicitly about closing the gap and reconciling ab title and rights with those of the Crown.

References

Adams, Howard. 1975. *Prison of Grass: Canada from the Native Point of View*. Toronto: New Press.

Adese, Jennifer. 2011. "'R' Is for Métis: Contradictions in Scrip and Census in the Construction of a Colonial Métis Identity." *TOPIA* 25: 203–12.

Ahousaht Indian Band and Nation v. Canada (Attorney General) 2018 BCSC 633.

Altamirano-Jiménez, Isabel. 2004. "North American First Peoples: Slipping up into Market Citizenship?" *Citizenship Studies* 8, no. 4: 349–65.

Altamirano-Jiménez, Isabel. 2014. *Indigenous Encounters with Neoliberalism: Place, Women, and the Environment in Canada and Mexico*. Vancouver: University of British Columbia Press.

Augustus, Camilla. 2005. *The Scrip Solution: The North West Metis Scrip Policy, 1885–1887*, University of Calgary (Canada), ProQuest Dissertations Publishing.

Auditor General of Canada. 2011. June Status Report.

Bains, Ravina. 2013. "Opportunities for First Nation prosperity through oil and gas development." Studies in Energy Transportation, Fraser Institute. November.

Bandhar, Brenna. 2019. *Colonial Lives of Property: Law, Land, and Racial Regimes of Ownership*. Durham: Duke University Press.

Barker, Joanne. 2018. "Territory as Analytic: The Dispossession of Lenapehoking and the Subprime Crisis." *Social Text*, no. 135: 19–39.

Blackstock. C. 2015. "Should Governments be Above the Law? The Canadian Human Rights Tribunal on First Nations Child Welfare." *Children Australia* 40, no. 2: 95–104.

British Columbia. 2019. Forest Consultation and Sharing Agreements. www2.gov.bc.ca/gov/content/environment/natural-resource-stewardship/consulting-with-first-nations/first-nations-negotiations/forest-consultation-and-revenue-sharing-agreements.

Browne, M. W., and Robertson, K. 2009. *Benefit Sharing Agreements in British Columbia: A Guide for First Nations, Businesses, and Governments*. Victoria, BC: Woodward.

Brownlie, Robin Jarvis. 2009. "A Persistent Antagonism: First Nations and the Liberal Order." In *Liberalism and Hegemony: Debating the Canadian Liberal Revolution*, edited by Jean-François Constant and Michel Ducharme, 298–321. Toronto: University of Toronto Press.

Calder v British Columbia (AG) [1973] S.C.R. 313.

Carter, Sarah. 1993. *Lost Harvests: Prairie Indian Reserve Farmers and Government Policy*. Montreal: McGill-Queen's University Press.

Cattelino, Jessica. 2005. Tribal Gaming and Indigenous Sovereignty, With Notes from Seminole Country, 46 AM. STUD. 193.

Christie, Gordon. 2004. "Aboriginal Resource and Subsistence Rights after *Delgamuukw* and *Marshall*." In *Advancing Aboriginal Claims: Visions, Strategies, Directions*, edited by Kerry Wilkins, 241–70. Saskatchewan: Purich.

Clark, Keith E. 2009. "Understanding the new BC resource revenue sharing policy with First Nations," June 2009, McMillan LLP.

Coates, Ken and Stephen Crozier. 2018. "Ontario, First Nations take giant step toward reconciliation with revenue-sharing deal." *Globe and Mail*, May 20.

Constitution Act, 1982, *being Schedule B to the* Canada Act 1982 *(UK), 1982, c. 11*.

Cornell, Stephen, and Joseph P. Kalt. 1998. "Sovereignty and Nation-Building: The Development Challenge in Indian Country Today." *American Indian Culture and Research Journal* 22, no. 3: 187–214.

Coulthard, Glen Sean. 2014. *Red Skin White Masks*. Minneapolis: University of Minnesota Press.

Daschuk, James. 2013. *Clearing the Plains: Disease, Politics of Starvation, and the Loss of Aboriginal Life*. Regina: University of Regina Press.

Day, Iyko. 2015. "Being or Nothingness: Indigeneity, Antiblackness, and Settler Colonial Critique." *Critical Ethnic Studies* 1, no. 2: 102–21.

Delgamuukw v. British Columbia, [1997] 3 S.C.R. 1010.

Doerfler, Jill. 2009. "An Anishinaabe Tribalography: Investigating and Interweaving Conceptions of Identity during the 1910s on the White Earth Reservation." *American Indian Quarterly* 33, no. 3: 295–324.

Du Bois, W. E. B. 1986. "Dusk of Dawn: The Concept of Race." In *Du Bois Writings*, 9th ed., 649. New York: Library of America.

Estes, Nick. 2019. *Our History Is the Future: Standing Rock Versus the Dakota Access Pipeline, and the Long Tradition of Indigenous Resistance*. New York: Verso.

Fasken. 2018. "Ontario Will Share Resource Revenue with Certain First Nations in the North." May 8. fasken.com/en/knowledge/2018/05/van-2018-05-07-indigenous-bulletin/.

Gabriel, Ellen. 2011. "Commentary Aboriginal Women's Movement; A Quest for Self-determination," *Aboriginal Policy Studies* 1, no. 1: 183–88.

Gehl, Lynn. 2000. "The Queen and I: Discrimination against Women in the Indian Act Continues." *Canadian Woman Studies* 20, no. 2: 64–69.

Goldstein, Alyosha. 2017. "Race, Capitalism, and Settler-Colonialism." In *Race and Capitalism: Global Territories, Transnational Histories*, edited by the Institute on Inequality and Democracy, 41–51. UCLA: Luskin.

High, Steven. 1996. "Native Wage Labour and Independent Commodity Production During the 'Era of Irrelevance.'" *Labour/Le Travail* 37: 243–64.

Hudson, Peter James. 2017. "To Remake the World: Slavery, Racial Capitalism, and Justice." In *Race Capitalism Justice*, edited by Walter Johnson with Robin D. G. Kelley, 59–65. *Boston Review, Forum 1*.

Jamieson, Stuart. 1962. "Native Indians and the Trade Union Movement in British Columbia." *Human Organization* 20, no. 4: 219–25.

Karuka, M. 2017. "Black and Native Visions of Self-Determination." *Journal of the Critical Ethnic Studies Association* 3, no. 2: 77–98.

Kelly, Dara. 2017. "Feed the People and You Will Never Go Hungry: Illuminating Coast Salish Economy of Affection." PhD thesis, University of Auckland.

Knight, Rolf. 1996. *Indians at Work: An Informal History of Native Labour in British Columbia 1858–1930*. Vancouver: New Star Books.

Kuyek, Joan. 2019. *Unearthing Justice*. Toronto: Between the Lines.

LaDuke, Winona. 1992. "We Are Still Here: The 500 Years Celebration." *Race, Poverty and the Environment* 3, no. 3: 3–21.

Laliberte, Ron, and Vic Satzewich. 1999. "Native Migrant Labour in the Southern Alberta Sugar-Beet Industry: Coercion and Paternalism in the Recruitment of labour." *Canadian Review of Sociology and Anthropology* 36, no. 1: 65–85.

Luk, Senwung. 2003. "Not So Many Hats: The Crown's Fiduciary Obligations to Aboriginal Communities since *Guerin*." *Saskatchewan Law Review* 76: 1–49.

Lutz, John. 1992. "After the Fur Trade: The Aboriginal Labouring Class of British Columbia, 1849–1890." *Journal of the Canadian Historical Association* 3, no. 1: 69–93.

Macdougall, B. 2016. "The Power of Legal and Historical Fiction(s): The Daniels Decision and the Enduring Influence of Colonial Ideology." *International Indigenous Policy Journal* 7, no. 3: 1–6.

Maracle, Lee. 1975. *Bobbi Lee: Indian Rebel: Struggles of a Native Canadian Woman*. Richmond, BC: LSM Information Center.

Marx, Karl. 1990. *Capital*, vol. 1. New York: Penguin.

McGregor, Deborah. 2005. "Traditional Ecological Knowledge: An Anishnabe Woman's Perspective." *Atlantis* 29, no 2: 103–9.

McGregor, Deborah. 2014. "Traditional Knowledge and Water Governance: the Ethic of Responsibility." *AlterNATIVE: An International Journal of Indigenous Peoples. Special Issue: Indigenous Knowledges Impacting the Environment* 10, no. 5: 493–507.

McGregor, Deborah. 2015–2016. "Indigenous Women, Water Justice, and Zaagidowin (Love)." *Canadian Woman Studies/les cahiers de la femme* 30, nos. 2–3.

McIvor, Sharon, Shelagh Day, and Pamela Palmater. 2018. "Equality Delayed Is Equality Denied." *Canadian Woman Studies* 33, nos. 1–2: 171–73

McLean, Kevin, and Grant Karwacki. 2019. "Meeting: Proactive Disclosure of RRS documents." Unpublished interview, ENDM, Deputy Minister's Breakout room, 5th Floor, Whitney Block, 99 Wellesley St. W. Wed. April 17.

McNeil, Kent. 1997. "How Can Infringements of the Constitutional Rights of Aboriginal Peoples Be Justified?" *Constitutional Forum* 8, no. 2: 33–39.

McNeil, Kent. 2004. "Continuity of Aboriginal Rights," In *Advancing Aboriginal Claims: Visions/Strategies/Directions*, edited by Kerry Wilkins, 127–50. Saskatoon: Purich.

McNeil, Kent. 2015. "Fiduciary Obligations and Aboriginal Peoples." In *The Law of Trusts: A Contextual Approach*, 2nd ed., edited by Jeffrey Berryman, Mark R. Gillen, and Faye Woodman, 907–76. Toronto: Emond Montgomery.

McNeil, Kent. 2016. "Aboriginal Title and Indigenous Governance: Identifying the Holders of Rights and Authority," *Osgoode Legal Studies Research Paper Series* 182: 17. digitalcommons.osgoode.yorku.ca/olsrps/182/.

Melamed, Jodi. 2015. "Racial Capitalism," *Critical Ethnic Studies* 1 no. 1: 76–85.

MEMD (Minister of Energy, Mines, Development). 2019. Resource Revenue Sharing. www .mndm.gov.on.ca/en/mines-and-minerals/resource-revenue-sharing.

Metallic, Naiomi Walqwan. 2018. "A Human Right to Self-Government over First Nations Child and Family Services and Beyond: Implications of the Caring Society Case." *Journal of Law and Social Policy* 28: 4–41.

Milloy, J. S. 1991. "The Early Indian Acts: Development Strategies and Constitutional Change." In *Sweet Promises: A Reader on Indian-White Relations in Canada*, edited by J. R. Miller, 145–56. Toronto: University of Toronto Press.

Morse, Bradford W. 1997. "Permafrost Rights: Aboriginal Self-Government and the Supreme Court in *R. v. Pamajewon*." *McGill Law Journal* 42, no. 4: 1011–42.

Palmater, Pamela. 2018. "Canada's Criminalization of the Indigenous Tobacco Trade." *Lawyer's Daily*, April 4.

Panitch, Leo. 1981. "Dependency and Class in Canadian Political Economy." *Studies in Political Economy* 6: 7–33.

Pasternak, Shiri. 2014. "Jurisdiction and Settler Colonialism: Where Do Laws Meet?" *Canadian Journal of Law and Society* 29, no. 2: 145–61.

Pasternak, Shiri. 2017a. *Grounded Authority: the Algonquins of Barriere Lake Against the State*. Minneapolis: University of Minnesota Press.

Pasternak, Shiri. 2017b. "Transfer payments impose permanent austerity on Indigenous communities," Series: Resistance 150: Unsettling Canada's Hidden Economic Apartheid, *Ricochet*, June 28.

Pasternak, Shiri, and Dafnos, Tia. 2017. "How Does a Settler State Secure the Circuitry of Capital?" *Environment and Planning D: Society and Space* 36, no. 4: 739–57.

Pendakur, Kala, and Adam Fiser. 2017. *Options and Opportunities: Resource Revenue Sharing Between the Crown and Indigenous Groups in Canada*. Ottawa: The Conference Board of Canada.

Perleman, Michael. 2000. *The Invention of Capitalism*. Durham, NC: Duke University Press.

Plain, Sylvia. 2019. Anishinaabe Inaakonigewin: Indigenous Governance, Laws, and Lifeways. Public Event. April 8. Toronto City Hall.

Povinelli, Elizabeth. 2002. *The Cunning of Recognition: Indigenous Alterities and the Making of Australian Multiculturalism*. Durham, NC: Duke University Press.

Pratt, Anna C., and Jessica Templeman. 2018. "Jurisdiction, Sovereignties and Akwesasne: Shiprider and the Re-crafting of Canada-US Cross-Border Maritime Law Enforcement." *Canadian Journal of Law and Society* 33, no. 3: 335–57.

R. v. Van der Peet [1996] 2 R.C.S.

R. v. Gladstone, [1996] 2 S.C.R. 723.

R. v. Marshall (No 1) [1999] 3 S.C.R. 456.

R. v. Marshall (No 2) [1999] 3 S.C.R. 533.

R. v. Pamajewon [1996] 2 R.C.S.

Robinson, Cedric. 1983. *Black Marxism*. London: Zed Books.

Scott, Dayna Nadine, and Andrée Boisselle. Forthcoming. "If There Can Only Be 'One Law,' It Must Be Treaty Law: Learning from Kanawayandan D'aaki." *UNB Law Review*, Special Issue on "Puzzles of Pipelines and Riddles of Resources." dx.doi.org/10.2139/ssrn .3410499.

Senate Standing Committee on Aboriginal Peoples. 2015. *On-Reserve Housing and Infrastructure: Recommendations for Change Standing Senate Committee on Aboriginal Peoples*, June.

Simpson, Audra. 2008. "Subjects of Sovereignty: Indigeneity, the Revenue Rule, and Juridics of Failed Consent." *Law and Contemporary Problems* 71: 191–216.

Simpson, Leanne Betasamosake. 2017. *As We Have Always Done: Indigenous Freedom through Radical Resistance*. Minneapolis: University of Minnesota Press.

Sparrow v. R., [1990] 1 S.C.R. 1075.

Statistics Canada. 2016. 2016 Census topic: Aboriginal peoples: www12.statcan.gc.ca/census -recensement/2016/rt-td/ap-pa-eng.cfm.

Todd, Zoe. 2014. "Fish Pluralities: Human-Animal Relations and Sites of Engagement in Paulatuuq, Arctic Canada." *Études/Inuit/Studies* 38, nos. 1–2: 217–38.

Tsilhqot'in v. British Columbia, 2014, SCC 44. R. v. Van der Peet [1996] 2 R.C.S. [Van Der Peet].

Waisberg, L., and T. Holzkamm. 1993. "'A Tendency to Discourage Them from Cultivating': Ojibwa Agriculture and Indian Affairs Administration in Northwestern Ontario." *Ethnohistory* 40, no. 2: 175–211.

Wiber, Melanie, and Chris Milley. 2007. "After *Marshall*: Implementation of Aboriginal Fishing Rights in Atlantic Canada." *Journal of Legal Pluralism and Unofficial Law* 39, no. 55: 163–86.

Wilson, Alex. 2015. "Our Coming in Stories: Cree Identity, Body Sovereignty, and Gender Self-Determination." *Journal of Global Indigeneity* 1, no. 1: 1–5.

Wilson, Bobby M. 2002. "Critically Understanding Race-Connected Practices: A Reading of W. E. B. Du Bois and Richard Wright." *Professional Geographer* 54, no. 1: 31–41.

Wilson Gilmore, Ruth. 2002. "Race and Globalization." In *Geographies of Global Change: Remapping the World*, edited by R. J. Johnston et al., 261–74. New York: Wiley-Blackwell.

Wilt, James. 2018. "Canada's Mining Giants Pay Billions Less in Taxes in Canada than Abroad." *Narwhal*, July 16.

Yazzie, Melanie K. 2018. "Decolonizing Development in Diné Bikeyah: Resource Extraction, Anti-Capitalism, and Relational Futures." *Environment and Society: Advances in Research* 9: 25–39.

Kylie Benton-Connell and D. T. Cochrane

"Canada Has a Pipeline Problem": Valuation and Vulnerability of Extractive Infrastructure

From the earliest days of opposition to tar sands extraction, Indigenous organizers and their supporters have targeted both pipeline companies and the financiers that fund them. According to the Indigenous Environment Network, "existing, approved and currently planned" tar sands extraction projects cover two thousand square kilometers, almost the area of 28,500 NFL football fields. Together, they make up the most prominent and visible process of destructive resource extraction that can be found across Indigenous territories claimed by Canada (Indigenous Environmental Network (2019a).

Apart from the danger pipelines pose to the communities and lands through which they run, they represent a crucial infrastructural bottleneck in getting tar sands oil to market. The Treaty Alliance against Tar Sands affirms that "Tar Sands expansion can't happen without new outlets" (Treaty Alliance Against Tar Sands Expansion 2019). In turn, such new outlets cannot happen without money. Through sustained campaigning, including confrontations with pipeline financiers, Indigenous-led movements have shifted oil transport infrastructure from the margins to the center of political contestation throughout North

The South Atlantic Quarterly 119:2, April 2020
DOI 10.1215/00382876-8177783   © 2020 Duke University Press

America. Finance and infrastructure are entangled in complex ways that strengthen extractive industries, but also generate vulnerabilities. Practices of financial valuation are central to capitalist decision-making about pipeline construction and extractive infrastructure more broadly. As such, these practices are worthy of detailed investigation and analysis by movement organizers and scholars.

The fruits of movement efforts targeting pipelines are clear: all new proposed tar sands pipelines over the past decade have been delayed or canceled, leading the *Wall Street Journal* to declare, in 2015, that "Canada has a pipeline problem" (Harder 2015). A number of banks have announced limits on the lending they will provide to tar sands projects, some excluding pipelines altogether (BankTrack 2018a). In order to demonstrate their support for continued tar sands expansion, in 2018 the Canadian government spent Can\$4.4 billion to buy the Trans Mountain pipeline outright, after its US owner walked away from a planned expansion project to double the pipeline's capacity. The company's about-face shows us that financial evaluation is an ongoing process, and political interventions can have meaningful impacts upon it.

In critical accounts, it is common to see descriptions of Canada as, for instance, a "colonial, capitalist petro-state" (Gunster 2019). This kind of account is useful, insofar as it underscores the strength of the connections between extractive industries and government decision-makers. However, instinctive use of such shorthand risks erasing important particularities. There are distinctions and divergences between various actors that have important consequences for political strategy. There are also distinctions between the financial tools that comprise capital, which have consequences for the relationships among these actors. Over the past decade, organizers and researchers have successfully traced some of the detailed contours of this landscape, and the opportunities they present for intervention. We hope, in this article, to detail and emphasize the strategic importance of this work.

In the first section of the article, we will make our case for why it is worth examining the relationship between finance and extractive infrastructure in granular detail: in short, because it helps us find opportunities for effective political interventions. In the second section, we will begin to flesh out a description of this relationship. We will start with a brief overview of the significance of finance in an analysis of colonial expansion and resource extraction, with an outline of the Canadian context generally and the tar sands specifically. We will continue with an examination of the link between the banking sector and resource extraction in Canada, and the history of financing arrangements for the first major pipelines built across Indigenous territories claimed by colonizers, and the basics of pipeline financing today. In the final section, we will give an overview of contemporary efforts to stop pipelines by constraining companies' access to money, and of how detailed understandings of industry dynamics strengthen such work.

Mapping Vulnerabilities and Widening Breaches

Our reflections on tar sands pipeline finance face a challenge shared by much critical work on possibilities for contesting corporate power. How should we explore openings for movement work, without minimizing the overwhelming strength of forces that organizers confront? In the final section of this article, we will outline political work opposing pipeline finance in more detail, arguing that the significant inroads achieved demonstrate the prospect of transformation. But first, we will briefly outline the main features of our response to this challenge.

We start from the commonly shared premise that categories like "capital" and "industry" are not monoliths, that is, that capitalists are in fact distinct and distinguishable in important ways. This is in many ways an obvious point, but much critical work—by both organizers and scholars— minimizes or contradicts it. In fact, a capital-as-monolith perspective has dominated critical political economy since Marx, and this has been reflected in theory and strategy. We instead concur with analyses showing that alliances among capitalists form and dissolve over time, as actors move into and out of alignment. William Carroll's (2017: 254) detailed work on relationships around fossil fuel executives illustrates how, although corporate Canadian networks are very tight, there is nonetheless friction between groups of capitalists in this arena.

We maintain that differences exist not only *between* sectors, but also *within* them; as our discussion of Canadian pipeline financing over time will show, there are often visible tensions and breaches between companies in the same sector. This may take the shape of capitalist competition for profits—as with the first pipeline companies to operate in territory claimed by Canada who fought each other tooth and nail over which project would win government support—or other kinds of differentiation, such as the banks that have broken ranks with the rest of their sector, and stopped making loans to tar sands operations. These breaches exist, in part, because capitalism is malleable and capitalists can make major shifts without causing systemic collapse. We propose that such gaps should be acknowledged and investigated, in all their contingency.

Second, we argue that greater knowledge of the historical contingencies that cause capitalist coalitions to form, align, misalign, and dissolve can inform movement strategies. We draw here on the work of Erik Olin Wright (2010: 291), in his description of long-term political work that generates "cracks and openings." Facing the monstrous, overwhelming edifice of extraction, we look both to identify such fissures and make them wider. Strategies to dismantle and weaken the forces and relationships that drive extraction might be located somewhere between what Olin Wright called the "ruptural" and what he called the "interstitial." The former strategies constitute revolutionary, radical breaks that overturn the existing order, while the latter are more gradual transformations involving the construction and expansion of alternative, noncapitalist social relations. While he used "interstitial" mostly in relation to prefigurative projects to "build the new society in the shell of the old," we find the term helpful as a way to frame the search for weaknesses in the financial support for extractive infrastructure. Our work in this arena is driven not merely by academic curiosity, but by the implications the work has for informing movement strategy. We contend that mapping the limitations and vulnerabilities of present-day settler colonial capitalism can be a practical project in support of communities resisting extractive infrastructure.

Finally, we assume that financial decision-making and financial valuation are profoundly social processes (Muniesa 2011; Çalışkan and Callon 2009), and as such, these breaches between companies, between sectors, and between people working in them can be observed and acted upon. Neither banks nor pipeline companies are machines that maximize profit according to unchanging rules. Contrary to the dominant value theories from both mainstream and Marxist political economy, value should not be understood in terms of mechanistic laws (for critical discussions of value theories, see Nitzan and Bichler 2009; Grossberg, Hardin, and Palm 2014; Mann 2010; Bryan, Rafferty, and Jefferis 2015). Value does not emerge as the outcome of perfectly rational actors engaged in market exchange. Nor is it simply determined by labor and production. Although labor, production, and markets pertain to processes of financial valuation, they are only part of the entangled web of relevant social relations. Capitalist processes of valuation can indeed be the object of explicit political interventions (Pasternak, Mazer, and Cochrane 2019; Cochrane and Manuel, forthcoming).

When company officers decide between going ahead with a pipeline construction project or abandoning it, they are most certainly assessing spreadsheets full of numbers. But we emphasize that these numbers are made, and that the processes of estimation, accounting, and calculation that produce them are neither impartial nor fully determined. The practices of value construction exist within a network of entities. Across the network there are zones of greater and lesser solidity. Some parts of the network are tightly linked, protected by powerful regularities that offer few—if any—openings for resistance. However, elsewhere there are cracks, contradictions, and vulnerabilities, as Indigenous organizers and their supporters have shown.

Finance and Colonial Extraction

Left thinkers have long acknowledged that resource extraction in the colonial world was crucial to capitalist wealth accumulation. There was no singular imperial process; European actors used a range of techniques as they scrambled to accumulate wealth from territorial conquest across the globe. Spanish conquistador armies operated from the outset with direct military accountability to the Crown; early British and Dutch forays were mediated through corporate entities such as the Dutch East India Company and the British East India Company, which were more autonomous. The actors, governance structures, and institutions varied over five centuries of colonial expansion, but a common thread remains; the accumulation of capitalist wealth derived from colonial resource extraction. Interpretations range from the dependency theory critique that Eduardo Galeano ([1973] 1997) popularized in *Open Veins of Latin America*, to more recent accounts of the deep connections between cotton plantations—staffed by enslaved people, on stolen or conquered land—and northern manufacturing, that iconic site of industrial capitalism (Beckert and Zafirovski 2013). The story of capitalism should not be told without centering the commodities derived from extraction, be they silver, tin, sugar, coffee, tea, spices, rubber, cotton, buffalo hides, or beaver pelts. Colonial expansion was not peripheral to these industries, but entirely integral to them.

The specific relationship of the *financial* sector to early colonial resource extraction is not always given sufficient attention. Many liberal and socialist critics in the early twentieth century saw colonialism as driven entirely by finance capital (Hobson [1902] 2018; Lenin [1917] 1963; Hilferding [1910] 1981; Luxemburg [1913] 1951). Less emphasis has been placed on the specific institutional history of colonial imbrication with the growth of the modern financial sector (Haiven 2018). Arguably the most important institutional form that shapes contemporary finance, the first shareholder corporations were built in service of imperial resource acquisition (Reamer and Downing

2016). Later, sales of North American railroad securities on capital markets—along with government support of various kinds—financed the web of rail lines spread across the continent, facilitating wide-reaching and rapid settler colonial incursions into Indigenous land. But it was not only railroad networks that grew; the market in railroad stocks and bonds fueled the growth of financial markets in North America and Europe (Chernow 2010; Morris 2006; White 2011; Chambers, Sarkissian, and Schill 2012)

Finance, Colonial Extraction, and the Tar Sands

While natural resources pulled Europeans into the Indigenous lands that would be claimed for Canada, the financial sector enabled and incentivized these violent colonial forays. The first shareholder corporation in North America was the Hudson's Bay Company, continuing the links between that specific corporate form and colonial expansion; the core of its business was expanding both the fur trade and territorial control (Dolin 2010). Canadian finance mirrored its US counterparts in its provision of loans to the Canadian Pacific Railway (CPR), completed in 1885. A massive government land grant to CPR made the project possible but was not sufficient; the president of CPR was continually scrambling to secure additional financing from British, US, and Canadian banks (Masters 1943). The CPR dealt a serious blow to Indigenous nations that still controlled large segments of land claimed as Canada's dominion, and opened access to vast areas for resource extraction (Cowen 2014). The colonial project that made this extraction possible allowed financial market participants to accumulate vast wealth.

The tar sands are the highest-profile example of the extractivism that remains central to Canada's economy. They have become emblematic of Canadian resource extraction and its roots in colonial violence. Their dystopically spectacular extraction zones have been characterized variously as an instance of "racial extractivism" (Preston 2017), "a slow industrial genocide" (Huseman and Short 2012), and "Mordor" (Vasil 2016). Tar sands mines are located mostly on Treaty 8 land claimed by the Canadian province of Alberta, and make up some of the world's largest oil deposits. But this oil is expensive and difficult to extract. Producers first raze boreal forest to access what is underneath—a combination of sand, clay, water, and bitumen. They then heat this mixture with water, making it liquid and pumping it to the surface for refining. The wastewater left behind creates vast toxic lakes. The Indigenous Environmental Network (2019b) describes the impacts of tar sands development as follows:

The cultural heritage, land, ecosystems and human health of First Nation communities including the Mikisew Cree First Nation, Athabasca Chipewyan First Nation, Fort McMurray First Nation, Fort McKay Cree Nation, Beaver Lake Cree First Nation Chipewyan Prairie First Nation, and the Métis, are being sacrificed for oil money. . . . Infrastructure projects linked to the tar sands expansion such as the Enbridge Northern Gateway pipeline and the Keystone XL pipeline, threaten First Nation communities in British Columbia, Canada and American Indian communities throughout the United States.

Pipelines are not a sideshow when it comes to tar sands extraction politics; in many ways, they have become the main event. Supporters of industry expansion—including banks (Canadian Press 2012), Alberta's provincial government (Neufeld 2018), and the major trade association of oil extraction companies (Canadian Press 2019)—have pushed relentlessly for new pipeline capacity. Critics suggest that expansion on the scale represented by all new proposed pipeline projects would be likely to produce an unnecessary glut (Vettese 2017; Gunton 2017); nevertheless, for the most part, parties in support of tar sands expansion have likewise supported new pipeline build-out. When two Canadian banks warned that without the Keystone XL pipeline, tar sands expansion would be stymied, anti-pipeline organizers listened and worked to let the world know where the banks stood (350.org 2012).

Canadian Banks and Finance for Extraction

Often, the specificity and the history of the links between finance and extraction collapse into blunt categories, such as in Kristian Gareau's (2016: 109) concept of "petro-finance." In such depictions, the relationships between finance and extraction are so close that the entities become almost indistinguishable from each other. The relationships between finance and extraction have many entangled threads. However, the complexities of these relationships—as well as the distinctions between the various entities—must be identified empirically and not just theoretically. We have chosen the relationship between pipelines and finance as a site of inquiry where such distinctions might be investigated.

Before delving into the details of pipeline finance, it is worth spending some time on the position of Canadian banks in the landscape of extraction more generally. Certainly, acquiring resources to sell in commodity markets was a key motivation for settler colonial expansion, and remains an important economic activity. But we should be mindful that much of the money that flowed into and out of early extractive activities necessarily passed through

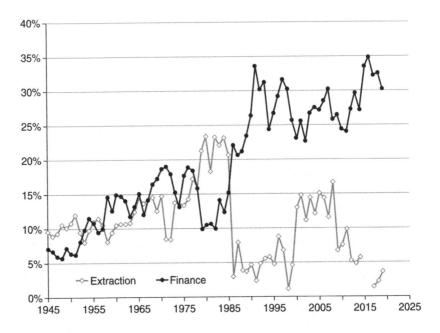

Figure 1. Finance and extraction share of Canadian corporate profits, 1945-2019Q1 (Statistics Canada 2018a, 2018b).
Note: Negative values for extraction in 2015-2016 excluded.

Canadian financial intermediaries (Naylor 1975). They offered basic financial services like deposit taking and check cashing. Such activities seem quaint and banal compared to credit default swaps, private equity, hedge funds, and other components of today's intricate financial sector. Nonetheless, Canadian financial companies were instrumental to colonial expansion and extraction, and they continue to be so today.

The characterization of Canada's as a "resource economy"—that is, dependent on extraction—can obscure the central role played by finance and banking in Canadian economic life. The scale of financial activity in Canada remains small relative to that in New York or London, and the country's financial markets are tied to both foreign centers. The finance sector does not provide the largest share of economic activity in Canada, but does provide the largest share of Canadian *profits*. Since 2000, more than 25 percent of profits in Canada have come from the country's financial sector. By contrast, Canada's extractive sector—following Statistics Canada's categories of "mining and quarrying (except oil and gas)" and "oil and gas extraction and support activities"—has contributed only 3.5 percent of corporate profits since 2009 (see Figure 1).

Canadian finance is centered around banks, which hold 70 percent of the assets in the sector (International Trade Administration 2018). These holdings are concentrated among the so-called Big Five banks: Bank of Montreal (BMO), Bank of Nova Scotia (Scotia), Canadian Imperial Bank of Commerce (CIBC), Royal Bank of Canada (RBC), and Toronto-Dominion (TD). All five are among the hundred largest banks in the world. They have deep roots in the Canadian political economy; they were all founded before or during the year of Canada's confederation in 1867. Together they hold almost US$4 trillion in assets (Garrido and Chaudhry 2019).

Many industry commentators consider Canada's finance sector to be thoroughly entangled with extraction, despite banks' protestations to the contrary (Trichur 2015; Posadzki 2018). This is reinforced by Carroll's (2017: 247) work tracking the overlaps of board membership between Canadian fossil fuel companies and financial sector companies.

According to research by D. T. Cochrane (seen in Appendix), the relationship between the Canadian finance sector and extraction is stronger than at any point over the previous ninety years. There is a strong positive correlation between the profits of Canadian banks and commodity prices: in other words, when commodity prices are increasing, the returns to Canadian banks are increasing. This echoes analyses arguing that Canadian capital is in a new version of the "staples trap" (Pineault 2018). The staples thesis has long been a point of contention in Canadian political economic debate, ever since Harold Innis ([1930] 2017, [1940] 2017) argued that the country's economy was shaped around the resources it extracted. Mel Watkins (1963) introduced a reformulation of Innis's thesis as a "trap," with recent critical accounts in this vein suggesting that Canada's political economy has indeed become dependent on its extractive industries (Watkins 2007; Stanford 2014).

The mechanisms through which Canadian banks are enmeshed with extraction vary, but one of the most important services they offer is the rotating line of credit. Extraction is a boom-and-bust business; commodity prices fluctuate up and down over short timelines, while extractive projects require massive capital investments that only pay for themselves over long timelines (Pineault 2018). Financial intermediaries are key to sustaining extraction companies through periods when commodity prices are low. A caveat must be noted for pipeline infrastructure: a substantial portion of pipeline capacity is dedicated to long-term "firm service agreements" where companies agree to pay for pipeline space at a fixed price whether they use it or not (Stockman and Trout 2017). This gives pipeline companies a stream of income that is not dependent on commodity price highs and lows. (And as

Troy Vettese [2017] has helpfully noted, drawing on the work of Jennifer Hocking, this can lead to major tensions between oil producers and pipeline companies.)

Rotating lines of credit—which can be extended essentially at the will of bankers—can mean the difference between a project continuing or going bankrupt. Building extractive infrastructure has enormous up-front costs, with significant uncertainty. Quick and easy access to money is essential. Canadian banks have been front and center in guaranteeing that pipeline construction projects have the cash they need on hand when unexpected costs emerge (Collins 2016; Bloomberg News 2016). Coverage in 2016 by Bloomberg News notes that the Big Five plus National Bank reported Can\$50 billion in outstanding loans to the oil and gas industry in their financial disclosures. But that was less than half the Can\$107 billion figure that emerged when unused credit lines were included (Bloomberg News 2016).

In addition to participating in rotating lines of credit, the banks also offer asset management services. This means managing other people's money through investment in a variety of assets, including pipeline companies and other companies involved in extraction. According to analysis by the Corporate Mapping Project, the Big Five banks are consistently among the top fifteen owners of fossil fuel extraction, processing, and transport companies; together, they own over 10 percent of the sector (Carroll and Huijzer 2018: 14–15).

Early Canadian Pipeline Finance: Conflict and Contingency

When oil was first made to gush at the Leduc-Woodbend field in 1947, it was the beginning of the Albertan petroleum industry. This set of economic relationships has incentivized a wave of destruction on Indigenous lands, displacement of Indigenous people, and devastation of Indigenous lives ever since (Preston 2017). To transport vast quantities of oil as quickly and cheaply as possible, industry and government actors began major pipeline projects (Kheraj 2015: 4). Examining the financial arrangements that enabled these early projects can provide insights for today's struggles.

Looking at the historical profile of the three companies behind current attempts to build new tar sands pipelines—Enbridge, TransCanada, and Trans Mountain—we see three things. First, far from a seamless alignment between state and industry, there were actually strong tensions between actors—such as between those who prioritized "nation building" and those who wanted access to more profitable US markets. These tensions were resolved in uneven ways. Second, financial valuation was a crucial mechanism through which decisions were made about pipeline construction. Third, the vulnerability of these projects rendered them contingent, not inevitable. Government support varied in degree and kind but was always present, and in some cases it was critical to a project's survival. This last point is particularly salient when we look at the precedents for the Trudeau government's intervention in support of the Trans Mountain pipeline expansion.

Pipeline projects—particularly those that connected the east and west coasts—were often framed in terms of nation building or national defense (Wilson and Taylor 1954: 13–14; Bothwell 1976: 700; White 2011; Kheraj 2015). The violent project of carving out the nation-state from Indigenous territories was not straightforward. As Deborah Cowen (2014: 16) notes, provinces literally demanded the building of long-distance rail as a condition of joining the Canadian federation, thereby "materializing settler colonial jurisdiction" in the physical infrastructure of the railway. Industry executive and writer Earle Gray (1970: 202) described it as follows:

> Canada wanted to build a nation east to west. The railway lines were built east to west, cutting across the grain of geography, at great expense, and had to be subsidized by the nation. If this was vital to the nation in the case of railways, the reasoning was, then it would be of the same importance in the case of pipelines.

As commentators note, contemporary pro–tar sands campaigns celebrate this colonial-frontier / "nation-building" history (Preston 2017: 19; Vieira 2013). Engineering and financial difficulties appear in the industry histories as problems to be solved by determined technicians, domineering statesmen, and gutsy engineers (Bott 1989; Wilson and Taylor 1954; Trans Mountain 1953; Gray 1970).

The genocidal project of conquest in which these projects were embedded is never far from view. In the official history of the Interprovincial Pipe Line Company (the precursor to Enbridge), the erasure of Indigenous sovereignty is casual: the author writes of how pipelines, as with transport systems based on rivers and railways, played "major roles in creating Canada and the United States from what was wilderness" (Bott 1989: 6). In Trans Mountain's official history, the author gleefully notes an early expedition into the territory where the pipeline would eventually be built, featuring "the first white girl born in the interior wilds of British Columbia" (Wilson and Taylor 1954: 19).

In a 2018 piece, pro–tar sands commentator Peter Shawn Taylor (2018) summarized the story of Canadian government involvement in pipeline infrastructure, explaining: "Canada was once a very large country with a very small population that could never generate the necessary market demand to make grand infrastructure projects a paying concern, as was the case in the United States." His depiction—of the US pipelines as a private affair, and of Canadians reluctantly forced to use government money—is misleading. While the configuration of relationships in each country was different, the government was present in the build-out of US pipeline infrastructure, as private capital—both US and Canadian—was likewise present throughout equivalent processes in Canada. In fact, from an international perspective, the similarities between the US and Canada are far more significant than their differences; according to industry consultant and historian Jeff Makholm, in the rest of the world "every major gas pipeline, and most oil pipelines, were built by governments" (Makholm 2012: 17).

But as Gray's commentary above implies, the project of Canadian nation building did not necessarily align smoothly with plans by profit-seeking pipeline entrepreneurs. A recurring theme throughout the early history of pipeline building is a nationalist push to build "all-Canadian" pipeline routes that would facilitate Canadian oil being sold to other Canadians. Public controversy enveloped Canada's first major pipeline, the Interprovincial (later Enbridge)—instead of running pipe to a Canadian destination, the company opted for the more lucrative option of selling oil to the US market in Wisconsin (Gray 1970: 209). The company would later run into more regulatory problems in Washington; according to Gray (1970: 209), US oil producers were unhappy about facing competition from cheap Canadian imports and strongly opposed a pipeline expansion. The original Trans Mountain pipeline route was far less controversial, due to its route across territory claimed entirely by Canada, though the company later added a spur crossing the border into Washington State.

A spectacular clash of nationalist desires and financial valuation was seen in the efforts to build TransCanada, a gas pipeline project from Alberta to Quebec. Companies had been fighting bitterly among themselves with competing projects to service the east for years; some Canadian capitalists had pushed for government approval of competing pipeline routes through the US (Kilbourne 1970: 105–6). Albertan suppliers wanted direct pipelines to Tennessee; purchasing companies on the east coast wanted gas from the US side of Niagara Falls (Kilbourne 1970: 94). C. D. Howe, a federal cabinet member known as the "minister for everything," due to his heavy involvement in Canadian industrial policy, forced two major companies into a "shotgun marriage" in 1954 on the proviso that they build an all-Canadian pipeline.

The project was plagued by years of delay and setbacks. East–west overland routes were much more expensive to build than north–south pipelines that would serve US markets, and TransCanada struggled to get either shippers or financiers to commit. Two attempts at government support failed, first when the cabinet declined to guarantee TransCanada debt, and then when a deal with the government-managed Bank of Canada fell apart. The latter debacle occurred when one of the main suppliers refused to do business with a company at the mercy of government shareholders. In the end, the government had to create an entirely new government-owned company to build the "uneconomic" section—amounting to about one-third of the whole project's cost—and extend a massive short-term loan to build the rest of the pipeline (Kilbourne 1970: 89, 119).

The eventual flow of private capital to fund all-Canadian pipeline routes resulted from evaluative exercises: financiers looked at pipeline proposals, made calculations, and assigned divergent, but comparative values. The fraught politics of Canadian nationalism were not outside, or in opposition to, the calculative practices of finance; rather, financial valuation occurred in relation to those politics. In each case, successful financing was not a foregone conclusion but an achieved outcome, with a mix of protagonists. Actors leading the formation of pipeline companies ranged from oil-producing companies to engineering companies and investment banks.

Imperial Oil was majority-owned by the US corporate heirs of Standard Oil and John D. Rockefeller when it formed the Interprovincial Pipe Line Company, in 1949. Most of the money to build this first major pipeline came from mortgage bonds, an arrangement where bond buyers lent money to the company through a mortgage on the pipeline. If the company collapsed, the owners of these bonds would, notionally, have ownership rights to the pipeline itself. The rest of the construction money would come from ownership shares in the Interprovincial company; about 25 percent would be bought by other oil companies (Bott 1989: 23).

According to company historians, the Trans Mountain project began at a meeting of oil and pipeline executives in an elite members-only club on the Upper West Side of New York City in February 1951 (Wilson and Taylor 1954: 10). The Trans Mountain Pipe Line Company was incorporated in March, and by August there were five shareholder companies; these were mostly oil producers (Wilson and Taylor 1954: 15), though Bechtel, the California engineering company—which would decades later become a despised target of anti-globalization movements for its role in Bolivian water privatization—was the most prominent actor identified with the project. Despite its many corporate partners, Trans Mountain needed a further Can$82 million to build the pipeline (Gray 1970: 215). As with the Interprovincial, the largest share of financing was raised through mortgage bonds, which were guaranteed by the oil companies involved (Wilson and Taylor 1954). With the backing of Canadian "underwriting houses" (merchant bankers that market the shares of a company when they are issued, also guaranteeing they will buy any unsold shares), 1.5 million shares were sold: many of these were bought by oil producers in Alberta, with some others going to small-scale investors (Wilson and Taylor 1954: 31).

In the case of TransCanada, Lehman Brothers—the US investment bank whose collapse would trigger the worst of the 2008 global financial upheaval—played a key role in forming the company, split 50/50 between US and Canadian owners (Kilbourne 1970: xiii). As noted above, TransCanada could not get capital market backing before the government stepped in; financial valuations deemed the pipeline unworthy of investment. But after the government stepped in with generous support, private investment followed; suppliers signed up, Canadian banks were involved in the first extension of private credit to the company, and a US insurance company provided a large chunk of the money through a deal similar to those used for two previous pipelines, involving mortgage bonds, debentures, and stock (Kilbourne 1970: 87, 144–46).

We must note here that the government support for TransCanada was incredibly unpopular, and faced heavy opposition in the Canadian Parliament, where the opposition railed against the government's "touching solicitude for U.S. business" (Kilbourne 1970: 101). The ruling Liberal party rushed the relevant legislation through in 1956 with the unusually autocratic use of parliamentary procedure, which was followed by its first electoral defeat in two decades (Bothwell 1979; Anonymous 2008; Kheraj 2018; Kilbourne 1970). As environmental historian Sean Kheraj (2018) notes, the parallels to the current situation with the Trans Mountain pipeline are clear.

Even this brief look at the precursors to Enbridge, Trans Mountain, and TransCanada shows that early pipeline building in Canada was far from a smooth process where state and capital were always aligned. Rather, disparate entities performed numerous calculations that informed corporate and political maneuvers that created interlocks and disjunctures. The petroleum "industry" can rarely be said to have been a totally coherent, unitary entity— it has been riddled with divisions, competing projects, and shifting allegiances. As Dayna Scott (2013: 58) notes, "the category of 'big oil' sometimes employed in these debates needs to be disaggregated to account adequately for the degree to which specific industrial actors stand to gain and lose from particular spatial configurations of privately-owned infrastructure."

The history of early pipeline construction sketched in this article (with pipeliners engaged in bitterly fought attempts to undermine each other's projects) provides ample illustration of this point. Not only was industry riven by factions with competing projects; state governments often represented diverging viewpoints; US-based actors (whether government regulators, oil producers, or bankers) sometimes supported and sometimes opposed the project at hand; in the case of TransCanada the federal government faced not only virulent opposition parties but doubt within its own party ranks (Kilbourne 1970: 156). In short: the construction of these pipelines was not preordained, but rather the result of messy and contingent processes. As we move into the discussion of pipeline finance and resistance today, we would do well to bear this aspect of Canadian pipeline history in mind.

Canadian Pipeline Finance Today: A Complex Battlefield

In the mid-century pipeline projects discussed above, managers created a new corporation to build each individual pipeline. By contrast, the North American midstream industry is now dominated by big umbrella companies like Kinder Morgan, TransCanada, and Enbridge, which own multiple pipelines through elaborate corporate structures. Many US pipeline companies (such as Energy Transfer Partners, the company in charge of the Dakota Access Pipeline) take the form of a Master Limited Partnerships (MLP), a complex and opaque corporate structure described by *Economist* journalists as a "distorporation" (*Economist* 2013). Created during the Reagan era, MLPs pass their profits through to "unitholders," who get a significant tax break (Koplow 2013). MLP unitholders are investors positioned somewhat like shareholders, but who have no voting rights with which to influence decisions by company management. MLP companies generally do not have much available cash, as they distribute most of it to unitholders. Therefore, they have been reliant on debt to finance new pipeline projects (DeWitt Capital Management 2015).

As a result, debt financiers of the pipeline companies have been heavily targeted by organizers, such as a group mobilizing against the Dakota Access Pipeline that noted: "$3.75 of the $3.8 billion it costs to build the pipeline is on credit. Without the money there is no pipeline" (Molinar 2016). But the debt used to build pipelines is not often as straightforward as a simple bank loan. For instance, the following is a list of the kinds of debt Enbridge has issued since 1995: senior bonds and notes, senior secured bonds and notes, senior unsecured bonds and notes, senior secured loans, senior secured debt, revolving credit, fixed rate debt, variable rate debt, term loans, convertible debt, commercial paper, trust preferred, capital leases, senior subordinated debt, junior subordinated debt, subordinated bonds and notes, nonrecourse debt, unamortized discount debt, unamortized premium debt, second lien bonds and notes, securitized facilities, and zero coupon debt.[1] It is not possible nor necessary here to detail all aspects of each of these kinds of debt. But it is important to note that each kind of debt may involve different lenders, and different conditions, which present different opportunities for movement pressure. One example: some loan agreements have clauses that state that if construction is delayed past a certain point, the loan can be cancelled—a key factor, analyst Robyn Allan (2018) suspects, in Kinder Morgan's decision to withdraw from building the Trans Mountain expansion.

Canadian companies that operate in the US (such as TransCanada and Enbridge) have historically had a US MLP as part of their corporate family tree. But in recent years, pipeline companies in North America have started to move away from this structure (Hsieh 2018). Kinder Morgan and Enbridge have both eliminated their MLPs in favor of a more conventional company structure, and TransCanada has only part of its business still channeled through its MLP in the US. This will increase these companies' ability to fund more of their new projects through their own profits, rather than through borrowing money from banks and bondholders, or issuing new shares (Steffy 2014). The move away from MLPs thus has significant implications for Indigenous-led movements confronting new pipelines, as companies may come to rely less on debt.

Other details of a company's relationship to capital markets are worth investigating: for instance, the volume, speed, and volatility at which the company's shares are trading may have consequences for a company's ability to raise enough money through debt. If it has a low stock price, a company may have difficulty finding people and institutions willing to lend it money. And if a company is not borrowing money or holding onto profits, the only way it can raise cash is to issue shares, as Kinder Morgan initially did to finance the Trans Mountain pipeline expansion (Allan 2018). This is more difficult if the stock price is low. A stock that is constantly bouncing up and down and traded often presents different campaign opportunities to one with a more stable share price. We were unable to do comprehensive original research in this arena, but one industry commentator provides a promising hint for further investigation:

> The profusion of fund products that offered significant exposure to master limited partnerships (MLP) also contributed to the indiscriminate buying and selling of US midstream stocks. Shares of Canadian midstream operators didn't experience anything near this level of financialization. (Conrad 2016)

As such, the shape of financial sector *ownership* investment in pipeline companies is also worth tracking. The figures here are clear: over the last ten years, investment advisor companies owned a solid majority of shares (between 60 and 80 percent) of Kinder Morgan, TransCanada, and Enbridge.[2] It is harder to get deeper historical information about the companies' ownership profiles (it is telling in itself that the major information interface of the financial markets—the Bloomberg Terminal—considers five–ten years "long-term.") But even limited present-day information is useful. It is useful to draw out distinctions: investment advisors, hedge funds, pension funds, and investment banks are all financial companies. But they present very different opportunities to social movements. For example: hedge funds have recently taken increasing positions in midstream MLP companies (Ross 2018). These companies are much more likely to make sudden entries or exits than other market actors, but also often tolerate higher risk, and may have thicker corporate skins when subjected to public pressure.

Starving the Black Snake: Efforts to Limit Pipeline Companies' Access to Money

As we noted at the beginning of this article, Indigenous-led fights against North American pipelines have long targeted the banks and investors enabling their construction. The highest-profile effort came out of the mobilization against the Dakota Access Pipeline. Indigenous land defenders, with collaborators in environmental organizations, identified financial institutions providing financial resources to Energy Transfer Partners, the pipeline's owner. In 2016, as the Standing Rock fight reached its peak, groups started

DefundDAPL.org to track widespread personal and institutional divestment from the banks funding the pipeline, from Jane Fonda to the Seattle City Council (Cook and McMillan 2019). Some divestment campaigners called for individuals and organizers to "starve the black snake" (Koo 2017).

But Standing Rock was only one of several high-profile pipeline struggles: others preceded and followed it. Organizers have made these pipelines household names: Energy East, Northern Gateway, Keystone XL, Line 3, Trans Mountain, Coastal GasLink. The companies trying to build them are Canadian and US corporations worth billions of dollars on stock markets, backed by banks and investors worth even more. As early as 2011, those leading resistance efforts to stop Keystone XL encouraged people and institutions to "move their money" from tar sands financiers (Mendelson 2011). Organizers staged repeated protests and occupations at banks, including RBS (Arnott 2011), BNP Paribas (Hill 2012), TD Bank (Colaneri 2013), and JPMorgan Chase (Atkin 2013)

In 2017, in the wake of the mobilizations at Standing Rock, Mazaska Talks was founded as an Indigenous organization to focus and track work pressuring the banks behind all remaining tar sands pipeline projects. Divest, Invest, Protect organized multiple delegations of Indigenous women to meet with European investors about DAPL and tar sands expansion projects ("Divest, Invest, Protect" 2019; for a detailed account of DAPL divestment work, see Cook and McMillan 2019). The same year, Kanahus Manuel, one of the organizers of the Tiny House Warriors (a group reoccupying Secwepemc land in the path of the planned Trans Mountain expansion), joined with Cedar George-Parker of the Tsleil-Waututh Nation to meet with bankers in Europe (Johnson 2018). Projects facing fierce resistance—from blockades to court cases—have been delayed for years (Trans Mountain, Keystone XL, Coastal GasLink), withdrawn (Energy East), or denied government approval (Northern Gateway).

In this context, some financiers have decided that funding these companies is not worth the possible return and have openly announced they will exclude financing for these kinds of construction projects. Thirteen banks have policies stating they will not provide project finance to companies building tar sands pipelines (BankTrack 2018b). Three banks have ruled out providing any sort of financing to pipeline companies (BankTrack 2018a). This distinction is important; while some pipeline construction is funded by "project finance" tagged to a specific purpose, some is instead funded by lines of credit provided by banks for general use. This can provide an impressive loophole; US Bank was estimated to have lent over US$2 billion to DAPL owner Energy Transfer Partners after promising to get out of the pipeline business (Stockman, Olson, and McMillan 2018).

Industry decision makers, as well as their allies in government, have taken notice. International oil companies sold off more than Can$30 billion in tar sands assets in 2017, with industry analysts giving pipeline capacity shortage as a major reason (Varcoe 2019). But it is not just overseas players: Canada's Suncor, the world's largest tar sands operator, announced in 2018 that it would not be investing in further expansion of its tar sands operations until more pipelines were built (*Financial Post* 2018). We should note that an alternate position from tar sands critics argues that the drop in investment has less to do with pipeline capacity shortages than with weak oil prices (Vettese 2017).

But backers of tar sands expansion are not going quietly. The Canadian government's purchase of both the existing Trans Mountain pipeline and planned expansion is only the highest-profile sign of support for tar sands expansion. Politicians across the spectrum of Alberta politics have backed extractive industries with national publicity campaigns to promote the tar sands, aggressive public investigations into environmental groups, and promises to subsidize oil-by-rail shipments to enable expansion while pipelines are on hold. As Shiri Pasternak and Tia Dafnos (2017) note, government and companies have collaborated on aggressive surveillance initiatives to thwart Indigenous-led disruption of "critical infrastructure" (see also Pasternak 2013). The head of the country's largest bank, the Royal Bank of Canada, is openly campaigning for pipeline construction (Zivitz 2019). And financiers of Teck Resources are betting on the profitability of a massive new tar sands mine (Canadian Press 2019).

Pipeline struggles in Canada have yet to attract the same international attention as the battle at Standing Rock. But Indigenous land defenders continue to push back against incursions, and confrontations are escalating. The violent removal of land defenders from a checkpoint protecting Unist'ot'en land from construction by Coastal GasLink in 2018 constitutes just such an escalation. Union of British Columbia Indian Chiefs president Stewart Phillip and Serge Simon, Grand Chief of the Mohawk Council of Kanesatake, warned that if Ottawa insists on pushing through the expansion of Trans Mountain, it could precipitate an "Oka-like crisis," referencing the 1990 armed standoff between Mohawk warriors and the Canadian army (Phillip and Simon 2018).

The nonpartisan Parliamentary Budget Officer (PBO) has calculated the present value of the expanded Trans Mountain pipeline at Can$4.6 billion. However, that valuation is contingent on construction being completed by the end of 2021. If construction is delayed by just one year, PBO estimates the value of the pipeline will drop below Can$4 billion—less than the government paid (Giroux 2019). Estimates of losses due to delay have already been put on record in court filings by the pipeline's previous owner, Kinder Morgan (Pasternak, Mazer, and Cochrane 2019). Analysts are already assessing the impact of Indigenous assertions of sovereignty and their potential to further stall construction—not only in the department of the PBO, but in banks, insurers, and pipeline companies.

Indigenous land protectors looking for leverage in the capital markets face no simple task—the finance and extractive sectors are not easily pried apart, especially in resource-dependent settler colonial arenas like Canada. It is notable that, to date, most banks that have excluded tar sands from their project lending are European (BankTrack 2018b). We do not know the details of internal discussions behind the closed doors of these banks; but we do know that their calculations have changed in the face of sustained Indigenous-led campaigns. We do not assume that decisions to withdraw from pipeline projects were made when executives got squeamish about teargassing land defenders; but nor do we assume that the companies concerned are perfectly functioning machines of profit maximization. Instead, we start from the idea that these companies, and the industries of which they are a part, are complex. They exist within an ecosystem of uneven power distributions, contradictory interests, and shifting alliances. Capitalist decision-making is calculative, and the decision to back a pipeline project is based on evaluation. But political interventions can impact those processes of evaluation: as Shiri Pasternak, Katie Mazer. and D. T. Cochrane (2019: 223) note, "the NoDAPL campaign posed a clear and fundamental threat to Energy Transfer Partners' bottom line by conjoining disruption of pipeline construction with targeting of its financing; these combined tactics undermined the viability and profitability of the project on a number of fronts" (see also Cochrane and Manuel forthcoming). It is worth understanding as much as we can about how financial intermediaries relate to extractive infrastructure projects. The more detailed our understanding of these processes and dynamics, the more strategic our interventions might come to be.

Conclusion

Indigenous organizers and their supporters have already changed the terrain on which industry decision makers are making calculations. We have argued in this article that it is helpful to read this terrain not as a tidy, predictable space where all governments collude with all capitalists, but rather as a situation where the relationships among various sectors and actors solidify, transform, and disappear. Looking at the historical background we provided in this article, we see that the connections among the financial sector, extraction, and settler colonial governments have not been smooth. The first major expansions of pipeline infrastructure were not seamless, well-organized attempts to expand corporate or state power; instead, they were somewhat chaotic processes in which all kinds of things could (and did) go wrong. This illustrates an important feature of capitalist accumulation: it is not automatic, but painstakingly achieved.

As Indigenous people and their supporters confront another wave of land alienation at the hands of both government and industry actors, this aspect of capitalist accumulation remains crucial. We would do well to look at the ways in which these actors are subject to tensions and conflicts that render them vulnerable. Financing of resource extraction projects is an important arena in which to assess these vulnerabilities. Indigenous-led movements, as we outlined in the final section of this article, have begun to find what Olin Wright called "cracks and openings" in the financial scaffolding that makes Canada's extractive industries viable. As a result, they are facing a vicious backlash.

The Trans Mountain buyout can be read as an attempt to quell the uncertainty faced by Canadian pipeline projects—and in turn, tar sands expansion—over the last decade. Despite the current Trudeau government's aggressive support for tar sands expansion, it aims to govern a state that is to some extent a fragmented entity, beset by factional squabbles and people working at cross-purposes. After all, the same government killed the Northern Gateway pipeline in 2016; then, less than two years later, it authorized a multi-billion-dollar payout to try to ensure the building of the Trans Mountain expansion. The current purchase certainly offers evidence of a historically contingent alignment among the current government, oil companies, pipeline companies, and the Canadian financial sector. But perhaps the most important word here is *contingent*.

There is no singular prescription that follows from the current strength of the bond between the Canadian financial sector and resource extraction. Capitalist actors in these industries are not invincible, but they are often cunning, strategic, and driven. Instead of definite proposals, we hope to contribute more detail to movement understandings of the industries they face.

Organizing to defeat colonial extraction and finance benefits from ongoing research and analysis, but the battles are entirely possible to win.

Appendix

Table 1 contains the correlation between returns on Canadian capital and the change in commodity prices.[3] A positive correlation means that rising commodity prices are coincident with higher returns, and vice versa. A correlation near zero means there is no statistical relationship. The current correlation is tighter than any point since the Great Depression. From 1930 to 1939, the correlation between the two series was 0.83. This fell to 0.07 for 1940 to 1979. It has been climbing since January 1980, and since January 2012, the correlation has been back above 0.80. This need not be the case. Indeed, it would be reasonable to assume that falling prices result in greater sales volume, generating higher profits.

Table 1. Correlation with Thompson Reuters Commodity Index

Years	S&P/TSX Composite	S&P/TSX Banks
August 1915 to December 1929	0.01	0.07
January 1930 to December 1939	0.88	0.70
January 1940 to December 1979	0.08	0.00
January 1980 to December 1999	0.48	0.18
January 2000 to December 2012	0.69	0.48
January 2012 to December 2019	0.81	0.80

This shift could be due to the changing presence of commodity-producing corporations within the S&P/TSX Composite Index. However, the same pattern can be seen with Canadian banks. The second column of Table 1 contains the correlations between changes in the Thompsons Reuters commodity index and returns on the TSX Banks Index. Indeed, for the banks, the correlation is currently higher than it was during the Great Depression. To state this again: the data shows that when commodity prices are increasing, the market capitalization of Canadian banks are also increasing, and vice versa.

Notes

1   Original research by Kylie Benton-Connell using Wharton Research Data Services.
2   Original research by Kylie Benton-Connell through *Bloomberg*.
3   Commodity prices are contained in the Thompson Reuters equal weighted Core Commodity Index. Returns to Canadian capital are the year-over-year monthly change in the S&P/TSX Composite Index.

References

350.org. 2012. "Big Banks Admit No Keystone XL, Limited Expansion of Tar Sands Development." *350.org* (blog), December 19. 350.org/big-banks-admit-no-keystone-xl-no-expanded-tar-sands-development/.

Allan, Robyn. 2018. "What's behind Kinder Morgan's May 31 Ultimatum? Follow the Money." *National Observer*, May 15. www.nationalobserver.com/2018/05/15/opinion/whats-behind-kinder-morgans-may-31-ultimatum-follow-money.

Anonymous. 2008. "The Minister of Everything." *Oilweek* 59, no. 6: 33–37.

Arnott, Sarah. 2011. "RBS Faces AGM Protests over Tar Sands Cash." *Independent*, April 19. www.independent.co.uk/news/business/news/rbs-faces-agm-protests-over-tar-sands-cash-2269713.html.

Atkin, Emily. 2013. "Man Faces One Year in Jail for Protesting JPMorgan's Fossil Fuel Investments." November 25. thinkprogress.org/man-faces-one-year-in-jail-for-protesting-jp morgans-fossil-fuel-investments-a9cb489f9df3/.

BankTrack. 2018a. "Banks' Policies on Tar Sands Companies." December 20. www.banktrack .org/page/banks_policies_on_tar_sands_companies.

BankTrack. 2018b. "Banks That Ended Direct Finance for Tar Sands." December 20. www .banktrack.org/page/banks_that_ended_direct_finance_for_tar_sands.

Beckert, Jens, and Milan Zafirovski, eds. 2013. *International Encyclopedia of Economic Sociology*. XXX: Routledge.

Bloomberg News. 2016. "Untapped Loans Double Canadian Banks Oil Exposure to $107 Billion." *Financial Post*, March 2. business.financialpost.com/news/fp-street/untapped -loans-double-canadian-banks-oil-exposure-to-107-billion.

Bothwell, Robert. 1976. "Minister of Everything." *International Journal* 31, no. 4: 692–702.

Bothwell, Robert. 1979. *C. D. Howe, a Biography*. Toronto: McClelland and Stewart.

Bott, Robert. 1989. *Mileposts: The Story of The World's Longest Petroleum Pipeline*. Edmonton: Interprovincial Pipeline Co.

Bryan, Dick, Michael Rafferty, and Chris Jefferis. 2015. "Risk and Value: Finance, Labor, and Production." *South Atlantic Quarterly* 114, no. 2: 307–29. doi.org/10.1215/00382876-2862729.

Çalışkan, Koray, and Michel Callon. 2009. "Economization, Part 1: Shifting Attention from the Economy towards Processes of Economization." *Economy and Society* 38, no. 3: 369–98. doi.org/10.1080/03085140903020580.

Canadian Press. 2012. "Oil Industry Faced with 'Serious Challenge' as Pipelines Fill Up, TD Warns." *Financial Post*, December 18. financialpost.com/commodities/energy/oil -industry-faced-with-serious-challenge-as-pipelines-fill-up-td-warns.

Canadian Press. 2019. "Teck Resource's 260,000-Bpd Oilsands Mine in Public Interest despite 'Significant Adverse' Effects: Panel." *Financial Post*, July 26. business.financialpost.com /commodities/teck-resources-260000-bpd-oilsands-mine-in-public-interest-despite -significant-adverse-effects-panel.

Carroll, William K. 2017. "Canada's Carbon-Capital Elite: A Tangled Web of Corporate Power." *Canadian Journal of Sociology/Cahiers Canadiens de Sociologie* 42, no. 3: 225–60.

Carroll, William K., and M. Jouke Huijzer. 2018. *Who Owns Canada's Fossil-Fuel Sector? Mapping the Network of Ownership*. Vancouver, BC: Canadian Centre for Policy Alternatives. www.policyalternatives.ca/publications/reports/who-owns-canada%E2%80%99s-fossil -fuel-sector.

Chambers, David, Sergei Sarkissian, and Michael J. Schill. 2012. "Geography and Capital: Explaining Foreign Listings of U.S. Railroad Securities during the First Era of Financial Globalization." *eh.net*, September 11. eh.net/eha/wp-content/uploads/2013/11 /Chambersetal.pdf.

Chernow, Ron. 2010. *The House of Morgan: An American Banking Dynasty and the Rise of Modern Finance.* New York: Grove Press.

Cochrane, D. T., and Kanahus Manuel. Forthcoming. "Confronting the Immanent Value of the Trans Mountain Pipeline Expansion." *Scapegoat.*

Colaneri, Katie. 2013. "Pipeline Protest Targets Bank HQ In South Jersey." *StateImpact Pennsylvania* (blog). August 12. stateimpact.npr.org/pennsylvania/2013/08/12/pipeline-protest -targets-bank-hq-in-south-jersey/.

Collins, Cory. 2016. "Canadian Banks Fund Dakota Access Pipeline Companies: Investigation." *Ricochet.* September 9. ricochet.media/en/1386.

Conrad, Roger. 2016. "The Canadian Invasion and Other Trends in MLP M&A." *Capitalist Times* (blog). September 9. www.capitalisttimes.com/the-canadian-invasion-and-other -trends-in-mlp-ma/.

Cook, Michelle, and Hugh McMillan. 2019. "Faire parler l'argent quand les banques se paient de mots" ("Money Talks, Banks Are Talking: Dakota Access Pipeline Finance Lessons "). *Mouvements* (blog), March 13. mouvements.info/defund-dapl/.

Cowen, Deborah. 2014. "The Jurisdiction of Infrastructure: Circulation and Canadian Settler Colonialism." *Funambulist*, no. 17: 14–19.

DeWitt Capital Management. 2015. "The Wrong Metric: Why Some Investors May Miss Out on a Great Investment." *MLP Blog*, August 3. www.dewittcm.com/mlp-blog/blog/the -wrong-metric-why-some-investors-may-miss-out-on-a-great-investment.

"Divest, Invest, Protect." 2019. WECAN International. www.wecaninternational.org/divest -invest-protect (accessed June 26, 2019).

Dolin, Eric Jay. 2010. *Fur, Fortune, and Empire: The Epic History of the Fur Trade in America.* New York: W. W. Norton.

Economist. 2013. "Rise of the Distorporation." October 26. www.economist.com/briefing /2013/10/26/rise-of-the-distorporation.

Financial Post. 2018. "Suncor Won't Approve More Oil Production Expansions until Canada Makes Progress on Approving Pipelines." September 5. business.financialpost.com /commodities/energy/suncor-wont-approve-more-oil-production-expansions-until -pipeline-progress-ceo.

Galeano, Eduardo. (1973) 1997. *Open Veins of Latin America: Five Centuries of the Pillage of a Continent.* New York: Monthly Review Press.

Gareau, Kristian. 2016. "Pipeline Politics: Capitalism, Extractivism, and Resistance in Canada." PhD diss., Concordia University, Montréal, Québec, Canada.

Garrido, Francis, and Saqib Chaudhry. 2019. "The World's 100 Largest Banks." S&P Global Market Intelligence, April 5. www.spglobal.com/marketintelligence/en/news-insights /latest-news-headlines/50964984.

Giroux, Yves. 2019. "Canada's purchase of the Trans Mountain Pipeline – Financial and Economic Considerations." February 12. Parliamentary Budget Officer. pbo-dpb.gc.ca/web /default/files/Documents/Reports/2019/Transmountain/Trans_Mountain_Report_EN _FINAL2.pdf.

Gray, Earle. 1970. *The Great Canadian Oil Patch.* Toronto: Maclean-Hunter.

Grossberg, Lawrence, Carolyn Hardin, and Michael Palm. 2014. "Contributions to a Conjunctural Theory of Valuation." *Rethinking Marxism* 26, no. 3: 306–35. doi.org/10.1080/089 35696.2014.895543.

Gunster, Shane. 2019. "Extractive Populism and the Future of Canada." *Canadian Centre for Policy Alternatives,* July 2. www.policyalternatives.ca/publications/monitor/extractive -populism-and-future-canada.

Gunton, Thomas. 2017. "Is Canada Setting Itself up for a Pipeline Glut?" *Globe and Mail,* January 12. theglobeandmail.com/report-on-business/rob-commentary/is-canada-setting -itself-up-for-a-pipeline-glut/article33603108/.

Haiven, Max. 2018. "CFP: Colonial Debts, Extractive Nostalgias, Imperial Insolvencies." *RiVAL—The ReImagining Value Action Lab* (blog). May 24. rival.lakeheadu.ca/colonial -debts-cfp/.

Harder, Christopher. 2015. "Canada Has a Pipeline Problem." *Wall Street Journal,* April 20. blogs.wsj.com/moneybeat/2015/04/20/canada-has-a-pipeline-problem-energy-journal/.

Hilferding, Rudolf. (1910) 1981. *Finance Capital: A Study of the Latest Phase of Capitalist Development.* London: Routledge and Kegan Paul. www.marxists.org/archive/hilferding/1910 /finkap/index.htm.

Hill, David. 2012. "Doesn't David Hockney See the Irony?" *New Internationalist,* March 22. newint.org/blog/2012/03/22/david-hockney-bnp-paribas-sponsorship.

Hobson, J. A. (1902) 2018. *Imperialism: A Study.* New York: Routledge.

Hsieh, Emily. 2018. "Alerian Explains It All: C Corps, MLPs, and the Midstream Indices That Contain Them." Alerian, August 14. www.alerian.com/alerian-explains-it-all-c-corps -mlps-and-the-midstream-indices-that-contain-them/.

Huseman, Jennifer, and Damien Short. 2012. "'A Slow Industrial Genocide': Tar Sands and the Indigenous Peoples of Northern Alberta." *International Journal of Human Rights* 16, no. 1: 216–37.

Indigenous Environmental Network. 2019a. "Tar Sands Facts." ienearth.org/tar-sands-facts / (accessed November 6, 2019).

Indigenous Environmental Network. 2019b. "Tar Sands." ienearth.org/what-we-do/tar-sands / (accessed November 6, 2019).

Innis, Harold A. (1940) 2017. *The Cod Fisheries: The History of an International Economy.* Toronto: University of Toronto Press.

Innis, Harold A. (1930) 2017. *The Fur Trade in Canada: An Introduction to Canadian Economic History.* Toronto: University of Toronto Press.

International Trade Administration. 2018. "Canada—Banking Systems." Export.Gov. December 14. www.export.gov/article?id=Canada-Banking-Systems.

Johnson, Ron. 2018. "Tiny Houses, Big Resistance." *Earth Island Journal,* January 2. www .earthisland.org/journal/index.php/articles/entry/tiny_houses_resistance_pipeline/.

Kheraj, Sean. 2015. "Historical Background Report: Trans Mountain Pipeline, 1947–2013." Report commissioned by the City of Vancouver. vancouver.ca/images/web/pipeline /Sean-Kheraj-history-of-TMP.pdf.

Kheraj, Sean. 2018. "The Complicated History of Building Pipelines in Canada." *The Conversation,* May 30. theconversation.com/the-complicated-history-of-building-pipelines -in-canada-97450.

Kilbourne, William. 1970. *PipeLine: Transcanada and the Great Debate, A History of Business.* Toronto: Clark, Irwin.

Koo, David. 2017. "Starve the Black Snake." Issuu, February 14. issuu.com/davidkoo/docs/sub-mission_thomas_church_2017.

Koplow, Doug. 2013. "Too Big to Ignore: Subsidies to Fossil Fuel Master Limited Partnerships." Washington, DC: Oil Change International. priceofoil.org/content/uploads/2013/07/OCI_MLP_2013.pdf.

Kusnetz, Nicholas. 2019. "Canada's Tar Sands Province Elects a Combative New Leader Promising Oil and Pipeline Revival." InsideClimate News, April 18. insideclimatenews.org/news/18042019/tar-sands-future-alberta-premier-conservative-jason-kenney-pipelines-carbon-tax-trudeau.

Lenin, Vladimir Ilyich. (1917) 1963. "Imperialism, the Highest Stage of Capitalism." In *Lenin Selected Works*. Moscow: Progress Publishers. www.marxists.org/archive/lenin/works/1916/imp-hsc/.

Luxemburg, Rosa. (1913) 1951. *The Accumulation of Capital*. London: Routledge and Kegan Paul. www.marxists.org/archive/luxemburg/1913/accumulation-capital/.

Makholm, Jeff D. 2012. *The Political Economy of Pipelines: A Century of Comparative Institutional Development*. Chicago: University of Chicago Press.

Mann, Geoff. 2010. "Value after Lehman." *Historical Materialism* 18, no. 4: 172–88. doi.org/10.1163/156920610X550640.

Masters, D. C. 1943. "Financing the C. P. R., 1880–5." *Canadian Historical Review* 24, no. 4: 350–61. doi.org/10.3138/CHR-024-04-02.

Mendelson, Zoe. 2011. "A Massive Positive Impact Potential: 5 Reasons Colleges and Universities Should Move Their Money." *HuffPost*, November 18. www.huffpost.com/entry/move-your-money_b_1101247.

Molinar, Jackie. 2016. "NoDapl Demonstration." December. actionnetwork.org/events/nodapl-demonstration-2.

Morris, Charles R. 2006. *The Tycoons: How Andrew Carnegie, John D. Rockefeller, Jay Gould, and J. P. Morgan Invented the American Supereconomy*. New York: Owl Books.

Muniesa, Fabian. 2011. "A Flank Movement in the Understanding of Valuation." *Sociological Review* 59, no. S2: 24–38. doi.org/10.1111/j.1467–954X.2012.02056.x.

Naylor, R. T. 1975. *The History of Canadian Business, 1867–1914*. Toronto: James Lorimer.

Neufeld, Lydia. 2018. "Alberta Launches Lost-Revenue Counter in Campaign for Trans Mountain Pipeline Expansion | CBC News." *CBC*, November 14. cbc.ca/news/canada/edmonton/trans-mountain-pipeline-expansion-digital-counter-alberta-government-1.4905387.

Nitzan, Jonathan, and Shimshon Bichler. 2009. *Capital as Power: A Study of Order and Creorder*. London: Routledge.

Pasternak, Shiri. 2013. "The Economics of Insurgency: Thoughts on Idle No More and Critical Infrastructure." January 14. www.shiripasternak.com/the-economics-of-insurgency-thoughts-on-idle-no-more-and-critical-infrastructure/.

Pasternak, Shiri, and Tia Dafnos. 2017. "How Does a Settler State Secure the Circuitry of Capital?" *Environment and Planning D: Society and Space*, June 7. doi.org/10.1177/0263775817713209.

Pasternak, Shiri, Katie Mazer, and D. T. Cochrane. 2019. "The Financing Problem of Colonialism: How Indigenous Jurisdiction Is Valued in Pipeline Politics." In *Standing with Standing Rock: Voices from the #NoDAPL Movement*, edited by Jaskiran Dhillon and Nick Estes, 222–34. Minneapolis: University of Minnesota Press.

Phillip, Stewart, and Serge Simon. 2018. "If Ottawa Rams through Trans Mountain, It Could Set up an Oka-like Crisis." *Globe and Mail*, April 12. www.theglobeandmail.com/opinion/article-if-ottawa-rams-through-trans-mountain-it-could-set-up-an-oka-like/.

Pineault, Éric. 2018. "The Capitalist Pressure to Extract: The Ecological and Political Economy of Extreme Oil in Canada." *Studies in Political Economy* 99, no. 2: 130–50. doi.org/10.1080 /07078552.2018.1492063.

Posadzki, Alexandra. 2018. "What Crisis? Canada's Big Six Banks Brush off Oil-Price Crash." *Globe and Mail*, December 9. www.theglobeandmail.com/business/streetwise/article -what-crisis-canadas-big-six-banks-brush-off-oil-price-crash-as/.

Preston, Jen. 2017. "Racial Extractivism and White Settler Colonialism: An Examination of the Canadian Tar Sands Mega-Projects." *Cultural Studies* 31, no. 2–3: 353–75. doi.org/10.1080 /09502386.2017.1303432.

Reamer, Norton, and Jesse Downing. 2016. "The Democratization of Investment: Joint-Stock Companies, the Industrial Revolution, and Public Markets." Chap. 2 in *Investment: A History*. New York: Columbia University Press.

Ross, Chris. 2018. "Back to The Basics: Evolution of the Midstream Sector." *Forbes*, January 22. www.forbes.com/sites/uhenergy/2018/01/22/back-to-the-basics-evolution-of-the -midstream-sector/.

Scott, Dayna Nadine. 2013. "The Networked Infrastructure of Fossil Capitalism: Implications of the New Pipeline Debates for Environmental Justice in Canada." *Revue* générale de *droit* 47, no. 57: 11–66. digitalcommons.osgoode.yorku.ca/cgi/viewcontent.cgi?referer =&httpsredir=1&article=1831&context=scholarly_works.

Stanford, Jim, ed. 2014. "The Staple Theory @ 50: Reflections on the Lasting Significance of Mel Watkins' 'A Staple Theory of Economic Growth.'" Canadian Centre for Policy Alternatives. policyalternatives.ca/sites/default/files/uploads/publications/National%20Office /2014/03/Staple_Theory_at_50.pdf.

Statistics Canada. 2018a. "Corporation Profits before Taxes, by Industry, Annual, 1926–1989." April 4. www150.statcan.gc.ca/t1/tbl1/en/tv.action?pid=3610028501.

Statistics Canada. 2018b. "Quarterly Balance Sheet and Income Statement, by Industry." April 17. www150.statcan.gc.ca/t1/tbl1/en/tv.action?pid=3310000701.

Steffy, Loren. 2014. "Kinder Morgan Eats Its Own; Will Other MLPs Follow Its Lead?" *Forbes*, August 10. www.forbes.com/sites/lorensteffy/2014/08/10/kinder-morgan-eats-its -own-will-other-mlps-follow-its-lead/#569fd29118a1.

Stockman, Lorne, Brant Olson, and Hugh McMillan. 2018. "Empty Promise: US Bank Continues Pipeline Finance." Washington, DC: Oil Change International. priceofoil.org /content/uploads/2018/04/EmptyPromise-USBANK-web.pdf.

Stockman, Lorne, and Kelly Trout. 2017. "Art of the Self-Deal: How Regulatory Failure Lets Gas Pipeline Companies Fabricate Need and Fleece Ratepayers." Washington, DC: Oil Change International. priceofoil.org/content/uploads/2017/09/Gas_Pipeline_Ratepayer _Report.pdf.

Taylor, Peter Shawn. 2018. "Buying a Pipeline? It's a Great Canadian Tradition." *Maclean's*, June 18. www.macleans.ca/politics/ottawa/buying-a-pipeline-its-a-great-canadian -tradition/.

Trans Mountain. 1953. *Oil across the Rockies*. Written by Richard S. Finnie. 16mm, 38 min. www.youtube.com/watch?v=vk-2EzTSAsg.

Treaty Alliance against Tar Sands Expansion. 2019. "About." www.treatyalliance.org/ (accessed July 30, 2019).

Trichur, Rita. 2015. "Canada's Banks Try to Downplay Exposure to Energy; Chief Executives Say Protracted Period of Lower Oil Prices Would Be Manageable." *Wall Street Journal*, January 14, Markets.

Varcoe, Chris. 2019. "Varcoe: International Stampede Out of Oilsands Grows, as Devon Energy Set to Exit Canada." *Calgary Herald,* February 21. calgaryherald.com/business /energy/varcoe-a-sign-of-the-times-oilsands-exodus-expands-petrochemical-incentives -spread.

Vasil, Adria. 2016. "Mordor Comparison Stirs Tempest in the Oil Sands." *NOW Magazine,* July 19. nowtoronto.com/lifestyle/ecoholic/mordor-comparison-stirs-tempest-in-the -oil-sands/.

Vettese, Troy. 2017. "Black Snake in the Grass." *Alternatives Journal* 43, no. 1. www.alternative sjournal.ca/energy-and-resources/black-snake-grass.

Vieira, Paul. 2013. "Canadian Government Invokes History to Build Support for Pipeline Projects." *Wall Street Journal,* August 26. blogs.wsj.com/canadarealtime/2013/08/26 /canadian-government-invokes-history-to-build-support-for-pipeline-projects/.

Watkins, Melville H. 1963. "A Staple Theory of Economic Growth." *Canadian Journal of Economics and Political Science* 29, no. 2: 141–58.

Watkins, Melville H. 2007. "Comment Staples Redux." *Studies in Political Economy* 79, no. 1: 213–26. doi.org/10.1080/19187033.2007.11675098.

White, Richard. 2011. *Railroaded: The Transcontinentals and the Making of Modern America.* New York: W. W. Norton.

Wilson, Neill Compton, and Frank J. Taylor. 1954. *The Building of Trans Mountain: Canada's First Oil Pipeline across the Rockies.* Vancouver, BC: Trans Mountain Oil Pipe Line Company.

Wright, Erik Olin. 2010. *Envisioning Real Utopias.* New York: Verso.

Zivitz, Noah. 2019. "RBC CEO Calls for Pipelines at 'Critical Time' for Canada." BNN Bloomberg, April 4. bnnbloomberg.ca/rbc-ceo-pounds-the-table-for-pipelines-at-critical -time-for-canada-1.1239584.

Irina Ceric

Beyond Contempt: Injunctions, Land Defense, and the Criminalization of Indigenous Resistance

There is much that can be gleaned from the lawyers of our opponents. In a 2017 law journal article, four commercial litigators from one of Canada's largest law firms contended that because the "criminal justice system will generally not intervene to prohibit civil disobedience," injunctions have become the "new normal" (Williams et al. 2017: 286). Their conclusion is clearly both description and prescription, as it is directed at their corporate clients: "an injunction has emerged as the only practical remedy available to project proponents who may be impacted by civil disobedience" (286). These lawyers argued—and I have to agree, even if I do not see it as a welcome development—that recent jurisprudence suggests that any reservations that judges had about "whether civil injunctions are an appropriate means of resolving civil disobedience" appear to have largely dissipated. But whereas these lawyers spend the rest of the article explaining how to exploit the current state of the law from the perspective of resource extraction companies, I want to think about how to challenge the pervasive use of injunctions and contempt in struggles over resource extraction by Indigenous peoples, their allies, and environmental justice movements.

The South Atlantic Quarterly 119:2, April 2020
DOI 10.1215/00382876-8177795 © 2020 Duke University Press

Even a cursory review of protest policing in Canada reveals that state intervention in resistance movements is alive and well and that Indigenous peoples and allied social movements are made subject to repression, surveillance, and criminalization through the mechanism of injunctions, among other legal tools. The reliance on injunctions by extractive industries embroils the courts and police in struggles over public and/or collectively held lands and resources that are nonetheless constructed by the law as private disputes, largely insulated from the reach of constitutionally-derived Aboriginal rights. In this article, I address the claim that injunctions are the "new normal"—and the policy prescriptions that flow from it—based on my direct experience with injunctions and contempt in British Columbia (BC) as an activist legal support organizer and a settler ally. The combined impacts of injunctions and the subsequent use of contempt charges carve out a distinctly colonial space within Canadian law for the criminalization of Indigenous resistance. I begin by outlining the basic operation of injunction and contempt law in the context of protest and land defense. I proceed to zero in on BC to demonstrate the long history of that province's "injunction habit," examining the judicial and policy practices that make the "new normal" claim possible—and show how it is ultimately not accurate. Finally, I argue that injunctions and contempt serve as crucial tools in the legal arsenal of settler-colonial states, facilitating access to resources and lands and easing the operation of extractive capitalism. I conclude by considering how to break BC's injunction habit by uncovering and challenging the doctrinal and procedural underpinnings of the so-called "new normal."

Injunctions 101

An *injunction* is a court order issued by a judge after an application is filed by a party to a lawsuit and is meant to protect the interests or rights of that applicant while the case is pending. In most of the cases discussed in this article, the applicant is a corporation worried that people, such as Indigenous land defenders or environmental activists, will do certain things adverse to their interests (e.g., block a particular road or impede access to a project site). If the injunction application is successful, the court issues an order forbidding the feared actions. An injunction can be interim (temporary) or interlocutory, meaning that it will stay in effect until trial. In cases involving protests or blockades, injunctions will usually bind not only the named defendants in the underlying lawsuit (however tenuous), but also "John and Jane Doe and persons unknown"—meaning anyone who becomes aware of the injunction (Lawn 1998; Ward 1993).

In deciding whether to issue an injunction, the court's key concern is whether doing so would be "just and equitable" given the circumstances of the case. A 1994 decision of the Supreme Court of Canada [SCC], *RJR-Mac-Donald Inc. v. Canada (Attorney General)*, [1994] 1 S.C.R. 311, set out the most widely applied test for the issuance of an interim or interlocutory injunction. It requires the applicant seeking an injunction to satisfy the court that: (1) there exists a serious or fair question to be tried in the underlying lawsuit (even if it is unlikely to ever get to trial); (2) the applicant will suffer irreparable harm if the injunction is not granted (usually, this means damage that cannot be financially compensated); and (3) the balance of convenience between the parties favors granting the injunction (at 334). In deciding the balance of convenience, the court asks which side would suffer more harm if the injunction was granted or refused, weighing the "maintenance of the status quo" among factors. In cases involving struggles over resource extraction, the balance of convenience often turns on how the court identifies the status quo; what is to be maintained, the unimpeded progress of the extractive project or the pre-development status of the lands and waters? Most often, the answer is the former and as a result, the *RJR-Macdonald* test for whether an injunction is warranted has generally proven to be a very low bar and as detailed below, this balancing of proprietary claims to lands and resources against Aboriginal rights ought be understood as a key component of the legal framework that underpins the "new normal" claim of Williams et al. (2017).

Violating the terms of an injunction generally results in contempt of court charges. In BC, the general practice with injunctions targeting land and water defense is to include an enforcement order empowering police to arrest such alleged "contemnors." There are two types of contempt—civil and criminal—and both remain common law (judge-made) offences not found in Canada's *Criminal Code*. Contempt of court is the only remaining common law offence permitted by the *Code*, an unreconstructed legal relic deriving directly from ancient British law. Since the twelfth century, the SCC notes, courts have exercised the right to punish contempt "to maintain their process and respect" (*United Nurses of Alberta v. Alberta (Attorney General)*, (1992) 71 CCC (3d) 225: 252; see also Miller 2016: 1). Then, as now, a perceived attack on the rule of law lies at the heart of both the contempt sanction generally and the distinction between criminal contempt of court and the less serious civil version. Criminal contempt requires an "element of public defiance of the court's process in a way calculated to lessen societal respect for the courts" and is proven by evidence of "open, continuous and flagrant violation of a court order without regard for the effect that may have on the respect accorded to edicts of the court" (*United Nurses*: 252).

How We Got to the "New Normal":
A Brief History of BC's "Injunction Habit"

My first direct encounter with what I would come to call BC's "injunction habit" was in 2014, when an injunction prohibiting obstructing or interfering with exploratory drilling for the proposed Trans Mountain Pipeline expansion project was issued. In the midst of mounting opposition to the pipeline expansion, Kinder Morgan, a Texas-based energy company, filed a multi-million-dollar lawsuit against five named defendants, all of them vocal pipeline opponents, as well a local community organization and "John and Jane Doe and persons unknown" (*Trans Mountain Pipeline ULC v. Gold*, 2014 BCSC 2133). The company sought damages (for nuisance, assault by threat, trespass, intimidation, and interference with contractual obligations), costs, and most crucially, an injunction prohibiting interference with its drilling site on Burnaby Mountain, just east of Vancouver. The resulting civil disobedience campaign, in which protesters deliberately violated the injunction by stepping onto the prohibited drilling site, led to 112 arrests over six days. During the course of that campaign, I was among several *pro bono* lawyers who appeared in court to represent two Indigenous arrestees charged with civil contempt of court, who, unlike most of the participants, had not been released by police pending trial. Our opposing counsel were not Crown prosecutors, but Kinder Morgan's high-priced corporate lawyers, and as we stood in the cavernous Vancouver courtroom built for the Air India terrorism trial, it turned out that all of us were unsure what the court's unwritten "summary procedure" for contempt charges would actually entail. Once the not-quite-criminal, not-quite-civil hearing began, the province's Chief Justice quickly released both accused on promises to appear but the court's contempt process remained opaque. The contempt charges against all arrestees were later dropped after it was revealed that the GPS coordinates setting out the injunction zone were inaccurate, rendering further court appearances unnecessary.

This brief glimpse into the strange world of injunction and contempt procedure would come in handy four years later, when Kinder Morgan obtained another injunction directed at opponents of the Trans Mountain project. This time, the injunction covered Kinder Morgan's existing facilities, restraining activists from blocking access to key sites, including a petroleum product "tank farm" on the shores of the Burrard Inlet. Another civil disobedience campaign followed, with a total of 229 people arrested for violating the injunction (Mazur 2019). Despite the long legacy of injunctions and subsequent contempt charges in BC, legal support organizers quickly realized that neither technical nor movement knowledge about these legal tools had been adequately preserved or passed down. As the number of arrests mounted and it became clear that—unlike in 2014—these charges would stick, a group of lawyers and legal support providers—some with injunction experience going back to the 1980s, most with none—met to strategize in Vancouver. Listening to a senior defense lawyer explain that the summary procedure for trying alleged "contemnors" was always somewhat *ad hoc*, I was relieved to learn that my confusion with the contempt process was entirely warranted. The lawyer went on to suggest that if, as in 2014, the company's corporate lawyers were still prosecuting contempt charges, we should throw all our criminal defense vocabulary and procedure at them—"they'll get scared," she chuckled. But apparently, that was a big "if"; the civil contempt of court charges activists arrested at Kinder Morgan's tank farm were facing could be converted into criminal contempt at any point during the trial process. The long-standing practice in BC was that lawyers for the corporation invite, either publicly or behind the scenes, the province (via the Attorney General) to take over prosecution in criminal contempt cases. This practice had evolved in the 1980s we were told, because it was not seen as right to see a private party put people in jail. A few weeks after the meeting, the Crown did step in to take over the prosecutions and a series of trials for criminal contempt followed in BC's Supreme Court, many resulting in jail sentences.

The need to reconstruct and revive both technical and movement knowledge about defending contempt charges required digging into the history of BC injunctions, starting with the mass arrests during the mid-1990s battle against old-growth logging in Clayoquot Sound. The group trials of the hundreds of people arrested over a summer of civil disobedience resulted in key legal precedents on the conduct of contempt cases, as well as the imposition of significant jail sentences (*MacMillan Bloedel Ltd. v. Simpson*, [1996] 2 SCR 1048), but there was a scant record of the activists' legal defense tactics in those cases or other anti-logging contempt trials. A memoir written by Betty Krawczyk, an activist known for enduring multiple prison stays during various environmental justice struggles, underscored that the absurd public-private partnership between the state and extractive industries on display in the contempt charges arising out of the Trans Mountain injunctions was nothing new in BC:

> If anti-logging protesters were treated like all other citizens, we would be arrested and charged under the *Criminal Code*, which makes provisions for an accused's defence. The reasons for the crime and the circumstances surround-

ing the crime would then be taken into consideration by a judge or jury. . . .
Instead, an unholy threesome—corporate companies like Interfor, the Attor-
ney General's office and the judiciary—circumvents justice in the province of
British Columbia by refusing protestors the protections of the *Criminal Code*.
They do this by arresting us under an injunction. (Krawczyk 2002: 12)

The most useful resources turned out to be materials written for lawyers,
especially those coming "from the perspective of counsel acting for a party
seeking to obtain or enforce an injunction" in a so-called "land use dispute,"
as a representative Continuing Legal Education guide from 2009 puts it
(Saul and Vanderburgh). Despite this orientation, R. Patrick Saul and Eileen
E. Vanderburgh acknowledged that criminalization of environmental and
Indigenous movements via injunctions often means that when struggles
over land and water are diverted to the courtroom, the "proceedings are the
protest" (§3.3). Their advice to counsel for project proponents rests on BC's
legal and policy approach to the management of Indigenous and environmental struggles as it has developed since the mid-1980s. By 1990, note
Saul and Vanderburgh, the BC Prosecution Service had initiated a policy to
"not criminalize civil disobedience *per se*," recognizing that the "the use of
the minor offence sections of the *Criminal Code* was found to be neither
effective nor efficient" (§3.43). This policy is still in effect today and states
that individuals whose interests are affected by civil disobedience "may be
advised to seek legal advice regarding the availability of a civil injunction"
and that "in the event that civil disobedience continues after an injunction is
granted, the party obtaining the injunction should be encouraged to proceed
with civil contempt proceedings in the court in which the injunction was
obtained" (BC Prosecution Service 2018: 2). Reflecting this policy, the BC
courts had standardized the wording of an enforcement order to be included
in protest-related injunctions by the late 1980s, at least partially in an attempt
to overcome Royal Canadian Mounted Police (RCMP) reluctance to interfere
in supposedly private, civil matters (Saul and Vanderburgh 2009: §3.43).
This comprehensive and now engrained policy approach is a key piece of the
legal framework underlying Williams et al.'s championing of injunctions as
the "new normal"—as well as an explicit rejoinder to the claim of newness.
The second—and related—component is the history of BC judicial pro-
nouncements critiquing the reliance on injunctions.

A review of BC case law on the use of injunctions and contempt
charges to criminalize protest activity reveals a surprising amount of judicial resentment of BC's injunction habit. The earliest such pronouncement

is from a 1990 case involving the contempt trials of anti-choice demonstrators arrested outside a Vancouver abortion clinic (*Everywoman's Health Centre v. Bridges* (1990), 62 C.C.C. (3d) 455 (BCCA)). Justice Southin lamented that no arguments about the applicability of case law developed in the context of labor disputes to the context of modern civil disobedience had been put before the court:

> There is today the grave question of whether public order should be maintained by the granting of an injunction which often leads thereafter to an application to commit for contempt or should be maintained by the Attorney General insisting that the police who are under his control do their duty by enforcing the relevant provisions of the *Criminal Code*. (467)

A few years later, in an appeal arising from one of the Clayoquot Sound contempt trials, Justice Wood (writing in dissent), argued that the inherent jurisdiction of the Supreme Court to punish contempt of court "is and always has been a jurisdiction to be exercised sparingly and as a last resort. It was never intended to be used to preserve law and order on our streets, or in our forests, any more than equity was ever intended to be used as an instrument of crowd control." (*Greenpeace Canada et al. v. MacMillan Bloedel Ltd.*, (1994) 118 D.L.R. (4th) 1 (BCCA): 49). In *Slocan Forest Products Ltd. v. John Doe*, 2000 BCSC 150, Justice McEwan took direct aim at BC's injunction habit after a detailed review of both RCMP and Crown Counsel policy, with a particular focus on the claims of police witnesses that injunctions ought to be preferred to criminal charges because they allow for a "cooling off" period, do not "criminalize" the process, and allow the police to remain "neutral" (para. 31). Rejecting all these claims, McEwan noted that *"by definition acts of civil disobedience are not in essence civil disputes between individuals"* (para. 35, emphasis in original) and concluded that he was

> simply not convinced that the rule of law is enhanced by the present [injunction] process which:
>
> (a) forces innocent bystanders to seek their own protection by manufacturing ill-fitting "civil" suits;
>
> (b) places the court in a position where it must fashion some remedy at the expense of repeatedly putting its authority in issue;
>
> (c) arguably deprives demonstrators of due process. (para. 49)

Justice McEwan reiterated his opposition most recently in 2014, stating that the "Crown's apparent preference for turning these [environmental] matters into contests not between those who have committed an illegal act and society, but with the judge, is highly regrettable. It is the standard in our law that injunctions are a last resort, not a first resort" (*Galena Contractors Ltd. v. Zarelli*, 2014 BCSC 324: para. 20). But Justice McEwan is now something of a lone holdout and as Williams et al. demonstrate, this thread of judicial critique is no longer evident in the case law (2017: 293–4). Recent decisions, they say, "tend to adopt the civil injunction framework without criticism of police refusal to intervene" under their criminal law powers alone (293) and injunctions remain the only "practical recourse" for private parties faced with civil disobedience (315).

The apparent acquiescence of BC's judiciary to the injunction habit is buttressed by tacit legislative approval. Despite the fact that civil lawsuits filed against Indigenous land and water defenders and environmental activists are, for all intents and purposes, merely a means to an injunction, the province's new anti-SLAPP (Strategic Lawsuits Against Public Participation) legislation, introduced in March of 2019, allows applications for injunctions even while a motion to dismiss a lawsuit as a SLAPP is pending (*Protection of Public Participation Act*, SBC 2019, ch 3, s. 5(2)). BC's famed 2001 SLAPP legislation, the first of its kind introduced in Canada, included a similar provision. Like the current statute, that law stated that an application to dismiss a lawsuit as a SLAPP did not prevent a "court from granting an injunction pending a determination of the rights under this Act of the parties to a proceeding" (*Protection of Public Participation Act*, SBC 2001, ch 19, s. 4(3) (repealed)). These are astonishingly brazen exceptions, given that as early as 1992, one BC judge presiding over an injunction application by a logging company noted that "I expect that the only reasons for the actions is to build a foundation for the injunction applications" (quoted in Ward 1993: 863).

I do not want to suggest however, that the path of BC's injunction habit has been a straightforward one. Just as a judicial critique of the use of injunctions and contempt has waxed and waned, the orientation of First Nations' engagement with this legal tool has shifted as well. The still evolving "new normal" of injunctions in BC has tread a convoluted path and injunctions have not always been a tool only in the hands of corporations. Lawyer John Hunter writes that

> Between 1985 and May 1990, the interlocutory injunction was the primary remedy in Aboriginal rights litigation in British Columbia. It was used to stop activities, primarily resource-based projects seen to be inconsistent with Aboriginal rights claims. During those years, Aboriginal people enjoyed considerable success in obtaining injunctions to halt resource activity on claimed lands. (2009: §4.1)

Nick Blomley's study of First Nations' blockades in BC between 1980 and 1995 finds similar evidence for the use of counter-injunctions against logging companies and other extractive industries during the same period (1996). This practice ended, argues Hunter, after the SCC issued its landmark decision in *R. v. Sparrow*, [1990] 1 S.C.R. 1075, in which the court interpreted the Aboriginal rights "guaranteed and affirmed" by section 35(1) of the *Constitution Act, 1982* for the first time, holding that fishing rights claimed by the Musqueam people had not been "extinguished" (terminated) and were in fact constitutionally protected. Rather than further expanding the use of injunctions to assert and protect Indigenous rights claims however, the *Sparrow* decision largely marked the end of the successful use of injunctions by First Nations. Two years after *Sparrow*, the BC Supreme Court issued its ruling in *Delgamuukw v. British Columbia*, [1991] 3 W.W.R. 97, holding that rights to Aboriginal title in BC had been extinguished prior to Confederation. Although the BC Court of Appeal and ultimately the SCC (*Delgamuukw v. British Columbia*, [1997] 3 SCR 1010) overturned this decision, all land-based injunction claims made by First Nations in the ensuing years were unsuccessful (Hunter 2009: §4.5). Hunter attributes this change to several factors, most of which center on how the balance of convenience in injunction applications has been shaped by shifting understandings of the scope of Indigenous rights in Canadian state law. As the SCC's section 35 jurisprudence has evolved, the court has itself recognized the limitations of injunctions sought by First Nations: "the balance of convenience test tips the scales in favour of protecting jobs and government revenues, with the result that Aboriginal interests tend to 'lose' outright pending a final determination of the issue, instead of being balanced appropriately against conflicting concerns" (*Haida Nation v. British Columbia (Minister of Forests)*, 2004 SCC 73: para. 14).

Toward a "Newer Normal": Breaking the Injunction Habit

The legal and policy framework of BC's injunction and contempt habit is a formidable one, but it can and must be challenged. In the remainder of this article, I explore the operation of "the new normal" on the ground as a means of contributing to the project of breaking this habit: first, situating the injunction process as a specific technique of settler-colonial legality that plays a key role in maintaining Canada state control and jurisdiction over Indigenous territories, and second, recognizing—and responding to—the subsequent use of contempt charges as a similarly specific, and especially pernicious, form of criminalization. I do not suggest that the solution to the criminalization and marginalization of Indigenous and allied resistance is going to be found inside Canadian state law, but I do argue that the contempt power is vulnerable and can be made unenforceable.

Breaking BC's injunction habit requires understanding it as more than a series of misguided policy decision and bad precedents. Injunctions are unavoidably implicated in what Brenna Bhandar refers to as racial regimes of property ownership in modern settler colonial states and in those states' need for "flexibility in the legal devices and rationales" used to "maintain state control—and possession—of indigenous lands" (2018: 14). The injunction, coupled with contempt charges and flexibly interpreted and applied by settler courts with shifting rationales, has proven to be a near-perfect legal device for the maintenance of settler colonial property relations. Recent injunction cases that preclude the consideration of Aboriginal and Treaty rights during the injunction process have effectively insulated these mechanisms from the reach of section 35 constitutional scrutiny, including the duty to consult. A 2017 decision of the Ontario Superior Court involving allegations of interference with pipeline work by members of the Haudenosaunee Confederacy canvasses this line of reasoning, concluding that "the question of whether the Crown has made efforts to comply with its duty to consult and accommodate is not relevant to the exercise of the court's decision to deny an injunction sought by a private party such as Enbridge with an interest in land" (*Enbridge Pipelines Inc. v. Williams et al*, 2017 ONSC 1642: para. 23). *Enbridge* relies on a previous injunction decision arising from the struggle over the Muskrat Falls dam project in Labrador, in which an appeal court held

> that the principles applicable to the granting of an injunction are no different just because aboriginal claims for consultation and accommodation may be involved in the issues regarding the cause of action being asserted and the specific remedy being sought. There is no pre-condition to application of the general principles for granting or refusing an injunction that the claimant satisfy the court that the duty to consult and accommodate has been exhausted and that the court must take steps to facilitate such consultation and accommodation. If there were such pre-conditions, a defendant resisting a remedy for vindication of claimed rights would always be able to stymie, or at least significantly delay, an injunction by simply asserting that the duty to consult has not been exhausted. That result would run counter to reassertion in *Behn* that the duty to consult does not give aboriginal peoples "a veto." (*NunatuKavut Community Council Inc. v. Nalcor Energy*, 2014 NLCA 46: para. 41)

Behn was not an injunction case but rather addressed the ability of Indigenous defendants in a civil suit to assert Treaty rights and the duty of consult in their defense after being sued by a logging company for blocking access to the company's work sites (*Behn v. Moulton Contracting Ltd.*, 2013 SCC 26). Yet the SCC's conclusion that allowing such a defense "would be tantamount to condoning self-help remedies [a blockade] and would bring the administration of justice into disrepute" has had an enormous impact on subsequent injunction cases (para. 42). The *Behn* decision has effectively carved out a space within an area of Canadian law inextricably bound up with the exercise of Aboriginal rights that is nonetheless shielded from the application of those same rights. Injunction decisions issued in its wake have also rejected the application of a more nuanced, multi-dimensional conception of the rule of law, potentially encompassing "reconciliation of Aboriginal and non-Aboriginal interests through negotiations," that had been tentatively articulated by the Ontario Court of Appeal in two cases decided in 2006 (*Henco Industries Limited v. Haudenosaunee Six Nations Confederacy Council*, 2006 CanLII 41649 (ON CA)) and 2008 (*Frontenac Ventures Corporation v. Ardoch Algonquin First Nation*, 2008 ONCA 534; see also Newell 2012: 54).

These recent cases have also engaged with the rarely applied exception to the first part of *RJR-MacDonald* test which states that "when the result of the interlocutory motion will in effect amount to a final determination of the action," a judge should undertake a "more extensive review of the merits of the case" while determining if there is a serious issue to be tried (338–39). Although injunctions seeking to restrain picketing in the labor context are specifically cited by the SCC as cases that "may well fall within the scope of this exception" (338), Naiomi Metallic's research indicates that "for reasons unknown, [this] exception has largely been ignored in the picketing and protest contexts," particularly in cases involving Indigenous resistance to extractive projects (2015: 7–8, 10). The injunction decision will often amount to a determination of the action in instances where project work will be completed during the life of the interlocutory injunction, yet most such cases have failed to engage in a "more extensive review" at the first stage of the *RJR-MacDonald* test before moving on to the irreparable harm and balance of convenience calculations (Metallic 2015: 24). A number of the post-*Behn* cases do apply this exception, assessing the injunction claimant's case according to the standard of a "strong *prima facie* case" rather that the lower "serious question to be tried" threshold (see, e.g., *Enbridge*: para. 40), yet the exclusion of substantive Aboriginal rights claims from the injunction process effectively cancels out the potential impact of a slightly more demanding assessment.

The "new normal" injunction is, in sum, a "legal billy club," the means by which "assertion of [Indigenous] rights on the ground is instantly criminalized by the Canadian state," as Art Manuel put it (2018: 215). At the enforcement stage of the injunction process, however—a stage anticipated and shaped inside BC courtrooms, where counsel for the RCMP are routinely granted leave to make submissions—the club is often not metaphorical. Both the case law and legal commentary on contempt of court rely on the reification of non-violent civil disobedience, eliding the use of force inherent in the "public-private" partnership between resource extraction industries and the state, with its police and its courts. Understanding contempt charges and the enforcement process as "legal devices and rationales" of the settler colonial state foregrounds enforcement as criminalization. In something of a postscript to the now defunct judicial critique of injunctions in BC, an Ontario judge expressed discontent with the *lack of force* used by police tasked with enforcing injunctions aimed at dismantling blockades set up under the banner of Idle No More, inadvertently contradicting the claim that civil injunctions, unlike criminal law, allow police to remain neutral (Scott 2013).

As a technique of criminalization, the contempt charges that enforcement portends, whether civil or criminal, operate differently from the use of *Criminal Code* or other statutory charges against protesters and land defenders. My experiences providing legal support to movements caught up in BC's injunction habit have revealed that this legal tool gives rise to a specific set of access-to-justice problems. As alluded to above, the "summary procedure" used to try contempt cases is confusing and difficult to navigate, even for lawyers. Alleged "contemnors"—even the term is anachronistic and baffling!—have an even harder time understanding and effectively engaging in the process, even when they are represented by counsel. Contempt charges lie within the exclusive jurisdiction of provincial superior courts, leading to practical difficulties based on geography (there are fewer superior courts, and the closest one may not be all that close) and reduced access to on-site legal assistance. Even civil contempt charges are in effect criminal or quasi-criminal (Miller 2016: 37), but especially given the very real possibility of jail time for criminal contempt convictions, contempt defendants are generally surprised by the limited application of the *Charter*. Alleged contemnors are "charged with an offence" and the prosecution (whether corporate or Crown counsel) must prove their guilt to the criminal standard of guilty beyond a reasonable doubt (37), but they have no right to a jury trial (*MacMillan Bloedel Ltd. v. Simpson*) and almost no viable defenses, including necessity (Mazur 2019: 6). Applying long-established criminal law doctrine in the contempt context can be a fight. In the on-going struggle over the Muskrat Falls dam in Labrador, some land defenders faced both *Criminal Code* and contempt charges for more than two and a half years until the Crown finally withdrew the criminal charges, citing the clearly applicable doctrine of "double jeopardy" (Barker 2019). While this length of time is unusual (perhaps the only good thing that can be said of the summary procedure is that it is generally faster than the *Criminal Code* trial process), the imposition of any charges imposes costs—financial, psychological, and practical—on activists and movements and as in SLAPP suits, diverts energy and resources from organizing into courtroom battles.

But for most contempt defendants, the most contentious and disappointing element of the contempt process is the "collateral attack" doctrine that precludes any challenge to the basis for the injunction itself. This rule rests on the notion that a court order is to be obeyed until it is set aside, varied, or reversed on appeal and that the validity of an injunction cannot be attacked in any other proceeding, including a contempt of court trial (hence the term collateral—or indirect—attack) (Saul and Vanderburgh 2009: §3.55; Mazur 2019: 7). In the contempt trials arising out of the 2018 Trans Mountain pipeline injunction, the collateral attack doctrine was used to exclude defenses based on the inadequacy of the National Energy Board's regulatory and approval processes, climate change, and in a variation of the *Behn* ruling, the applicability of Indigenous law. The BC Supreme Court's rejection of Indigenous sovereignty-based challenges to its jurisdiction in contempt cases is long-standing. In a 1991 decision, the court held that the "issue of Indian sovereignty may not be raised or argued" in contempt proceedings, rejecting the argument that the questions about the jurisdiction of the court over sovereign nations and unceded territories is an exception to the collateral attack doctrine (*British Columbia (Attorney General) v. Mount Currie Indian Band*, (1991) 54 BCLR (2d) 129 (BCSC): para. 53; see also Newell 2012: 59–61).

The imperative to challenge the procedural and doctrinal foundations of BC's injunction habit is illustrated by the Coastal GasLink injunction issued in late 2018. The injunction targeted a blockade established in 2012 on the traditional territories of the Unist'ot'en clan, one of the house groups making up the Dark House (Yex T'sa wil_k'us) of the Gilseyhu or Big Frog clan of the Wet'suwet'en nation. Coastal GasLink's injunction application claimed that that blockade, generally referred to as the Unist'ot'en camp, now stood in the way of the company's proposed liquefied natural gas (LNG) pipeline. The Unist'ot'en response argued that their actions "are fully in accordance with Wet'suwet'en law and the Wet'suwet'en legal process, and the actions of the plaintiff are not" (*Coastal GasLink Pipeline Ltd. v. Huson*, 2018 BCSC 2343: para. 28). To no one's surprise, the court issued an interim injunction, later expanding its reach to the Gidimt'en Access Point blockade erected by another Wet'suwet'en clan to support of the Unist'ot'en camp. The Wet'suwet'en nation, in conjunction with the Gitxsan, had brought the suit that resulted in the SCC's landmark 1997 *Delgamuukw* decision recognizing the existence of Aboriginal title on the very territories now being encroached upon via a simple interlocutory injunction. Shiri Pasternak (Forthcoming) puts it this way: "the very nation that first succeeded in defining Aboriginal title as an underlying proprietary interest was now being removed from these same lands through a low-level lever—the equivalent of an emergency stop cord on a train." As the RCMP prepared to enforce the Coastal GasLink injunction, it invoked the *Delgamuukw* decision in a press release issued on the eve of the police raid on the Gidimt'en Access Point:

> For the land in question, where the Unist'ot'en camp is currently located near Houston, BC, it is our understanding that there has been no declaration of Aboriginal title in the Courts of Canada. In 1997, the Supreme Court of Canada issued an important decision, Delgamuukw v. British Columbia, that considered Aboriginal title to Gitxsan and Wet'suwet'en traditional territories. The Supreme Court of Canada decided that a new trial was required to determine whether Aboriginal title had been established for these lands, and to hear from other Indigenous nations which have a stake in the territory claimed. The new trial has never been held, meaning that Aboriginal title to this land, and which Indigenous nation holds it, has not been determined. Regardless of the outcome of any such trial in the future, the RCMP is the police agency with jurisdiction. (RCMP 2019a)

The next day, in the aftermath of the violent arrest of fourteen people at the access point (Bellrichard and Ghoussoub 2019), the RCMP issued another press release, which read in part:

> The RCMP respects the Indigenous rights and titles in BC and across Canada. It was inappropriate for the RCMP to make any reference to the materials provided to the court during the injunction application process. Our role is to enforce the injunction and not to interfere with any ongoing discussion between our Indigenous communities and any other level of government. (RCMP 2019b)

There is a deep irony at work here. The *Behn* precedent insulated Coastal GasLink's injunction application from the impact of the exponentially more significant precedent in *Delgamuukw* and the collateral attack doctrine would have excluded defenses based on Aboriginal title during a contempt trial. In the meantime, the RCMP invoke *Delgamuukw* and the law on Aboriginal title (or at least the gas company's interpretation of it), as justification for the use of force and incursion on unceded Wet'suwet'en territory.

I say "would have" because after the province took over prosecution of the contempt charges arising out of the raid on the Gidimt'en Access Point, Crown prosecutor Trevor Shaw "told the Supreme Court of British Columbia in Prince George that after a "detailed review of the evidence" there wasn't sufficient evidence for convictions on criminal contempt charges" (Trumpener 2019). A lawyer for Coastal GasLink then stated the company would follow the Crown's lead and would not proceed with civil contempt proceedings. The judge acquiesced to this joint state-corporate prosecution decision, stating that "There is high public interest, but it is not appropriate to proceed. . . . I accept that Coastal GasLink does not wish to proceed" (Trumpener 2019). In the aftermath of the raid and the withdrawal of contempt charges, the Unist'ot'en camp continued its challenge to the issuance of interlocutory injunction, arguing in court that Wet'suwet'en law must be upheld on unceded Wet'suwet'en lands (Unist'ot'en Camp 2019). More recently, the Gidimt'en clan sued Coast GasLink for damages in relation to the destruction of property during the Access Point raid in January, stating that the "spiritual and emotional traumas these companies have inflicted on the Wet'suwet'en are tremendous and grave. These acts of violence must not go unpunished or unrecognized in the courts" (Barker 2019).

Such challenges to the "new normal" of injunctions and contempt by Indigenous land defenders and allied movements ought to be understood as praxis-based resistance to settler-colonial legality. After the 2014 Trans Mountain pipeline injunction was issued, activists known as caretakers chained themselves to the doors of the Vancouver courthouse "to draw attention to the role of the courts in ongoing colonial occupation of Indigenous territory on Burnaby Mountain and across the country" (Burnaby Mountain Updates 2014). Following an all too rare instance of a declined injunction application, Alliance Against Displacement organizer Maria Wallstam argued that successful challenges to injunctions by grassroots movements turn "slightly against the general and fundamental colonial rule of Canadian law that private property is more important than people's lives" (Wallstam 2017). By revealing the foundational role of law in mediating between extractive industry and the settler colonial state, such resistance also shows the beginning of a way out of BC's injunction habit.

References

Barker, Jordan. 2019. "Criminal Charges Dropped against Group that Occupied Muskrat Falls in 2016." *CBC News*, May 29. cbc.ca/news/canada/newfoundland-labrador/charges -dropped-muskrat-falls-occupation-1.5154345.

Barker, Thom. 2019. "Wet'suwet'en Clan Launches Civil Lawsuit against Coastal GasLink." *Williams Lake Tribune*, July 23. wltribune.com/news/wetsuweten-clan-launches-civil -lawsuit-against-coastal-gaslink/.

Bellrichard, Chantelle, and Michelle Ghoussoub. 2019. "Fourteen Arrested as RCMP Break Gate at Gidimt'en Camp Checkpoint Set Up to Stop Pipeline Company Access." *CBC News*, January 7. cbc.ca/news/indigenous/rcmp-injunction-gidimten-checkpoint -bc-1.4968391.

Bhandar, Brenna. 2018. *Colonial Lives of Property: Law, Land, and Racial Regimes of Ownership.* Durham, NC: Duke University Press.

Blomley, Nicholas. 1996. "'Shut the Province Down': First Nations Blockades in British Columbia, 1984–1995." *BC Studies* III: 5.

British Columbia Prosecution Service. 2018. "Civil Disobedience and Contempt of Related Court Orders" In *Crown Counsel Policy Manual.* www2.gov.bc.ca/gov/content/justice /criminal-justice/bc-prosecution-service/crown-counsel-policy-manual.

Burnaby Mountain Updates Facebook page. 2014. facebook.com/burnabymountain/photos /a.659497007504053.1073741827.659487880838299/665120590275028/?type=3 &theater.

Hunter, John J. L. 2009. "Aboriginal Rights Litigation." In *Injunctions—British Columbia Law and Practice*, 2nd ed. Vancouver: Continuing Legal Education Society of British Columbia.

Krawczyk, Betty. 2002. *Lock Me Up or Let Me Go: The Protests, Arrest, and Trial of an Environmental Activist.* Vancouver: Press Gang.

Lawn, Julia E. 1998 "The John Doe Injunction in Mass Protest Cases." *University of Toronto Faculty of Law Review* 56: 101.

Manuel, Arthur, with Grand Chief Ronald Derrickson. 2018. *The Reconciliation Manifesto: Recovering the Land, Rebuilding the Economy.* Toronto: Lorimer.

Mazur, Dylan. 2019. *Know Your Rights: Injunctions and Contempt of Court.* Vancouver: British Columbia Civil Liberties Association.

Metallic, Naiomi. 2015. "Injunctions against Pickets and Protests in the 21st Century: It's Time to Stop Applying the Three-Part *RJR-MacDonald Test*." Unpublished manuscript on file with the author.

Miller, Jeffrey. 2016. *The Law of Contempt in Canada.* 2nd ed. Toronto: Carswell.

Newell, Ryan. 2012. "Only One Law: Indigenous Land Disputes and the Contested Nature of the Rule of Law." *Indigenous Law Journal* 11, no. 1: 41.

Pasternak, Shiri. Forthcoming. "Why Does a Hat Need so Much Land?" In *Allotment Stories: Indigenous Responses to Settler Colonial Land Privatization*, edited by Jean O'Brien and Daniel Heath Justice.

Royal Canadian Mounted Police. 2019a. "Background on BC RCMP's Role in Enforcing Injunction Order" bc.rcmp-grc.gc.ca/ViewPage.action?languageId=1&siteNo-deId=2087&contentId=57805 (accessed January 6, 2019).

Royal Canadian Mounted Police. 2019b. "Fourteen Arrested during Enforcement of Injunction Order in Houston, BC." bc.rcmp-grc.gc.ca/ViewPage.action?siteNodeId=1075&lan-guageId=1&contentId=57830 (accessed January 7, 2019).

Saul, R. Patrick, and Eileen E. Vanderburgh. 2009. "Land Use Disputes." In *Injunctions: British Columbia Law and Practice*, 2nd ed. Vancouver: Continuing Legal Education Society of British Columbia.

Scott, Dayna Nadine. 2013. "Commentary: The Forces That Conspire to Keep Us 'Idle.'" *Canadian Journal of Law and Society* 28, no. 3: 425.

Trumpener, Betsy. 2019. "Contempt Charges Dropped against 14 Protesters Blocking B.C. Pipeline Project." *CBC News*, April 15. www.cbc.ca/news/canada/british-columbia/14-unist-ot-en-supporters-leave-court-1.5098760.

Unist'ot'en Camp. 2019. "Unist'ot'en Defends Indigenous Law at Injunction Hearing." unistoten.camp/june14/ (accessed August 20, 2019).

Wallstam, Maria. 2017. "Ten Year Tent City Beats Vancouver in Court!" *The Volcano*, May 22. thevolcano.org/2017/05/22/ten-year-tent-city-beats-vancouver-in-court-by-maria-wallstam/.

Ward, Cameron. 1993. "The Contemptuous Mr. Doe." *Advocate* (Vancouver) 51: 861.

Williams, Rick, et al. 2017. "The New Normal? Natural Resource Development, Civil Disobedience, and Injunctive Relief." *Alberta Law Review* 55, no. 2: 285–315.

Sherry Pictou

Decolonizing Decolonization:
An Indigenous Feminist Perspective on
the Recognition and Rights Framework

> I loved the land. Our people always lived on this
> land. . . . This is what our ancestors had done. . . .
> And there is something in us that always carry
> that thing of teaching the next generation.
> —Elder Agnes Potter

> It's our freedom to be who you want to be.
> —Elder Patricia Robar-Harlow[1]

On February 14, 2018, the prime minister of
Canada announced that a new "Recognition and
Implementation of Rights Framework" (Rights
Framework) would be developed "in full partnership with First Nations, Inuit, and Métis Peoples"
on a nation-to-nation basis (Canada 2018). The
Rights Framework was presented as a new form
of self-government outside of the *Indian Act* and
was initially hailed as a "decolonizing" approach
or as a process for decolonization by the federal
government. However, in the wake of the growing
dissent among Indigenous leaders and grassroots
organizations that followed, the Rights Framework was withdrawn in December of 2018.

Of major contention was how the Rights
Framework was being rushed through with very
limited engagement and consultation with Indigenous people. Yet there has been a host of related

The South Atlantic Quarterly 119:2, April 2020
DOI 10.1215/00382876-8177809   © 2020 Duke University Press

legislation and policy affecting Indigenous people moving forward, indicating a trajectory of implementing the framework with or without Indigenous consent (Yellowhead Institute 2019; APTN News 2019).

While this activity appeared to have been politically motivated by an upcoming federal election in 2019, there are critical implications for Indigenous people and for Indigenous women and gender diverse persons[2] in particular. The Final Report of the Missing and Murdered Indigenous Women and Girls Inquiry (MMIWG)[3] released on June 3, 2019, raises concern about how patriarchy and colonial governance systems are linked to the causes of gender discrimination and violence. The Final Report outlines 231 recommendations covering Indigenous women and gender diverse persons as Indigenous and human rights holders to culture, health, security and justice. Fundamental to the Inquiry's findings are recommendations for insuring there is gender equity and participation in political and governance systems, as well as policy requirements for gender-based socio-economic impact assessments in resource extractive and development industries (MMIWG 2019b: 26). While these recommendations should significantly alter the implementation of the Rights Framework, the MMIWG Inquiry—also launched as a process of state "decolonization" in 2016—has been criticized as being a state controlled process. This casts uncertainty as to what degree the recommendations will be taken seriously (Cervantes-Altamirano 2015; Pictou 2019a; Simpson 2017).

In this context, this paper seeks to open up a discussion about how decolonization is being conceptualized in the federal government's new Rights Framework from an Indigenous feminist perspective. While the paper does not specifically examine the legislation and policies that by all analyses appear to be moving the framework forward, it interrogates the overarching concept of the framework as a new form self-government and a process for decolonization. By comparison, the concept of decolonization for Indigenous scholars and activists has become a way for articulating strategies for exposing how settler colonialism, in both its historic and contemporary forms, impacts Indigenous people within settler states like Canada. At the same time, strategies for decolonization are complicated by three interrelated complex tensions within processes of settler colonialism and settler-state colonialism in particular, affecting Indigenous lives, especially for Indigenous women and gender diverse persons.

First, state-driven processes for negotiating Aboriginal title and Treaty rights are driven by neoliberal ideologies, i.e. exploiting natural resources as an imperative for self-government, under the guise that economic development will address complex social issues present in contemporary, trauma-tized Indigenous communities (Alfred 2009; Corntassel 2012; Coulthard 2014; Lloyd and Wolfe 2017). Patriarchy and neoliberalism intersect in ways that induce a colonial stratification of gender in economic development mainly to the advantage of males. Second, settler-state colonialism is also embedded in patriarchal power relations that are often internalized in Indig-enous politics in multiple and violent ways. Subsequently, Indigenous women and gender diverse persons struggling for gender and social justice find themselves having to navigate through the ways patriarchal colonialism is manifested by the state, as well as, within their own communities and related political organizations (Cervantes-Altamirano 2015; Ladner 2009; Kuokkanen 2019). The third tension has to do with how the term decoloni-zation itself has gained currency in recent years within both academic and policy circles but has taken on different and contradictory interpretations and meanings. Most often decolonization is confused with historic notions of colonization. This has led to conceptions of decolonization that prescribe rectifying or reconciling past injustices in the context of the present, without addressing the contemporary forms or extensions of settler colonialism (Pic-tou 2019b; Singh 2018; Tuck and Yang 2012).

By taking up these collusions between patriarchy, neoliberalism, and contradictory concepts of decolonization, I demonstrate how the Rights Framework manifests a contemporary form of patriarchal colonialism in state-Indigenous relations that will continue to negatively impact Indigenous women and gender diverse persons, especially if gender issues are sidelined. Equally important, I raise the issue about how settler-colonialism needs to be redefined in a way that will demand the eradication of gender violence and seek gender justice in strategies for decolonization.

In order to take up the complexity of these tensions, the paper is orga-nized in three sections. The first section examines how settler-colonialism and neoliberalism work together to instill violence against Indigenous land, water, and bodies. The second section delineates ways patriarchy is internalized within Indigenous communities in a way that serves neolib-eralism. The third section explores how strategies for decolonization can be reformulated from an Indigenous feminist perspective for achieving gender and social justice. I argue that this can only be achieved by fore-grounding the voices and experience of Indigenous women and gender diverse persons themselves, as active knowledge holders gained from expe-riences with patriarchal colonialism and land/water-based practices. This includes considerations of an intersectional, gender-based analysis + or

GBA+ (gender and gender diverse inclusive), and a human rights approach (with some precautions).

Neoliberal and Colonial Violence against Indigenous Land, Water, and Bodies

Indigenous societies are governed by systems that differ significantly from those that continue to be imposed by the settler state. Many ancestral Indigenous governance systems are inclusive of all human and non-human living relations. Leanne Simpson (2017:116) explains how Nishnaabeg political systems and governance were embedded in a "political and governing structure and process that facilitated a gentle and sustainable use of our lands and waters, a decentralized national leadership, and an intensification of personal and political relationships with a diversity of human and nonhuman nations." Tuma Young (2016:86) describes a similar system in Mi'kmaki (ancestral homelands of the Mi'kmaq) founded in creation stories that reinforce reciprocal relations that are characterized by

> both the extent of individual duty owed to immediate and extended family—including the dramatically extended family of other life forms and forces—and the extent of help one can expect to receive from one's kin and allies. Such reciprocity forms the basis of L'nuwey [Indigenous worldview] family law, a complex set of obligations and benefits structured around the proper treatment of women, children, elders and other (human and non-human) kin.

Simpson and Young theorize here how within Indigenous systems of governance, human relations of accountability and responsibility extend to land/water as sources of food and lifeways. In contrast, land/water in Western systems of governance is grounded in legal concepts of property or commodity, and ownership of land is regarded as a necessary premise for asserting sovereignty.

Western systems of governance and sovereignty operate within a matrix of domestic and international legal apparatuses for dispossessing land on the one hand, and replacing or repossessing land within capital relations, especially for extracting natural resources, on the other. For example, it has been well established how the legal concept of *terra nullius* (vacant or empty land), which derives from ancient Roman law, serves as a basis for devaluing Indigenous people and their governance systems to claim space for colonial sovereignty over land and resources (Altamirano-Jiménez 2013; Bhandar 2018; Moreton-Robinson 2015). Virginia Marshall (2017) further argues how like terra nullius, *aqua nullius* is used to dispossess Indigenous people in Australia from their water rights, which applies to Indigenous people being dispossessed of water rights around the globe including Canada. These concepts of property ownership propel a form of legal governance marked by a possessive ownership of land/waters that also extends to the disposal and exploitation of bodies in the global economic system (Moreton-Robinson 2015; Altamirano-Jiménez 2013; Bhandar 2018; Goeman 2017; Simpson 2016, Simpson 2017; Women's Earth Alliance and Native Youth Sexual Health Network 2016).

Human rights law is another legal category of Western law where protection for economic actors, especially in resource extractive industries, are weighed far greater than those for Indigenous and human rights—even when Indigenous peoples rights are violated by those very same economic interests (Altamirano-Jiménez 2013; Cervantes-Altamirano 2015; Lloyd and Wolfe 2016; MMIWG 2019a). As Khoury and Whyte (2017) state:

> There is a highly controversial principle in human rights law that allows corporations and other "legal persons" to apply for the same protections as real persons at human rights courts. . . . But corporations cannot be held accountable for human rights violations. So, while corporations can be protected by human rights law, they can at the same time enjoy impunity for committing human rights violations.

In this sense, then, legal concepts of terra/aqua nullius intersect with human rights law in the formation of a hierarchy of rights by privileging neoliberal corporatism (Bhandar 2018; Goeman 2017; Kuokkanen 2019; Pictou 2019b).

In Canada, the control over bodies as well as ancestral lands is operationalized and normalized through the patriarchal underpinnings of the *Indian Act,* placing Indigenous women and gender diverse persons within this hierarchy with the very least of rights among all First Nation people (Barker 2006; Bhandar 2018; Kuokkanen 2019; Ladner 2009; Pictou 2019b; Simpson 2016; Simpson 2017). It is well known how the *Indian Act* has historically created state-controlled First Nation bodies as "wards" of the state and designated reserve lands as being entrusted to the "Crown." The *Indian Act* was also instrumental in initiating patriarchal power relations that dehumanized Indigenous women and children. This was achieved by limiting the criteria for Indian (First Nation) status along patrilineal lines, disqualifying women who married non-Indigenous men. Eligibility for programs and services was (and continues to be) determined by those registered by the government as having "Indian Status." Therefore, those women who lost status, and their children, regardless of gender, were denied programs and services and the right to participate in Indian Band (reserve) elections (ibid.). Despite several legal challenges brought forward by First Nation women, including a successful submission to the United Nations Human Rights Committee by a Wolastoqiyik (People of the Beautiful River or Maliseet) woman, Sandra Lovelace, in 1981 (Barker 2006; Kuokkanen 2019), Canadian attempts to amend the *Indian Act* have never fully remedied the systemic gender discrimination.[4]

Gender discrimination regarding status further prevented women and their children, later as adults, from exercising political rights. Even women who were not displaced by the *Indian Act* could not participate in Indian Band Chief and Council elections until this restriction was removed in 1951. An effect of this disenfranchisement, the MMIWG Final Report emphasizes how women and gender diverse persons remain grossly underrepresented in governance and decision-making systems especially in regard to natural resource development and extraction (MMIWG 2019a: 399, 591–93; also see Martin and Walia 2019). So even though the *Indian Act* was amended to include women as eligible voters, the authors of the MMIWG Final Report argue that the power relations manifesting gender discrimination did not change. To put it simply, the *Indian Act* creates a gender-based hierarchy of power relations through Indian status (see also Simpson 2017: 111).

The MMIWG Final Report links these forms of discrimination to "intergenerational trauma; social and economic marginalization; a lack of institutional and political will; and the failure to recognize the expertise and capacity of Indigenous women themselves in creating self-determined solutions" (MMIWG 2019a:124). In this sense, violence against Indigenous women, girls, and gender diverse persons is facilitated by regulating and controlling Indigenous bodies and is deeply connected to the acquisition of land and its natural resources in the interest of economic development. Moreover, this "particular mode of colonial governance points to a deeper structure of dispossession: the fusing together of identity and property ownership, encapsulated in the notion of Indian status" (Bhandar 2018:177). Within this structure of dispossession, the ability to enact decolonial options for Indigenous women and gender diverse persons are further affected by the complex ways in which gender discrimination along with neoliberal notions of governance, are also internalized in Indigenous politics explored in the next section. I argue how this will also be the case in recent efforts to implement the Rights Framework if gender issues are not addressed, posing a risk for increased discrimination and violence against Indigenous women, girls, and gender diverse persons.

Internalizing colonial patriarchy: The contradictions of Indigenous Self-Government and dismantling the *Indian Act*?

Narratives about self-government have been dominated by an espousal to economic development as essential for filling in the socio-economic gap or addressing poverty. Therefore, economic development is a driving factor in various forms of state-Indigenous negotiations whether they are over land, self-government agreements or implementing Treaty rights (Pictou 2019b). The neoliberal push towards the exploitation of natural resources has become an imperative for self-government under the guise that economic development will address social issues. Instead, development under this model entails a form of capitalism that "enables Indigenous elites (often male) to position themselves as the main beneficiaries of the profits derived from resources and businesses . . . while neglecting social issues affecting particularly women: domestic violence, lack of adequate housing and social services" (Kuokkanen 2011: 276). In this sense, the colonial constructions of masculinity are perpetuated through the colonial stratification of gender in economic activities where males are privileged as income earners.

Moreover, what is characterized, as "Indigenous" self-government in state-Indigenous relations, is in fact contingent on the recognition and authorization by the state. For example, self-government is defined by the federal government as "Negotiated agreements [that] put decision-making power into the hands of Indigenous governments who make their own choices about how to deliver programs and services to their communities" (CIRNA). Though these negotiated agreements are cast as alternatives to the *Indian Act,* they are very much restricted to program and service delivery, in conjunction with neoliberal interpretations of Aboriginal and Treaty rights as economic endeavours to "development and economic growth that generates benefits for Indigenous peoples" (ibid.). These articulations of self-government align with the patriarchal colonial power-relations described earlier in relation to the *Indian Act*. As Kiera L. Ladner (2009:69) argues, aspirations for Indigenous sovereignty have undertaken a "masculinist discourse" that reinforces gender discrimination. In other words, imposed patriarchal state systems for self-government are taken up and internalized in Indigenous politics. Further, economic development projects posited as potential investments or benefits for Indigenous people especially in the extractive industries, are in turn increasingly putting more Indigenous subsistence systems and livelihoods as well as, Indigenous health at risk with industrial forms of environmental degradation and pollution. At the same time, rates of youth suicide and MMIWG continue to accelerate (Cervantes-Altamirano 2015; Pictou 2019b; MMIWG 2019b). Just as important, there is emerging research exposing how extractive industries induce multiple forms of violence against women, girls, and gender diverse persons (MMIWG 2019a; KAIROS 2015; Martin and Walia 2019 For example the MMIWG Final Report (2019a: 593) states:

> There is substantial evidence of a serious problem demonstrated in the correlation between resource extraction and violence against Indigenous women, girls, and 2SLGBTQQIA people. Work camps, or "man camps," associated with the resource extraction industry are implicated in higher rates of violence against Indigenous women at the camps and in the neighbouring communities.

Of equal significance is how the Red Women Rising research project that centers the experiences of Indigenous women and gender diverse persons living in Vancouver's Downtown East Side, reveals other forms and threats of violence (Martin and Walia 2019). Though patriarchal colonial violence is often associated with rural, Band or reserve systems, urban formations of dispossession are just as complicit in systems of violence. However, there is a tendency for politicians to respond with a focus on the lives of Indigenous women and gender diverse persons as constitutive of social deficits (not unlike the socio-economic gaps on reserves) instead of the various state constructions and impacts of violence and discrimination. Martin and Walia (2019: 16) emphasize in the report, *Red Women Rising: Indigenous Women Survivors in Vancouver's Downtown Eastside*:

> Indigenous women in the DTES [Down Town East Side] are stigmatized as having 'high-risk lifestyles' and blamed for violence committed against them when, in fact, colonial poverty and patriarchy are the highest risk factors in Indigenous women's lives. Our report explores how individual experiences of violence are inseparable from state violence including loss of land, forced poverty, homelessness, child apprehension, criminalization within the justice system, and health disparities.

As with industrial neoliberalism, urban forms of development (land dispossession) also poses risks for harm to bodies and land such as gentrifying (displacing) poor neighborhoods and replacing them with rich ones (Martin and Walia 2019: 97). Thus activism against neoliberal colonial capitalism (in its many forms) involves a multifaceted response that addresses threats to the land/water while also addressing threats of violence (and death) against

Indigenous bodies described in the previous section. Therefore, it is difficult to reconcile how social issues are addressed by economic development (Alfred 2009).

Further, while dismantling the *Indian Act*—as touted by government and the Assembly of First Nations (AFN)—should to be a viable option for ending gender discrimination, without addressing the masculinist narratives of self-government and Indigenous rights gender discrimination and violence will continue. Without question, historically gender discrimination in the *Indian Act* created another hierarchy of power relations to the disadvantage of women, children, and gender diverse persons, as discussed earlier. This became very evident during Indigenous women's advocacy for gender equity and efforts to amend the Canadian *Constitution Act* and the *Indian Act* in the early 1980s (Barker, 2006). Indigenous women were put in the position of having to double their lobbying efforts with both state and Indigenous leadership. However, it was the pushback from Indigenous male leaders that condemned women "challenging the discriminatory provisions of the Indian Act as well as sexism and violence" as "being anti-Indian, selfish, individualistic, and charged of betrayal of the self-determination struggles and of co-optation into colonial, Western discourses of individualism" (Kuokkanen 2019:72; also see Barker 2006; Ladner 2009). In efforts to address the "histories of sexism then so firmly associated with the Indian Act" it was federal officials who pressured Indigenous leaders into accepting Indigenous women's appeals to amend the constitution and the *Indian Act* to reflect gender equity, including the removal of the patrilineal requirements for status (Barker 2006:144).

These types of patriarchal power relations were carried over and continue in Indigenous organizations like the Assembly of First Nations (AFN) that remain predominately controlled by male leaders (Barker 2006; Kuokkanen 2019; MMIWG 2019a; Monture-Angus 1995). Therefore, significant attention must be given to how patriarchal colonialism is manifested in "policy and development frameworks [that] tend to be uncritical of neoliberal capitalism and the role of the state in perpetuating inequalities, pushing for assimilation and encouraging the dispensability of Indigenous women's bodies" (Cervantes-Altamirano 2015:8). While the MMIWG recommendations have the potential to disrupt the ways colonial forms of patriarchy are internalized and the violence they produce in Indigenous politics, it is becoming apparent that the recommendations—especially those pertaining to governance—are far from being implemented anytime soon. This further poses a question about political concepts of decolonization as being proposed with the Rights Framework, without consideration for gender. I maintain, the Rights Framework will instead elevate the risk of violence for Indigenous women, girls, and gender diverse persons, unless gender discrimination and violence are fully addressed. In the next section I examine how from an Indigenous feminist perspective, applying concepts of Intersectionality, GBA+, and Human Rights pertaining to gender together, have the potential to *decolonize the concept of decolonization* as being proposed by the federal government.

Decolonizing Decolonization: An Indigenous Feminist Perspective

In order to better understand how the government is conceptualizing the Rights Framework Agreement as representing decolonization, I examine some of the preliminary actions taken in leading up to the announcement of the Rights Framework. There were several critical institutional and administrative changes that had taken place within the federal government concerning Indigenous people. Central to these was how the Department of Indigenous and Northern Affairs Canada was split into two separate entities: Crown-Indigenous Relations and Northern Affairs (CIRNA) and the Department of Indigenous Services Canada (DISC) (King and Pasternak 2018). Also in 2017, the federal government struck a Memorandum of Understanding (MOU) with AFN, "to jointly identify measures and priorities for closing the socio-economic gap between First Nations and other Canadians . . . [and] to decolonize and align federal laws and policies with the *United Nations Declaration on the Rights of Indigenous Peoples* [UNDRIP] and First Nations' inherent and Treaty rights" (AFN 2017: 4). Similar reference to "decolonizing" federal laws and policies and "closing the socio-economic gap" is emphasized in the current CIRNA departmental plan for 2019–2020 (CIRNA 2019:11). Another notable change prior to announcing the Rights Framework was re-naming land claim and modern Treaty negotiations as "exploratory tables" in 2016 to be renamed again in 2017 as "Recognition of Indigenous Rights and Self-Determination Discussion Tables" (King and Pasternak 2018:17). While there is no clear rationale why these changes were made, it implies a solidification of economic development with concepts of self-government in preparation for executing the Rights Framework (Yellowhead Institute 2019). At the same time, it is important to note that while it appears the Rights Framework is moving forward despite Indigenous dissent, this raises concern about how the principle of Free Prior and Informed Consent (FPIC) in UNDRIP is being sidelined. FPIC is required for any legislation or approval of projects that impact Indigenous people. Thus, even though the government has openly declared a commitment to implementing UNDRIP principles as written in the MOU with AFN, it appears the government holds a diluted conception of FPIC. Further, even the legal requirement to consult Indigenous people regarding any potential impacts to Aboriginal and Treaty rights only include the "official" leadership. In other words, there is no mechanism for consulting with the broader Indigenous population (Pictou 2019b).

At the same time, government actions in regard to the MMIWG Inquiry since its launch in 2016 appear to be relegating gender issues as social deficits (as the Red Woman Rising report describes, noted earlier) to the realm of Indigenous services. For example, the MMIWG Inquiry is listed on the CIRNA website under "services and information" and outlines actions taken since launching the inquiry as providing funding to service areas.[5] These focus on prevention in health and support services for survivors and families; improving safety and security; monitoring and creating awareness in policing. While these initiatives are important, they do not elicit the broader structural changes that are necessary to address gender injustice and violence. Further, though the CIRNA plan (CIRNA 2019:9) does include considerations for a gender-based-analysis or GBA+, to what degree it will impact its goal in "co-developing modern treaties and self-government agreements" is uncertain in the sense that consultation is limited to Indigenous leadership that remains predominantly male, as previously discussed. It is important to note that even though the CIRNA plan makes reference to a GBA+, women and gender issues are not even mentioned in the Joint Priorities MOU of 2017 with the AFN mentioned earlier. AFN did recently pass a resolution at its General Assembly that mandates the AFN to work toward the "Implementation of Recommendations from the National Inquiry into Missing and Murdered Indigenous Women and Girls" (AFN 2019). However, to what degree the AFN will make this a priority or how this will impact the MOU or the Rights Framework remains to be seen.

Given these political dynamics, are there ways to propel the MMIWG Final Report recommendations to having a substantive impact for disrupting the way the Rights Framework appears to be moving forward? Furthermore, is there any way to disrupt the inadequate concept of decolonization that the Rights Framework is suggesting? In this context, I propose that some consideration be given to how the concepts of Intersectionality, GBA+ and a Human Rights approach from an Indigenous feminist perspective constitute a way to decolonize decolonization, but with some precautions.

The wisdom of applying the tools provided in mainstream feminist scholarship to issues of gender within the context of Indigenous self-government and sovereignty has been greatly debated (Altamirano-Jiménez 2013; Barker 2006; Cervantes-Altamirano 2015; Kuokkanen 2019; Ladner 2009; Wier 2017). On one end of the spectrum you have criticisms of mainstream feminism as being too focused on equal rights as human rights within the context of state sovereignty and thereby undermining Indigenous sovereignty. On the other, you have resurging Indigenous ways of knowing rooted in land/based practices where Indigenous women play a significant role that hold possibilities for disrupting the current trajectory of internalized patriarchal notions of Indigenous sovereignty and self-government (MMIWG 2019a; Simpson 2017; also see Wier 2017). There are valid concerns that the inclusionary aims of mainstream 'white' feminist politics might be pursued without addressing colonialism, which borders on tokenism and risks a re-subjugation, if not re-colonization, of Indigenous gender concerns (Arvin, Tuck, and Morrill 2013; Kuokkanen 2019; Simpson 2017). On the other hand, I agree with Rauna Kuokkanen's (2019: 175) argument about how useful and important western feminist theory is for "examining Indigenous political institutions shaped by and embedded in the Western conceptions of power and structures of decision-making . . . if we are to fully comprehend the character and scope of heteropatriarchy's effects in Indigenous institutions and gender relations. Such an examination forms the core of relational analysis required for restructuring of relations" (Also see Moreton-Robinson 2015; Ladner 2009). To put it another way, how do we find decolonial options within Indigenous experience rooted in ancestral knowledges but profoundly impacted by centuries of experience with patriarchal coloniality? I propose that by centering Indigenous women's and gender diverse persons' experiences and knowledge rooted in land/water-based practices for food and lifeways we could potentially open up Intersectionality, GBA+, and Human Rights together as a decolonial process.

An Indigenous Intersectional Gender Based Analysis (IIGBA)

African American scholar Kimberlé Crenshaw is credited with coining the term *intersectionality* as a way to examine how race, class, and gender intersect in the lived experiences of discrimination against women of color. In feminist scholarship, intersectional theory has been expanded to include the socioeconomic, political, and legal power dimensions that diversely impact women's lives (Hankivsky and Mussell 2018). Feminist literature also takes up these various intersections in women's lives to understand gender-based discrimination and gender-based violence is produced. In the past decade, governmental policy has increasingly engaged with feminist theory in developing a mainstreaming strategy of a GBA+ in its programs and policies, as included in the current CIRNA plan discussed above. However, Olena Hankisky and Linda Mussell (2018: 308), argue there are some tensions between GBA+ and intersectional theory. They contend that GBA+ "alone does not address processes of structures . . . and maintains a unitary analysis of difference. Intersectionality [on the other hand] . . . leaves open, as a matter of investigation, the content and implications of co-constituting relationships between power structures and social locations." Thus, it cannot be assumed that GBA+ will also take on the critical features of intersectional theory that are useful in demanding institutional change.

Though the MMIWG Inquiry undertakes both a GBA+ and intersectional analysis, there still remains a real danger of approaching the report recommendations without an understanding of the confines of its patriarchal colonial-political and economic institutions, and thus, without effectively addressing structural forms of dispossession and violence against land/water and bodies. For example, though the recommendations include a "call upon all governments to equitably support and promote the role of Indigenous women, girls, and 2SLGBTQQIA people in governance and leadership" (MMIWG 2019b: 6), they also call for the inclusion of Indigenous women and gender diverse persons in extractive and development industries to ensure they "equitably benefit from the projects" (26). The presumption here is that gender discrimination and violence can be mitigated within neoliberal notions of addressing social issues with economic benefits derived from resource extractive industries. Indeed, Simpson (2017: 42) writes, "'Fixing' the 'social ills' without addressing the politics of land and body dispossession serves only to reinforce settler colonialism, because it doesn't stop the system that causes the harm in the first place while also creating the opportunity for neoliberalism to benevolently provide just enough ill-conceived programming and 'funding' to keep us in a constant state of crisis."

Further, while GBA+ is gaining a foothold in government directives, it does not guarantee that it will address the structures of patriarchy and colonialism. On the other hand, it is imperative that intersectionality theory too, must also include the intersection of colonialism and how it impacts both bodies and land in decolonial work (Arvin, Tuck, and Morrill 2013;

Cervantes-Altamirano 2015; Kuokkanen 2019; MMIWG 2019a). I propose that by foregrounding the voices of Indigenous women and gender diverse persons, this can open up both GBA+ and an intersectional approach with possibilities for disrupting structures of patriarchal colonialism. In other words, in order to ensure patriarchal colonialism is taken into consideration, GBA+ and Intersectionality must be approached together from an Indigenous feminist perspective or as an Indigenous Intersectional Gender Based Analysis + (IIGBA+) approach. The Red Women Rising research project is important in this sense in how the shared experiences of Indigenous women and gender diverse persons were instrumental in forming solution-based recommendations. Participants were not considered "anonymous research subjects; they created and drove the process, incorporated diverse Indigenous methodologies in the research design, and are the central knowledge holders. [The] report, and the 200 recommendations contained within it, is based on their leadership, lived experience, and expertise as Indigenous women in the DTES" (Martin and Walia 2019: 5).

As others have argued, there can be no decolonization without addressing colonialism. I also suggest, that the MMIWG report cannot be mobilized as a tool for decolonization in seeking social justice for Indigenous women and gender diverse persons without their active knowledge and experience, especially in directing how the recommendations are implemented. It is important to point out, that both the Red Women Rising and MMIWG reports emphasize how women and gender diverse persons traditionally, and in many ways still, have significant roles in the governance of food and lifeways. These food and lifeways encompass Indigenous understandings where all of life is respected, especially sources of food and water. In other words, Indigenous women and gender diverse persons themselves are capable as critical actors in resisting patriarchal colonialism.

Furthermore, it important to also point out that while larger socio-political and neoliberal economic dynamics that characterize state-Indigenous relations has excluded Indigenous women and gender diverse persons, this exclusion has propelled Indigenous women led-movements to protect sources of food, land, and water against resource extraction (Coulthard 2014; Pictou 2019a; Simpson 2017). Movements such as the Tiny House Warrior Resistance Campaign against the TMX pipeline and the Unist'ot'en Camp Campaign, have been instrumental in exposing how in addition to environmental harms, extractive industries pose real physical harm, especially sexual violence against Indigenous women and gender diverse persons with the influx of male workers or man camps discussed earlier (Kuokkanen 2019;

MMIWG 2019a). Thus, if we are to move beyond the position of victimhood induced by settler colonialism, it is also critical to recenter experiences of resistance within processes of decolonization.

Though patriarchal colonialism has had concerted impacts on Indigenous lifeways, traditional approaches to governance and resistance can play a significant role in informing decolonizing strategies for a resurgence, especially through those values pertaining to ensuring the health of humans by ensuring the health natural resources and foods (Alfred 2009; Corntassel 2012; Coulthard 2014; Pictou 2019a; 2019b; Simpson 2017).

Therefore, by reaching out to Indigenous women and gender diverse persons, this can serve as a way to inform and disrupt hetero-patriarchal colonialism inherent in coalescing Indigenous and Non-Indigenous governance processes. In applying both an Intersectional and GBA+ from an Indigenous feminist perspective or IIGBA+ in all aspects of the Rights Framework, open up possible decolonial possibilities for mobilizing and implementing the recommendations of the MMIWG Inquiry. Gender concerns, especially concerns about colonial violence, cannot just be mitigated in the interest of moving neoliberal economic projects ahead. Instead, gender justice is founded in decolonizing ways that specifically address structural gender discrimination and violence.

A Word about a Human Rights–Based Approach

The MMIWG Final Report emphasizes how Indigenous women and gender diverse persons hold human rights as well as Indigenous rights. Therefore, Indigenous and human rights must work in tandem to insure more substantive forms of self-governance that include Indigenous laws while at the same time, hold all governments legally accountable in addressing gender discrimination and violence:

> In addition, the evidence makes clear that changing the structures and the systems that sustain violence in daily encounters is not only necessary to combat violence, but is an essential legal obligation of all governments in Canada. We target many of our Calls for Justice at governments for this reason, and identify how governments can work to honour Indigenous women, girls, and 2SLGBTQQIA people, and to protect their human and Indigenous rights, in the thematic areas examined within the *Final Report* (MMIWG 2019b: 1).

A main concern with human rights-based approaches is the obvious compatibility of the approach with neoliberal corporatism as discussed earlier.

Neoliberalism is perceived "as a 'friend' to human rights, gender equality and cultural rights. The relationship is sold as that of a natural process of capitalist-neoliberal-democratic-governmentality . . . and has co-opted resistance" (Cervantes-Altamirano 2015:11). Furthermore, Indigenous activists and scholars interrogating neoliberal colonial capitalism and issues of gender equity are quickly condemned (if not criminalized) as being anti-development or "as angry radicals who are unwilling to work together for the betterment of Indigenous peoples and Canadians" (Simpson 2017:46). Moreover, other related literature suggests that individualist values that premise human rights law threatens the collective nature of Indigenous Rights, which was the rationale for Indigenous leaders to dismiss gender equity in the 1980s (Cervantes-Altamirano, 2015; Kuokkanen, 2019). Yet as previously noted, Indigenous aspirations to self-government and sovereignty too continue to be subjugated to patriarchal state colonialism.

At the same time, it is important to remember that in 1981, it was the United Nations Human Rights Committee that reaffirmed that the *Indian Act* facilitates gender inequality in the Sandra Lovelace case discussed earlier. Also, in 2016, the Canadian Human Rights Tribunal rendered federal government child welfare policies as being discriminatory against Indigenous children living on reserve (Pictou 2019b; Kuokkanen 2019). More recently the United Nations report, *Human Rights Council Report of the Special Rapporteur on Violence Against Women, its Causes and Consequences* (Šimonović 2019: 16) supports the MMIWG Inquiry recommendations regarding how it is "crucial to provide a human rights-based approach to discrimination and violence against Indigenous women and to promptly investigate all the cases of missing and murdered women in the country." Thus, domestic and international human rights law indeed serve a role in directing government in addressing gender discrimination and violence. Rauna Kuokkanen (2019: 221) proposes that rather than reject human rights, "we need to reframe and rearticulate it to demonstrate that without Indigenous gender justice, there is no Indigenous self-determination."

Furthermore, collective self-determination cannot be achieved without individual self-determination or without sovereignty over our own bodies (Simpson 2017; Simpson 2016). In other words, only with sovereignty over our own bodies can there be collective sovereignty. In this regard, I contend that a Human Rights–based approach has the capacity to become an important tool in seeking gender justice that is often regarded as separate from Indigenous aspirations for sovereignty and self-governance. Yet as discussed earlier, "current models of Indigenous sovereignty merely replicate masculinist and patriarchal political structures and ideologies" (Kuokkanen 2011). We cannot simply ignore the fact that hetero-patriarchy and settler colonialism is a part of who we are and we will never be able to have an effective process for decolonization without fully addressing gender injustice.

Indigenous approaches to self-governance and sovereignty, especially through state-driven processes, cannot just merely dismiss other Indigenous concerns as Indigenous male leaders did with Indigenous women in the 1980s. Therefore, in order to achieve true social and gender justice, we must work toward transforming laws that currently uphold a hierarchy of rights to the advantage of neoliberalism in ways that centers and reprioritizes Indigenous and Human Rights. With this in mind, from and Indigenous-feminist perspective, a Human Rights–based approach along with an IIGBA+ described above, represent potential decolonial options for resurging Indigenous women's and gender diverse knowledge and practices of governance as a catalyst in achieving true decoloniality.

Conclusion

Though the Rights Framework was withdrawn in December 2018, a host of related policy and legislation has proceeded giving every indication that the Rights Framework is being implemented, despite growing Indigenous dissent about how there was not adequate consultation. This has raised serious questions about how the principle of FPIC in the UNDRIP is being sidelined even though the government claims a commitment to abiding by the principles of UNDRIP. Moreover, the Rights Framework was cast as setting out a process for decolonization by offering a mode of self-government outside of the *Indian Act*. This paper identifies three tensions playing out in this concept of decolonization that include: (1) neoliberalism within state-driven negotiation of Aboriginal title and Treaty rights, (2) patriarchal power relations and, (3) the contradictory concepts of decolonization itself. Instead of decolonization, the Rights Framework imposes a mechanism for consolidating neoliberal approaches to economic development with or as a form of self-government. What is critically important to reiterate is how these neoliberal approaches to development have been linked to historic and contemporary formations of patriarchal settler-colonialism, and settler-state colonialism in particular, with various forms of gender discrimination and violence (and death) against Indigenous women and gender diverse persons (living in both rural and urban areas). This was emphasized quite strongly in the MMIWG Final Report released on June 3, 2019, and included a call for gender equity in political and governance systems including policy reforms for gender-based socioeconomic impact assessments in resource extractive industries. Though to date there have been no actions taken in this regard, the government approach to issues of gender discrimination and violence so far, appears to have been conceptualized as social deficits to be addressed by programs and services. This raises a critical question about the degree to which the MMIWG Final Report recommendations will be taken seriously or in substantive ways that will also impact the way the Rights Framework is moving forward?

In this regard, this paper sets out to provoke a discussion about how the Rights Framework will perpetuate patriarchal colonial forms of gender discrimination and violence, if not addressed in effective ways. This is complicated by how legal mechanisms including human rights law privilege neoliberalism over other human rights, especially those pertaining to gender equality. Taking inspiration from the report on the Red Women Rising project, I propose that by foregrounding the knowledge and experience of Indigenous women and gender diverse persons, opens up the potential of Intersectionality, GBA+, and human rights approaches together as a decolonial option for addressing patriarchal forms of coloniality that also intersect with race, class, and gender in socio-economic, political and legal power relations. Both the Red Women Rising and MMIWG Inquiry reports emphasize how traditional forms of governance held values and land/water based practices and lifeways that attend to the health of Indigenous bodies and land/water or the ecological environments in which they live. I contend that this knowledge and experience as with the knowledge and experience gained in resisting patriarchal colonialism, is also actively required to ensure that the MMIWG Inquiry Final Report recommendations are not implemented in superficial ways that only serve to uphold patriarchal colonialism and neoliberalism. In this regard I offer two precautions. One is how recommendations calling for equal benefits in resource extraction industries have the potential of mitigating gender concerns while not addressing the structural ways in which gender discrimination and violence are produced, such as with mancamps. Second is how human rights law privileges neoliberalism. Therefore, there must be concerted efforts in applying an IIGBA that Human Rights approaches that strategically dismantle laws that create this hierarchy of rights to the disadvantage of Indigenous people, especially those pertaining to gender. Only then can we achieve a gender justice of asserting an Indigenous sovereignty over our bodies as well as over the land and waters in ways that are conducive to our resilience and freedom as Indigenous people.

Notes

1   Quoting Mi'kmaq Elders in *We Story the Land* film documentary by Martha Stiegman and Sherry Pictou (2016). See: http://westorytheland.ca/.

2   "Gender diverse persons" is used to also reference the acronym 2SLGBTQQIA (two-spirited, lesbian, gay, bisexual, transgender, queer, questioning, intersex, asexual) in the MMIWG Final Report 2019.

3   The MMIWG Inquiry Final Report, *Reclaiming Power and Place* consists of one volume in two parts: (a and b) and supplementary documents that include *Calls for Justice.* This paper references all of these as the Final Report and direct references or quotes cite the actual volume or document that can be found on the MMIWG website: https://www.mmiwg-ffada.ca/final-report/.

4   For example, Bill C 31 passed in 1985 to address loss of status through marriage fell short in the sense that only women and their children qualified for reinstatement of status but not their grandchildren. More recently Bill C 3 in 2017 was to address the shortcomings of Bill C 31, yet was limited to a specific timeframe from 1951 to1985 through which ancestral lineage could be traced. However, at the time of this writing this timeframe has been removed (see: https://www.canada.ca/en/indigenous-services-canada/news/2019/08/removal-of-all-sex-based-inequities-in-the-indian-act.html).

5   See the CIRNA website here: https://www.canada.ca/en/crown-indigenous-relations-northern-affairs.html.

References

Aboriginal Peoples Television Network (APTN). 2019. National News. Indigenous rights framework far from dead as Trudeau government rolls it out in pieces, February 1, 2019. aptnnews.ca/2019/02/01/indigenous-rights-framework-far-from-dead-as-trudeau-government-rolls-it-out-in-pieces/.

Alfred, Gerald Taiaiake. 2009. "Colonialism and State Dependency." *Journal of Aboriginal Health* 5, no. 2: 42–60.

Altamirano-Jiménez, Isabel. 2013. *Indigenous Encounters with Neoliberalism : Place, Women, and the Environment in Canada and Mexico.* Vancouver: University of British Columbia Press.

AFN (Assembly of First Nations). 2017. *Assembly of First Nations—Canada Memorandum of Understanding On Joint Priorities (June 12, 2017).* www.afn.ca/uploads/files/canada-afn-mou-final-eng.pdf.

AFN. 2019. "Implementation of Recommendations from the National Inquiry into Missing and Murdered Indigenous Women and Girls." Resolution no. 13/ 2019 AFN General Assembly, July 24, 2019. www.afn.ca/wp-content/uploads/2019/08/19–13–Implementation-of-Recommendations-from-the-National-Inquiry-into-Missing-and-Murdered-Indigenous-Women-and-Girls-3.pdf.

Arvin, Maile, Eve Tuck, and Angie Morrill. 2013. "Decolonizing Feminism: Challenging Connections between Settler Colonialism and Heteropatriarchy." *Feminist Formations* 25, no. 1: 8–34. doi.org/10.1353/ff.2013.0006.

Barker, Joanne. 2006. "Gender, Sovereignty, and the Discourse of Rights in Native Women's Activism." *Meridians* 7, no. 1: 127–61. www.jstor.org/stable/40338720.

Bhandar, Brenna. 2018. *Colonial Lives of Property : Law, Land, and Racial Regimes of Ownership.* Durham, NC: Duke University Press.

Bradley, K., and Herrera, H. 2016. "Decolonizing Food Justice: Naming, Resisting, and Researching Colonizing Forces in the Movement." *Antipode* 48, no. 1: 94–114. onlineli-brary.wiley.com/doi/full/10.1111/anti.12165.

Canada. 2018. *Remarks by the Prime Minister in the House of Commons on the Recognition and Implementation of Rights Framework, February 14, 2018.* pm.gc.ca/en/news/speeches /2018/02/14/remarks-prime-minister-house-commons-recognition-and-implementation -rights.

Corntassel, J. 2012. "Re-envisioning Resurgence: Indigenous Pathways to Decolonization and Sustainable Self-Determination." *Decolonization: Indigeneity, Education and Society* 1, no. 1: 86–101. jps.library.utoronto.ca/index.php/des/article/view/18627.

Crown Indigenous Relations and Northern Affairs (CRINA). *Self-Government.* www.rcaanc -cirnac.gc.ca/eng/1100100032275/1529354547314 (accessed August 14, 2019).

CIRNA. 2019. CIRNA Departmental Plan 2019–2020. rcaanc-cirnac.gc.ca/eng/155301694559 8/1553017051005.

Cervantes-Altamirano, Eren. 2015. "Sexual Violence against Indigenous Women: Policies, Human Rights and the Myth of Development." *ETopia*, no. 7. etopia.journals.yorku.ca /index.php/etopia/article/view/36752.

Coulthard, Glen Sean. 2014. *Red Skin, White Masks: Rejecting the Colonial Politics of Recognition.* Minneapolis: University of Minnesota Press.

Goeman, Mishuana R. 2017. "Ongoing Storms and Struggles: Gendered Violence and Resource Exploitation." In *Critically Sovereign: Indigenous Gender, Sexuality, and Feminist Studies,* edited by Joanne Barker, 99–126. Durham, NC: Duke University Press.

Hankivsky, Olena, and Linda Mussell. 2018. "Gender-Based Analysis Plus in Canada: Problems and Possibilities of Integrating Intersectionality." *Canadian Public Policy* 44, no. 4: 303–16. doi.org/10.3138/cpp.2017-058.

KAIROS Canada. 2014. Gendered Impacts: Indigenous Women and Resource Extraction. www.kairoscanada.org/wpcontent/uploads/2015/05/KAIROS_ExecutiveSummary _GenderedImpacts.pdf.

Khoury, Stefanie, and Whyte, David. 2017. "How Human Rights Law Has Been Used to Guarantee Corporations a 'Right to Profit.'" *Conversation,* March 15. theconversation.com /how-human-rights-law-has-been-used-to-guarantee-corporations-a-right-to-profit -74593.

King, Hayden, and Pasternak, Shiri. 2018. Canada's Emerging Indigenous Rights Framework: A Critical Analysis, June 5, 2018. Toronto, Yellowhead Institute. yellowheadinstitute. org/wp-content/uploads/2018/06/yi-rights-report-june-2018–final-5.4.pdf.

Kuokkanen, Rauna. 2011. "From Indigenous Economies to Market-Based Self-Governance: A Feminist Political Economic Analysis." *Canadian Journal of Political Science* 44, no. 2: 276–27. doi: 10.1017/S0008423911000126.

Kuokkanen, Rauna. 2019. *Restructuring Relations: Indigenous Self-Determination, Governance, and Gender.* New York: Oxford University Press.

Ladner, Kiera L. 2009. "Gendering Decolonisation, Decolonising Gender." *Australian Indigenous Law* Review 13, no. 1: 62–77. www.jstor.org/stable/26423117.

Lloyd, David, and Patrick Wolfe. 2016. "Settler Colonial Logics and the Neoliberal Regime." *Settler Colonial Studies* 6, no. 2: 109–18. doi.org/10.1080/2201473x.2015.1035361.

Marshall, Virginia. 2017. *Overturning Aqua Nullius: Securing Aboriginal Water Rights*. Canberra, A.C.T: Aboriginal Studies.

Martin, Carol Muree, and Walia Harsha. 2019. *Red Women Rising: Indigenous Women Survivors in Vancouver's Downtown Eastside*. Vancouver: Downtown Eastside Women's Centre. dewc.ca/wp-content/uploads/2019/03/MMIW-Report-Final-March-10-WEB.pdf.

MMIWG (Missing and Murdered Indigenous Women and Girls). 2019a. *Reclaiming Power and Place: The Final Report of the National Inquiry into Missing and Murdered Indigenous Women and Girls*. Vol. 1 a and b. www.mmiwg-ffada.ca/final-report/.

MMIWG. 2019b. Calls to Justice. http://www.mmiwg-ffada.ca/final-report/.

Monture-Angus, Patrica. 1995. *Thunder in My Soul: A Mohawk Woman Speaks*. Halifax, Nova Scotia: Fernwood.

Moreton-Robinson, Aileen. 2015. *The White Possessive: Property, Power, and Indigenous Sovereignty*. Minneapolis: University of Minnesota Press.

Pictou, Sherry. 2019a. "Beginnings and Renewal, Oppression and Fragmentation." In *Dis/Consent: Perspectives on Sexual Violence and Consensuality*, edited by KellyAnne Malinen, 18–30. Halifax, Nova Scotia: Fernwood.

Pictou, Sherry. 2019b. "What Is Decolonization? Mi'kmaw Ancestral Relational Understandings and Anthropological Perspectives on Treaty Relations." In *Transcontinental Dialogues: Activist Research and Alliances from and with Indigenous Peoples of Canada, Mexico and Australia*, edited by Rosalva Aída Hernández Castillo, Suzie Hutchings, and Brian Noble, 37–64. Tucson: University of Arizona Press.

Simpson, Audra. 2016. "The State Is a Man: Theresa Spence, Loretta Saunders and the Gender of Settler Sovereignty." *Canadian Journal of Women and the Law* 19, no. 4: muse.jhu.edu/article/633280.

Simpson, Leanne. 2017. *As We Have Always Done : Indigenous Freedom through Radical Resistance*. Minneapolis: University of Minnesota Press.

Singh, Jakeet. 2018. "Decolonizing Radical Democracy." *Contemporary Political Theory*, 1470–8914. doi.org/10.1057/s41296-018-0277-5.

Šimonović, Dubravka. 2019. *Report of the Special Rapporteur on Violence against Women, Its Causes and Consequences*. United Nations Human Rights Council Forty-First Session, 24 June–12 July 2019. ohchr.org/EN/Issues/Women/SRWomen/Pages/Annual Reports.aspx.

Tuck, Eve, and K. Wayne Yang. 2012. "Decolonization Is Not a Metaphor." *Decolonization: Indigeneity, Education and Society* 1, no. 1: 1–40.

Weir, Allison. 2017. "Decolonizing Feminist Freedom: Indigenous Relationalities." In *Decolonizing Feminism: Transnational Feminism and Globalization*, edited by Margaret A. McLaren, 257–88. London: Rowman and Littlefield.

Women's Earth Alliance and Native Youth Sexual Health Network. 2017. *Violence on the Land, Violence on Our Bodies Building an Indigenous Response to Environmental Violence*. landbody defense.org/uploads/files/VLVBReportToolkit2016.pdf

Yellowhead Institute. 2019. From the Rights Framework to the 2019 Election. yellowhead institute.org/from-the-rights-framework-to-the-2019-election/.

Young, Tuma W. 2016. "L'nuwita'simk: A Foundational Worldview for a L'nuwey Justice System." *Indigenous Law Journal* 13, no. 1: 75–102. jps.library.utoronto.ca/index.php/ilj/article /view/26700.

The Rise of Precarious Workers

Todd Wolfson, Editor

Todd Wolfson

Introduction: Class Struggle before Class

On May 8, 2019, the day before Uber released its IPO (initial public offering), app-based drivers across the world turned off their cell phones and went on strike. These strikes, which took place in dozens of cities from Sydney and Sao Paolo to London and Los Angeles, lasted anywhere from two hours to a full day. The goal of the global action was twofold: disrupt the IPO, showing investors and the company that all was not well for workers in the platform economy, while simultaneously illustrating the unified transnational nature of this emerging workers' struggle. One the eve of the strike, six driver-led grassroots organizations across the US released a joint statement titled "Why We Are on Strike" (New York Taxi Workers Alliance 2019) In the statement the authors outlined the rationale for the May 8 action:

> We are calling for a National Day of Action Against Uber, Lyft, and all other App-based For-Hire-Vehicle companies on Wednesday, May 8th to shine light on how Uber and Lyft's flawed business model pushes hard-working drivers across the US and the globe into poverty and desperation. . . . Driver-led grassroots organizations across the entire nation are unified in our call for a strike against Uber corporate greed. . . . Drivers will never back off or fade into the night. Our movement will only grow stronger.

This statement crystallized the militancy and growing solidarity among Uber and Lyft drivers as well as taxi drivers who feel they are being taken advantage of by an exploitative system. It is likely that we will look back at May 8, 2019, as the opening salvo of a protracted struggle between a growing class of precarious workers on the one hand and Silicon Valley elites and tech-focused venture capital firms on the other.

The South Atlantic Quarterly 119:2, April 2020
DOI 10.1215/00382876-8177959 © 2020 Duke University Press

The Shape of the Struggle

The growing struggle within the "gig" economy is taking place on two intertwined levels. From one vantage, the fight between platform workers and companies like Deliveroo, Lyft, Handy, Amazon, or Care.com is being fought over the rollback of the social contract and the devolving economic situation of workers clawing to survive in a callous economy. This aspect of the struggle was clearly brought to life on May 8, as drivers made cogent demands around bread-and-butter issues like a minimum wage and a more transparent process around driver deactivation (read: firing).

At the same time, however, if we step back and look at the broader historical sweep, we can also see May 8 as a critical moment in the ongoing cycle of "organization, disorganization, or reorganization" of the working class (Przeworski 1977: 377), or what Marx once called the "now hidden, now open fight" between classes. If we take this argument into account, the struggle between app drivers and Silicon Valley takes on a different hue.

To elaborate, using a historical lens, we can begin to make out the ways that the economic, political, and ideological logic of platform capitalism (Srnicek 2017) is a radical extension of the neoliberal logics of flexibilization, the casualization of labor, and the deregulation of corporate enterprises. And building on this, we can trace how the strategies employed by platform companies are an attempt to disorganize this growing segment of precarious workers by harnessing technology and other tools to deskill, disempower, and disaggregate.

Accordingly, if we take the same broader historical approach to the emerging fight of platform workers we can see similar patterns. Through the transnational organizing of May 8, and other worker actions such as the strike waves of food couriers throughout the UK and Europe (Cant 2017), we can see the outlines of a new worker-led resistance. This new figure of resistance has come into focus as platform workers have established new lines of communication, developed a collective understanding of their shared concerns, and ultimately worked to build new political organizations through which to advance their collective struggle.

The essays in this installment of Against the Day pick up on some of these broad historical questions of the struggle of workers, the logic of capitalism, and the possibility of building organization through different narratives and analyses. The articles detail the transformation in capital and the ways technology has been harnessed by platform companies. The essays also explore, from different vantages, the emerging struggle of platform workers in particular, as well as the conditions necessary for the development of nascent political organization. And importantly, the essays are written by people on the front lines of these struggles, whether in London, Hyderabad, or New York.

The underlying assumption in this series is that the structural dislocation of workers, which has accompanied the rise of platform capitalism, offers a critical moment to examine the dynamic processes of class struggle. More specifically, following E. P. Thompson's (1978) famous rejoinder, "class struggle before class," this special section of *SAQ* examines emergent processes of worker struggle that are a priori to workers' shared understanding of themselves as a class. Thompson's formulation is instructive, as it offers an orientation toward investigating the struggle between platform workers and Silicon Valley as one critical moment in a historical process.

In the remainder of this brief introduction, I will make two broad framing arguments that set up the articles to come. First, building on this argument that we need to see this struggle as part of a broader sweep of history, I detail the rise of platform capitalism not as the outcome of benign technology, as it is often argued, but rather as part of a historical legacy to disempower workers and working-class organizations. Following that, I look at how this moment of worker organizing can be seen as an initial stage of an emerging class or class segment. Workers in the platform economy are forging novel strategies to rebuild this segment of the working class.

The Invisible Hand of Technology

An age-old narrative has been deployed to explain the rise of the gig or platform economy. Simply put, platform companies developed in dialogue with technological advances ranging from the increase in the power of computing to expanded possibilities of communication and coordination. Recognizing the increased opportunities, entrepreneurs saw an opportunity to harness emerging technologies to wipe out inefficient markets. Thus, the breathless moniker, "market disruptor." As the story goes, through the development of networked apps and seizing on growing class of the un- and underemployed, new strategies around the delivery of service were deployed where customers were able receive goods and services at breakneck speed. Meanwhile a new "on-demand" workforce was cultivated, and workers were afforded the flexibility to operate as mini-entrepreneurs, working on their own time with the "freedom" to choose when and how to work. The underlying implication is that platform capitalism and the resulting labor relations were not the result of human intervention but instead that of the machines and big data sets that are prodding us forward toward a new societal age.

While this narrative is intoxicating, it conjures up a new "invisible hand"—this time the invisible hand of technology that silently guides social progress. We have heard this trope before. In his social history of automation (1984), historian David Noble discussed the development of technological innovation on the factory floor in New England. In reference to increasing automation in the factory Noble argued, "technology has come to be viewed as an autonomous process, having a life of its own which proceeds automatically, and almost naturally, along a singular path." Challenging this perspective Noble (1984: xiv-xv) continued:

> Rather than showing how social potential was shaped by technical constraints, . . . I examine how technical possibilities have been delimited by social constraints. . . . For when technological development is seen as politics, as it should be, the very notion of progress becomes ambiguous: What kind of progress? Progress for whom? Progress for what? And the awareness of the ambiguity, this indeterminacy, reduces the powerful hold that technology has had on our consciousness and imagination, and it reduces also the hold upon our lives enjoyed by those whose social power has long been concealed and dignified by seemingly technological agendas.

> Bringing this argument to life, Noble outlines how the process of automation within the factory was guided by the desire of managers to take control away from workers, which led to specific decisions about technological design. Thus, technological innovations were made with the specific intent to weaken the power of workers on the factory floor, in short, to disorganize the working class.

Following Noble, in her book on digital labor, Ursula Huws (2014) examines the rise of the gig economy and particularly the deteriorating work conditions of gig workers. Huws details three critical moments that have taken place within this broader economic sweep of the last forty years—from the Oil shock of 1973 and the fall the Berlin Wall in 1989 to the economic crisis of 2008. Each of these moments, she argues, has led to social and economic transformations that have altered labor processes, and further weakened the working class. This series of economic transformations set the stage for the gig economy, as gig work—low-wage, temporary, casualized, and precarious—quickly emerged as a preferred means of employment.

If we dive further into the transformation of the labor process in the gig economy, and consider the broader historical sweep, it becomes quite clear that many of the key features of the labor process are meant to disorganize and disaggregate the working class. This is made evident in multiple ways. The most obvious is the reclassification of workers as independent contractors without the right to collectively bargain. While this drives down costs, it also importantly hinders the ability of workers to organize and build working class institutions, like unions. Alongside the reclassification of workers is the isolation and alienation of workers in the gig economy. While many workers in past periods shared a collective space, whether it was a factory or a hotel, workers in the gig economy often work alone, and consequently their ability to connect with one another and build solidarity is compromised. The lack of connectivity and solidarity leads to an alienated and individualistic mindset among workers—which workers must fight against when attempting to build power.

While I don't have the space to elaborate on this argument, following Noble, it is clear that the emergence of the technologies and labor processes that have come to define the gig economy—independent contractor status, alienated labor process, algorithmic management, constant workplace surveillance—did not emerge independent of political needs of the owning class. Quite the opposite, the technologies and strategies have been developed that facilitate the accumulation of capital, the isolation and casualization of workers and the dismantling of working-class institutions like labor unions. In short, the disorganization of the working class.

Reorganization?

In Uber's S-1 filing to the SEC, the company outlined a series of risks investors should be aware of before buying their stock. These risks ranged from Uber's market position to their brand management and importantly legal cases challenging the independent contractor status of workers. The company also marked growing worker resistance as a critical challenge to the future of the company. Uber (2019: 30) explained in detail:

While we aim to provide an earnings opportunity comparable to that available in retail, wholesale, or restaurant services or other similar work, we continue to experience dissatisfaction with our platform from a significant number of Drivers. In particular, as we aim to reduce Driver incentives to improve our financial performance, we expect Driver dissatisfaction will generally increase. . . . Further, we are investing in our autonomous vehicle strategy, which may add to Driver dissatisfaction over time, as it may reduce the need for Drivers. Driver dissatisfaction has in the past resulted in protests by Drivers, most recently in India, the United Kingdom, and the United States. Such protests have resulted, and any future protests may result, in interruptions to our business.

Here, in dry legal terms, Uber outlines the possibility of worker organizing and driver-led resistance as one of the key risks to the long-term success of the company. And, as if rising at the appointed hour, drivers coordinated their transnational strike on May 8, in part countering Uber's S-1 filing and the launch of the IPO. From Nairobi to Nottingham, workers turned off their apps and withdrew their labor in an effort to exercise their collective power. As we seek to reckon with this moment as part of the cycle of class struggle, it is important to return to E. P. Thompson. Explaining his dynamic understanding of class, Thompson (1978: 149) argued that

classes do not exist as separate entities, look around, find an enemy class, and then start to struggle . . . on the contrary people find themselves in a society determined in structured ways (crucially, but not exclusively, in productive relations), they experience exploitation, (or the need to maintain power over those whom they exploit), they identify points of antagonistic interest, they commence to struggle around these issues, and in the process of struggling they discover themselves as classes, they come to know this discovery as class-consciousness. Class and class consciousness are always the last, not the first, stage in a real historical process.

Thompson's insight offers important context for understanding the emerging struggle of workers in the platform economy. First and foremost, the struggle in the gig economy is not foreordained, but rather it is a historical unfolding. This growing class of workers—from package delivery drivers to nannies and food couriers—find themselves in exploitative circumstances and they have begun to organize and fight back. The struggle is both against the exploitation, but it is also against a labor process that alienates and disorganizes workers. Traditional labor unions have moreover largely watched from the sidelines, and thus a new breed of worker organization has emerged. This new organizational form is indicative of the moment of struggle we are in. The organizations are nascent and militant, and they are forging novel lines of communication among workers as they fight Silicon Valley.

Whether platform workers are able to harness technology and their shared conditions to build novel worker-led organizations is a critical question. Moreover, whether this emerging class of platform workers can organize and build the power necessary to fight companies and the transforming logic of capital will determine future developments of the capitalist economy.

References

Cant, Callum. 2018. "The Wave of Worker Resistance in European Food Platforms 2016–2017." *Notes from Below*, January 29. notesfrombelow.org/article/european-food-platform -strike-wave.

Huws, Ursula. 2014. *Labor in the Global Digital Economy.* New York: Monthly Review.

New York Taxi Workers Alliance. 2019. "Why We Are on Strike!! A Joint Statement from May 8th Striking US Cities." *nytwa.org*, May 8. www.nytwa.org/statements/2019/5/13/joint -national-statement-on-why-we-strike-from-may-8th-2019-striking-cities-released-5819.

Noble, David. 1984. *Forces of Production: A Social history of Industrial Automation.* New York: Knopf.

Srnicek, Nick. 2017. *Platform Capitalism.* London: Polity.

Przeworski, Adam. 1977. "The Proletariat into a Class: The Process of Class Formation from Karl Kautsky's The Class Struggle to Recent Controversies," *Politics and Society* 7, no. 4: 343–401. journals.sagepub.com/doi/pdf/10.1177/003232927700700401.

Thompson, E. P. 1978. "Eighteenth Century English Society: Class Struggle before Class." *Social History* 3, no. 2: 133–65.

Uber Technologies, Inc. 2019. "Form S-1 Registration Statement under the Securities Act of 1933." *Sec.gov*, April 11. sec.gov/Archives/edgar/data/1543151/000119312519103850 /d647752ds1.htm.

Callum Cant and Clara Mogno

Platform Workers of the World, Unite! The Emergence of the Transnational Federation of Couriers

Twelve countries, sixty workers, thirty organizations, four languages spoken, one set of objectives: smashing platform capitalism, sharing tactics and strategies, exploring new ways to structure solidarity, making transnational connections.

Over the last five years food delivery platforms have spread all over the world. With this growth has come a rapid transformation in the way that urban residents consume commodities, reproduce their labor-power, and use space.

But most importantly of all, these platforms have recomposed the class antagonism at the heart of the capitalist mode of production on a new technical level. Huge quantities of surplus capital, unable to find significant returns in a low-profit post-crash environment (Roberts 2016), have flooded into the food delivery sector. This influx—which may yet prove to be a bubble (Srnicek 2017)—has led to a significant process of development, creating a new terrain of confrontation between labor and capital. In response, platform workers have developed new forms of organization and political imaginaries that address this new organization of capital.

The formation of the Transnational Federation of Couriers (TFC) at a meeting in Brussels in late 2018 was a watershed moment in the ongoing development of the platform workers' movement. For the first time couriers from different national contexts came together with the explicit intention of creating an organizational form that matched the global ambitions of "platform capitalism" (Srnicek 2017).

The South Atlantic Quarterly 119:2, April 2020
DOI 10.1215/00382876-8177971 © 2020 Duke University Press

This article provides an introduction to the TFC by presenting the results of ongoing processes of participant observation (Hammersley and Atkinson 2007; Marcus 2010) carried out by the authors. First, it gives an account of the background to the TFC in the spread of food delivery platforms and the specifics of the technical composition of the workforce therein. Second, it moves onto a discussion of how the TFC was able to formulate a set of demands that applied across the different contexts of its member organizations. Third, it discusses a case study of the federation in action in response to the death of a Glovo rider at work in Barcelona in 2019 and in organizing simultaneous strikes. The article finds that workers in platform capitalism have the capacity to generate new forms of collective self-organization that fit their recomposed technical and social composition (see Woodcock et al. 2018).

Before the TFC: Transnational Struggles, Links, and Alliances

Delivery platforms come in all shapes and sizes. Broadly, there are three tiers of platform: the global, the multinational, and the national. Deliveroo, Glovo and UberEats are globally active, often holding a dominant position in multiple national markets. Multinationally, platforms like Rappi and Pedidosya dominate in South America, and Foodora competes in Europe, whilst foodpanda is a significant player in Asia. At a national level, there is a great diversity of platforms, from small examples like MyMenù in Italy to colossal Chinese platform Meituan with 290 million monthly active users (Windsor 2018). In addition, there are also delivery platforms with slightly distinctive models, such as Stuart—a European platform that provides business-to-business logistics through a platform model, with significant contracts with food service players like Kentucky Fried Chicken. Even if the exact scale of the industry is hard to identify given the paucity of accurate data collection, it is increasingly clear that delivery platforms are a substantial component of the wider service sector, which provides commodified social reproduction through directly market mediated means (Endnotes 2013).

The pattern of expansion evident so far is of investment on a metropolis-by-metropolis basis, beginning in the most advanced capitalist urban spaces (like London and Paris) and spreading outwards from there. Global and multinational platforms, in particular, have gained market share through rapid expansion that reproduces a basic platform model over and over again in new areas. Investments in new markets can be made very rapidly due to the low-to-zero levels of constant capital required to start operating. This reproduction of a basic model has led to significant similarities in the class composition of delivery platform workers in urban contexts across the world.

Where differences do exist, a clear pattern of development can be observed, with modifications to the platform model such as the introduction of variable piece rates being applied first in the most "mature" and advanced cities, and then rolled out from there. The advanced metropolis is the laboratory of platform capitalism.

Platforms apply additional micro-variations to their models in order to adapt to national legislative frameworks and take advantage of potential wage differentials. UberEats, for instance, pays different boosts on a zone-by-zone basis within a city; Glovo in Italy varies both rates of pay and opening hours by the size of a local market; and Deliveroo in the UK historically paid different hourly rates depending on the state of the local labor market. The rapid spread of platform models has produced a transnational recomposition—with new fractions of the working class being introduced to the sector across different urban and national contexts and finding themselves in a common position.

All of these platforms, whatever their scale or specific model, have one thing in common: they require a constant pool of labor-power available to respond to spikes in demand. They maintain this pool through either the scheduling of shifts or incentives built into piece-rate wage systems. Workers spend much of their "working" time as part of this reserve while waiting for orders, often in common spaces (for instance, quiet side streets beside busy restaurants or designated "zone centers"). As they wait together, they create "informal work groups" (Weir 2004: 235) in which they socialize—discussing everything from working conditions to politics and life. It is out of these in-person groups that much of the "embryonic solidarity" (Atzeni 2010) on which collective action relies is generated.

However, workers also spend a lot of time watching their phones whilst they wait, particularly if they find themselves on their own. During this time they interact with friends and family—but also other members of their informal work groups. These interactions are usually structured in the form of encrypted messenger chats hosted on apps such as WhatsApp and Telegram, but can also emerge in other social media formats such as Facebook groups or even Strava clubs. In short, the requirement for a constant pool of surplus labor generates the conditions out of which what Wood (2015: 260) has characterized, in a different context, as "mass self-communication networks" arise.

Workers use these chats for a multitude of purposes: from requests for information and practical assistance to sharing memes. Informal work groups form through and reinforce themselves via these mass self communication networks, and therefore they function as an important avenue for collective worker identity formation. In most cases, when processes of self-organization develop in a direction antagonistic to platforms, these chats can change function to facilitate collective action. Sometimes entirely new chats are created with the explicit intention of forming the organizational backbone for a network/union hybrid. As such, mass self-communication networks form a crucial part of the "invisible organization" (Alquati 2013; Calder Williams 2013) of platform workers from which otherwise apparently spontaneous collective action can emerge.

Italian workerist Romano Alquati, according to Evan Calder William, conceptualized the circulation of struggle as workers hijacking "the architecture of capital circulation that has historically determined them. They exploit capital's determination of the factories, piazzas, houses, and all the zones between as a network of propulsive nodes and established paths through which to structure itself as an extensive force of material and social negation" (Calder Williams 2013). With this is mind, we argue that the transnational organization of platforms—which produces a similarly composed class subject across many different national contexts—has created the material basis for the global nature of platform worker struggle.

The rapid formation of the TFC relies on the fact that workers across different contexts experience a fundamentally similar labor process and their technical/social composition is very similar, in a manner that is less likely to occur, for instance, across the links in a south-north global value chain. This material basis in the network of capital has combined with the use of mass self-communication networks to facilitate solidarity amongst workers in different local contexts.

The first tentative links between workers in Europe were conducted by workers who wanted to understand their specific local situations through comparison. For instance, a UK workers' bulletin, *The Rebel Roo*, had an extensive record of communication with riders from France, Italy, and Germany. The issues contained a comparison of conditions from a worker-correspondent based in Marseilles, news of a strike in Turin, a translated statement from "Deliverance project" (a workers' collective in Turin), further news of a wildcat strike in Marseilles, and information on organization in Berlin. But the information being shared was not purely technical: whilst some issues highlighted differences in economic conditions—"If they can pay us €15 an hour here in France, they can pay you £15 an hour in the UK!" (Anon 2016: 1)—others also articulated a common class perspective on the political implications of the struggle:

> Our generation is deprived of its own future by the imposition of working conditions that, exploiting both the grey areas of the law and our desperation, trample on those rights won by workers through decades of struggles and sacrifice. It is time to say, enough! It is time to take back the dignity of work, and come together to demand what belongs to us. (Anon 2017: 3)

But as well as public-facing publications, extensive behind the scenes communication was underway from early 2017 onwards. At that early point, only six months after the first large-scale strikes in food platforms in 2016, workers from the UK, Italy, France, Belgium, Germany, and Spain were discussing common issues, strategies, and demands. This communication took on the form of collective inquiry, through which workers thrown into an unfamiliar composition of capital began to understand their contexts. This research from below presaged a process of mobilization, which would gradually spread, as workers from across Europe began to form a united front against the platforms and their political program of exploitation, extraction, and immiseration.

The Making of the Transnational Federation of Couriers

These companies operate on a transnational level, so we need to resist them on a transnational level.
—IWW Courier Network member from the UK (labournet.tv 2018 01:56)

In early 2018 an NGO, Alter Summit, decided to bring together platform workers and their organizations from across Europe with researchers, journalists and other supporters to discuss common strategies, approaches, and demands. A call out was written and circulated in English, French and Spanish. This meeting would become the founding congress of the TFC.

When the meeting took place in October 2018, thirty-four organizations were in attendance. These organizations ranged from official trade unions to self-organized rider collectives from twelve different countries: Austria, Belgium, Finland, France, Germany, Holland, Ireland, Italy, Norway, Spain, and the UK. All of them, in one way or another, represented actors and tendencies within a transnational cycle of platform worker struggle that had, over the previous two years, spread across the continent at remarkable speed (Cant 2018).

> We have to find a kind of common strategy because these companies have strategies: how to cope with us, how to deal with us, as workers or not workers, whatever, "people doing the job," but we also have to find something to . . . get some kind of balance of power. (Courier from Austria transcribed from labournet.tv 2018 02:54)

The primary objective of the meeting was to create a space for delivery riders to meet each other and organize their struggles. The presence of other actors was intended to create connections and allow for workers to enlarge their struggle by making ties with potential allies. In order to combine these two objectives, the participants were separated into two groups, which met largely in parallel: Food delivery riders (and ex-riders) and observers.

Throughout the meeting, workers expressed a common sentiment: that sharing information on the tendencies and strategies of platform capitalism was an essential prerequisite to organizing an adequate working class response that matched the global ambitions of platforms. While the tendency towards transnational organization had been evident for a long time, this meeting marked the first time that it resulted in a set of common demands. The participants reached agreement on the substance of a declaration:

> Fake free lancers or employees, but all under-employed, under-payed [*sic*], under-protected by Foodora, Deliveroo, Ubereats, Stuart, Glovo, have met in Brussels for a first transnational Assembly the 25th and 26th October 2018.
>
> We have decided to unite our numerous struggles in one international couriers struggle.
>
> We demand:

> - Freedom of association
> - Hourly minimum guaranteed wage
> - A fair definition of working time
> - Data and App Transparency
> - Job Security
> - Insurance
> - Workers choose employee/free-lance
> - Recognition of plateforms [*sic*] as employers
> - Participation for all riders
> - Regular negotiations mediated by city and municipal councils
> - Protection and legalisation of all plateform [*sic*] non EU migrant workers (who may not have resident permits)
> - Act to express solidarity with other precarious and gig economy workers
> - Respect
> - Common space for riders
> - Abolish internal ranking

These demands contained two key themes: first, an anti-legalistic conception of class and self-organization; and second, a desire for workers' control against the algorithmic manager's prerogative.

There is a new trend, new ways of working, the gig economy, these new platforms, everyone is fighting against something like a transformation of work, that has been imposed by companies, you know, these app-companies, and it needs to be a voice for those people who are working for these companies. (IWGB member from the UK transcribed from labournet.tv 2018 04:55)

For much of the last century, the dominant theorization of trade unionism amongst those concerned with industrial relations was that they were multiple parties involved in the orderly regulation of the employment relationship. Whilst the different parties with a stake in employment (state, capital, and labor) all had divergent interests, strong tripartite relational processes could produce mutual benefit. Indeed, the whole discipline of industrial relations emerged historically out of the realization that attempts to unilaterally maintain total capitalist domination of the employment relationship during periods of elevated class struggle could result in serious social disorder (Heery 2016).

But the platform workers who formed the TFC precisely did not demand to be made into full-time employees represented by mainstream trade unions. Instead, they made positive demands for freedom of association and collective bargaining, but expressly did not link those demands to their respective pre-existing legalist frameworks of employment. They expressed a conception of class and organization defined by workers themselves, who would retain the capacity to dictate what legal status they wanted but simultaneously be enabled to take part in associations and bargain collectively regardless of status. Simultaneously, they also expressed a similar extra-legal solidarity with platform workers who were migrants without the right to work. Instead of a nativist refusal to accept the legitimacy of workers without papers as part of the same category as workers with papers, they proactively demanded an extension of the category of worker along class lines.

Rather than creating a well-resourced central federation apparatus made up of paid staff and elected leadership, a combination of necessity and political desire has led to the TFC taking on a more lightweight form. This form attempts to maximize the ability to create coalitions and exert discursive power, whilst emerging out of the already-existing processes of self-organization on which the movement is built. On one level, it can operate as a simple communication technology, which allows and encourages workers from different contexts to discuss their actions and circumstances and continue the process of comparison from below. On another, it can be a network allowing for the coordination of collective action. This structure is well-suited to its role as a power amplifier. So far, this structure appears to allow for a highly-functional extension of the federation: since the October 2018 meeting, organizations from Argentina, Mexico, Chile, Australia, and Japan have all been brought into what started as a primarily European federation.

The Federation in Action

A desire for control over the technical means used to manage work has long been a feature of working class organization in the sphere of production (Baldi 1972; Goodrich 1975). However, in the context of platform capitalism, this desire takes on a new form. The informational asymmetries implied by algorithmic management go some way to inverting the knowledge dynamic implied by classical Taylorist perceptions of the workplace: rather than workers having knowledge of the labor process which needs to be extracted by managers in order to intensify the exploitation of labor-power, workers are operating within a process controlled by a black box that they never understood in the first place (Cant 2019). One group of workers do understand the black box intimately, the developers and tech workers in the platforms' centralized workforces, but as of yet no alliance among these isolated segments of the work force has been generated. As a result, workers' desire for control is primarily expressed as a drive to understand two things: the decisions and calculations made by the black box; and the data generated by and about them in the course of the labor-process. This entails a challenge to what has been called "data extractivism" (Mezzadra and Neilson 2019) and a technical composition which seeks to lock out workers from the decision making processes of an automated supervisor and the data collected on the basis of their concrete activity.

At the end of the October 2018 meeting, discussion turned towards how the newly-founded organization could facilitate collective action. Workers' perceived there to be a necessity to continue to link up their distinct national fights in order to amplify their collective power. The result of this discussion was an agreement to participate in a transnational day of action on Deliveroo founder Will Shu's birthday: the first of December. On the day, workers in Paris, Turin, Milan, and Bologna demonstrated and took strike action at the same time, explicitly linking their actions with common demands and slogans and communicating directly from picket line to picket line (Mogno 2018).

In 2019, a Glovo worker in Barcelona died whilst working for the platform. Again, the TFC was heavily involved in organizing a response to the continued deaths of couriers at work. The internal networks of the TFC were used as a channel through which to crowd-source a database of workers' killed on the job from different national contexts. Workers then sent in videos from across the federation, in which they spoke to the camera about their demands for safer working conditions. This was edited together into one short video by a member of the federation, and released to the public and promoted by federation members (RidersXDerechos BCN 2019). Through this collective action, workers were able to highlight an ongoing antagonism between workers and platforms on the question of safety. The result of working for piece rates (payment per drop rather than per hour) on the road is a significant incentive for auto-exploitation through working intensification and speed up, which then leads to workers' being forced into a choice: lower wages and lower risk, or higher wages and higher risk.

To understand exactly how the federation acts as a power amplifier, it is necessary to distinguish between forms of power workers' can exert in the workplace. Vandaele's analysis of the power resources of food couriers has correctly identified that the workplace bargaining power of food platform couriers is "fairly high" (Vandaele 2018: 10) due to the time and location specific nature of their labor process. This allows couriers to take significant direct action at the point of production, which can rapidly grind capital accumulation to a halt. However, this capacity for workplace power is not extended by a transnational division of labor. Each city operates as an island, with the only point of connection (the algorithmic manager) operating on a scale that cannot be immediately controlled through the action of delivery workers' on the street. Unlike the capacity of car factory workers in one workshop to bring a whole factory to a halt, the technical composition of the working class in this sector allows for no such consequential spill over.

However, this does not mean that transnational coordination has no impact on the power of workers' collective action. Vandaele has also identified the significance two further phenomena to food platform workers: coalitions of wider class interests and the exertion of discursive power (2018: 16). These forms of association and power are both aided significantly through the transnational organization of collective action, as relations of solidarity allows for a broader working class alliance to form around the political and social questions demands of platform workers.

Beyond shared demands and actions, groups of workers participating in the TFC are also developing common theorizations of the political significance of their struggle. At the TFC-linked 2019 "My Boss Is Not an Algorithm" conference in Barcelona, a pamphlet on "Red Sky Thinking" written by the Industrial Workers of the World (IWW) lead courier organizer in the UK and Ireland was distributed and discussed (Sharp 2019). In the pamphlet, he argued for a development from thinking defensively about protecting workers' interests to developing a "positive collective vision of the future we want." This effort, and the discussion that surrounded it, indicates the potential forward trajectory of food platform workers' struggle, and its potential significance for a political movement that aims at the abolition of capitalist social relations. To this end, we might think of the TFC as an incubator of some of the most advanced political ideas generated in this ongoing cycle of struggle.

The TFC will meet again in Paris in late 2019. It remains to be seen whether that meeting will represent a moment of further development for the federation.

Conclusion

The TFC emerged because of the confluence of an objective material basis in the class composition of delivery platforms and a subjective desire amongst the workers' involved to articulate their demands and their politics on a scale that goes beyond the national. Perhaps most importantly, however, these workers believe there is a potential for the multiplication of their associational power through transnational coordination.

The future of platform capitalism will be determined by the balance of class forces within it—and as ever, the varied subject that we call the working class will have to draw on strength and solidarity generated outside and across nations if it is to win out.

Note

We dedicate this essay to the memory of Mario García Fernández, sweet and energetic comrade. May you rest in power.

References

Anon. 2016. "Rebel Roo 1." *Notes from Below*, November. notesfrombelow.org/article/rebel-roo-1.

Anon. 2017. "Rebel Roo 3." *Notes from Below*, January. notesfrombelow.org/article/rebel-roo-3.

Atzeni, Maurizio. 2010. *Workplace Conflict: Mobilization and Solidarity in Argentina.* Basingstoke: Palgrave Macmillan.

Baldi, Guido. 1972. "Theses on Mass Worker and Social Capital." *Radical America* 6, no. 3: 3–21.

Calder Williams, Evan. 2013. "Invisible Organization: Reading Romano Alquati." *Viewpoint*, September 26. www.viewpointmag.com/2013/09/26/invisible-organization-reading-romano-alquati/.

Cant, Callum. 2018. "The Wave of Worker Resistance in European Food Platforms 2016–17." *Notes from Below*, January 29. notesfrombelow.org/article/european-food-platform -strike-wave.

Cant, Callum. 2019. *Riding for Deliveroo: Resistance in the New Economy.* Cambridge: Polity.

Endnotes. 2013. "The Logic of Gender." *Endnotes 3*, September. endnotes.org.uk/issues/3/en /endnotes-the-logic-of-gender.

Goodrich, Carter. 1975. *The Frontier of Control: A Study in British Workshop Politics.* London: Pluto.

Hammersley, Martyn, and Paul Atkinson. 2007. *Ethnography: Principles in Practice.* 3rd ed. London: Routledge.

Heery, Edmund. 2016. "British Industrial Relations Pluralism in the Era of Neoliberalism." *Journal of Industrial Relations* 58, no. 1: 3–24.

labournet.tv. 2018. "Riders across Europe Unite to Form the Transnational Federation of Couriers." *labournet.tv*, October 30. facebook.com/watch/?v=516413332161000.

Marcus, George E. 2010. *Ethnography through Thick and Thin.* Princeton, NJ: Princeton University Press.

Mezzadra, Sandro, and Brett Neilson. 2019. *The Politics of Operations: Excavating Contemporary Capitalism.* Durham, NC: Duke University Press.

Mogno, Clara. 2018. "Buon compleanno Will Shu! Note sullo sciopero transnazionale dei riders" ("Happy Birthday, Will Shu! Notes on the Transnational Strike of the Riders"). *Euro-Nomade*, December 3. www.euronomade.info/?p=11337.

RidersXDerechos BCN. 2019. "No More Riders Deaths." *YouTube*, June 8. youtube.com /watch?v=LM4PNg6QBx8.

Roberts, Michael. 2016. *The Long Depression.* Chicago: Haymarket.

Sharp, Sam. 2019. "Red Sky Thinking in the Platform Economy—Courier Organising Beyond Pay and Workers' Rights." *New Syndicalist*, April 30. newsyndicalist.org/2019/04/30/red -sky-thinking-in-the-platform-economy-courier-organising-beyond-pay-and-workers -rights/.

Srnicek, Nick. 2017. *Platform Capitalism.* London: Polity.

Vandaele, Kurt. 2018. *Will Trade Unions Survive in the Platform Economy? Emerging Patterns of Platform Workers' Collective Voice and Representation in Europe.* Brussels: European Trade Union Institute.

Weir, Stan. 2004. *Singlejack Solidarity.* Edited by G. Lipsitz. Minneapolis: University of Minnesota Press.

Windsor, Richard. 2018. "Meituan-Dianping: Finally, a Chinese Tech IPO with Some Value." *Forbes*, September 4. forbes.com/sites/richardwindsoreurope/2018/09/04/meituan -dianping-finally-a-chinese-tech-ipo-with-some-value/#26e8551bfee4.

Wood, Alex J. 2015. "Networks of Injustice and Worker Mobilisation at Walmart." *Industrial Relations Journal* 46, no. 4: 259–74.

Woodcock, Jamie, et al. 2018. "The Workers' Inquiry and Social Composition." *Notes from Below*, January 29. notesfrombelow.org/article/workers-inquiry-and-social-composition.

Yaseen Aslam and Jamie Woodcock

A History of Uber Organizing in the UK

This article details Yaseen Aslam's experience of organizing at Uber. Yaseen is the National General Secretary of UPHD (United Private Hire Drivers), a branch of the IWGB (Independent Workers Union of Great Britain). He is a co-claimant, with James Farrar, in the employment rights court cases against Uber in the UK. The article is the outcome of co-writing with Jamie Woodcock, presenting Yaseen's first-person perspective. It builds on the method of workers' inquiry (Woodcock 2014) and writing between workers and academics (Waters and Woodcock 2017).

In February 2019, I stood on London Bridge in the cold, the wind whipping up from the Thames. With a small number of volunteers clutching red flags, we start to block the usually busy bridge as the early signs of the evening rush hour began to appear. The Mayor of London had recently announced a new congestion charge for private hire drivers. As the cars began to arrive in convoy for the protest, drivers began to gather. We talked about issues they were having with Uber, as well as some of the new platforms that had recently started operating in London. The police arrived to block off access to the bridge, taking a very different tone to their often-friendly interactions with the anti-Uber Black Cab protests that had been taking place in Parliament Square that week. Despite our agreement for the protest, they refuse to let many drivers join, leading to threats they will shut down our protest.

Despite the attempted intimidation, there are now hundreds of mostly migrant workers gathered on the bridge. Supporters from the Deliveroo campaign have arrived on bicycles and the University of London workers branch of the IWGB has brought a sound system to liven things up. James

The South Atlantic Quarterly 119:2, April 2020
DOI 10.1215/00382876-8177983 © 2020 Duke University Press

Farrar and I, as co-claimants in the workers' rights case against Uber, give speeches about the campaign. We both argue that we need to fight Uber—on the streets and in the courts—as well as taking the fight to the regulator. Following more speeches and as darkness falls, a decision is made to march off to protest outside the City Hall. Banners are unfurled, placards handed out, and red flares are lit—the thick smoke drifting between cars. Someone shouts: "driver power?" the crowd bellows in response "union power!"

Standing on this bridge was the result of starting work at Uber six years before. During this time, I have organized with many drivers and organizations, and used different tactics and strategies. We have been on strike against Uber, fought them in the courts, and protested outside their offices. This has been as associations, networks, and in different trade unions. The campaign has grown and developed into a fight against companies like Uber, as well as regulators and politicians. This article covers the history of my Uber organizing in the UK, drawing out different lessons that we have learned along our journey.

The Arrival of Uber in London

I started working in the taxi industry in 2006, before Uber arrived in the UK. As other jobs were disappearing, factory and manual labor was drying up, restaurants and corner shops closing, this was the next industry that migrants or so-called low skilled workers could turn to. I had been made redundant from my job in IT 2006 and decided to try working as a private hire minicab driver. This kind of work is different from the famous London Black Cab Taxis that can pick up passengers from the side of the road. Instead, minicab drivers work for a company and a radio dispatcher hands out the jobs. The industry has long been divided between the Black Cabs and private hire drivers, often along racial and class lines.

In the UK, Uber drivers need a private hire license to operate. In London, these are issued by TfL (Transport for London). When UberX first launched in July 2013 it was the private hire drivers like me that they tried to recruit. When Uber came to town offering high fares and bonuses, and best of all the freedom from corrupt minicab controllers and operators, many drivers were quick to sign up. I wanted to find out what it would be like to work as a driver through an app.

It was my first job working without a human managing me. Like many drivers, I too was lured in by the promise of making money and the working flexibility I needed—or the supposed freedom to be my own boss. Early on, it was possible to make good money working for Uber. For example, I was paid bonuses of £10 for each job I completed, on top of getting 85 percent of what the customer paid for the journey. I started working four days a week, averaging about ten hours a day. After all my expenses, I was taking home about £1,000 a week. On top of that, if I referred a driver to the platform, I received another bonus of £200. I was telling all the drivers I knew to join, as well as my friends. However, I knew that it could not last. In other countries, since it became more established "Uber has taken a larger and larger slice of every fare" (Slee 2015: 65). Soon after, the hours I needed to work to earn enough money started increasing.

A typical week for me was driving Thursday to Sunday, as those were the busiest days to find work. Usually I would log in and start working as soon as I was in the car. This meant clipping my phone onto the dashboard, loading up the Uber app and turning it on. I would immediately start receiving trip requests from customers. These would ping and I would have fifteen seconds to confirm my availability before they were then sent to another driver. The trip request would show me the customer's location, their rating, and the estimated time it would take me to reach their pick-up point. Once I had confirmed a trip request I would then begin driving to the customer's pick-up location shown on the app.

Other than through the app, I did not have much contact with Uber. This became a problem with the rating system that Uber used. I felt that system was unfair and designed to benefit Uber at the expense of drivers. If a customer was rude, drunk, or made a mess in my car, I would often feel that I had to complete the journey because I could not risk a bad rating. This was great for Uber and their customers, but not for me. We were now managed by an algorithm and at the mercy of these star rating and we never realized this when we joined. However, there were no human dispatcher or controllers to deal with—which was one of the reasons we left other minicab companies. At Uber the power had transferred, and it seemed the customer had control based on how they rated us. This was used by both Uber and the customer to blackmail us as drivers. In trying to escape from the human controllers of the minicab industry, we ended up trapped by an algorithm (Rosenblat and Stark 2016).

When I first started working for Uber, I had never heard the term "gig economy." Uber claimed that I am self-employed and that drivers contract directly with customers to provide a service. I do not agree with this. I understood Uber as a company that offered a private hire service to customers and I worked for Uber as part of their service. However, Uber claimed to be a "tech startup" rather than "a labor company" (Scholz 2017: 44), meaning that I supposedly had a driving business myself. My experience was that Uber had the commercial relationship with the customer, not me: the customer paid Uber, not me (drivers were not allowed to take cash as payment as all customers have to pay Uber electronically for their journey); Uber decided on the fare and cancellation penalties that customers paid, not me; Uber paid me part of the fare, but also bonuses and incentives; the customer provided all their details to Uber and they had a policy of not giving this to drivers; Uber set the rules that we drivers had to follow. When changes were introduced, we were told we had to accept them.

Organizing at Uber

Before I started working for Uber, I had a WhatsApp group with 50–60 drivers. We used the group to talk about where demand was, or traffic to avoid. These networks, and many of them that we later brought in, were an early form of "invisible organization" (Alquati 2013). By December 2013, we started hearing more and more issues from drivers, particularly "deactivations" with drivers kicked off the platform for little or no reason. In response, we decided to start organizing. At first, Uber were keen to talk to us and I could walk into the office and sit down with the manager. By August 2014, Uber started significantly reducing the rates. It was at that point that I started to see the bigger picture. I reached out to drivers in New York and San Francisco on social media. Through our discussions I realized the process in London had already happened to them two years ago.

In September 2014, we started organizing meetings. We called drivers together in overcrowded community centers and started talking about our work. This quickly caught Uber's attention. While they would initially arrange meetings and say they would listen to our concerns, we thought we had achieved something. However, when they met with us, the tone was different. Our biggest concern was the reduction in fares. Pay was falling with commission going up—first to twenty percent then to twenty-five percent—and then the bonuses disappeared. Uber's argument was "you're going to get more work, so you'll make more money." We did not believe them, as this meant working harder to make the same amount. We wanted a tip option and a "going home" option so that if we worked all nights, we could get a job heading in the direction of our house not the opposite way.

The WhatsApp group and the meetings among drivers led to our first organization: LPHADA (London Private Hire App Based Drivers Association).

However, Uber quickly stopped talking to us. The association aimed to improve how Uber treated drivers, particularly in terms of communication and transparency. When I started driving for Uber, I felt that it was a good company to work for and I helped to recruit a lot of other drivers for that reason. However, I felt this had now changed. At the time, my main focus was getting respect for drivers. We started asking why the regulator was not helping drivers. Every day I was coming across more serious cases of verbal racism and physical abuse. We started trying to find ways to get justice for Uber drivers.

The conditions changed in February 2015. When I tried to log in, I found I had been "deactivated" for the first time. There was no reason given or warning. I believed that they did this to stop my organizing. After emailing and demanding an explanation, I was eventually "reactivated" and started working again. Around this time, issues at Uber started to be reported in the press—both around drivers being attacked and those—like me—who had been "deactivated." There was also speculation on social media that Uber was not checking insurance documents for drivers. I worked with a journalist to test this, submitting a blank document through Uber's system. Uber accepted the document and I became a whistleblower. Despite the fact I had active insurance, I was arrested and then permanently "deactivated" from working for Uber.

The GMB Experience

It was just before my last "deactivation" that I met James Farrar. He became another key Uber driver organizer in London. James had heard about what I had been doing, and he had been assaulted by a passenger too. Uber refused to give James the passenger information, so he started a legal case for disclosure (Temperton 2018). Through our discussions, James and I realized that we needed to make TfL a target for our campaign. James met with the law firm Leigh Day and we found out more about workers' rights to which we should be entitled. This was a watershed moment for us. If worker rights could be secured in the courts—not only would drivers be guaranteed minimum wage, but the obligation for occupational safety and duty of care could be put back on to Uber. This seemed to be the perfect answer to the struggles of Uber drivers. Through Leigh Day, we also came into contact with GMB, a large general union. At the time, GMB assured us they would help us with the regulator and politicians, meaning we could now fight politically and legally. We saw this as an important development of our organizing, moving from taking on Uber to also the regulator and policy makers.

We folded LPHADA to join GMB in May 2015. In the process of converting to paid membership, we lost the majority of members, going from five hundred members to fifty. While James and I had been prepared to fund the legal challenge against Uber, GMB stepped in to support it. Quickly, however, we ran into difficulties. The GMB branch also represented black-cab drivers, and was running a strong anti-Uber line, demanding TfL revoke its license. This was the opposite of what we wanted as Uber drivers. In addition to the legal case, we wanted to highlight issues of racism and discrimination at TfL. Instead, GMB fed into this narrative by supporting a false story of drivers defecating in gardens at Heathrow airport. They gave this story to the BBC and it was used in a legal case funded by Addison Lee (a rival minicab company) as a further argument for the revocation of Uber's license. Leigh Day were then asked to brief Addison Lee senior management on the workers' rights case against Uber, without consulting the Uber drivers like us who were members. Innocent drivers were used as cannon fodder in Addison Lee's dirty war with Uber and GMB is shamefully implicated in it.

We were deeply concerned by the behavior of our branch. We tried to meet with officials to address these problems. We wanted to see if we could form a new branch so that private hire drivers could advance their own cause, on their own terms. The officials went back and forth but would not agree. Instead, we started putting our ideas into practice. James and I were elected shop stewards for Addison Lee and Uber respectively. The election followed all of the GMB rules. We now had activists working at the grass roots, supported by elected officials. However, someone at GMB—I still do not know who—decided the elections were illegal. The first I knew of this was when new ballots for nominations came through my letterbox. Nobody ever communicated the decision to us, but the election had been invalidated. We felt that GMB never trusted us, as members, to decide for ourselves how we wanted to be organized and tackle the issues we faced. GMB failed us as drivers.

We launched UPHD the same year because we realized we were not making progress with GMB. We started holding regular meetings, making sure they worked for drivers. We did not want to meet in pubs, but instead put on food for drivers who could take a break between shifts. This is an important part of building a community. We hosted UPHD *iftar* meals for drivers during Ramadan. Drivers felt confident telling the representatives from UPHD (like me and James) that they needed to pray during meetings or demonstrations. This is not something that is common in other unions. In a context of widespread Islamophobia, we allow people to bring and integrate their own cultures into organizing.

Using the Law and Picking Targets

Despite what happened with GMB, they did support us taking Uber to employment tribunal in 2016. During this time, I could no longer work for Uber. Addison Lee found out I was organizing and pushed me out—which GMB again failed to support me. I went back to work for a local cab office, but they had no work due to the growth of Uber. I had to sell my car and used all my savings, spending the three months up to the tribunal date in summer 2016 working with Leigh Day to prepare evidence for the case.

The employment tribunal, *Uber BV v. Aslam*, involved myself and James Farrar. We claimed that we should be paid the minimum wage and receive paid annual leave. This meant arguing that we were "workers," an intermediate status between employee and self-employed, while Uber claimed we were "partners" and self-employed independent contractors. My experience of the tribunal was nerve wracking. In the courtroom we were faced by media and put under pressure by Uber's barristers. Before the case, we kept being told Uber will buy out the judges and we cannot compete against their lawyers, everyone thought we were fighting a lost battle and should give up. In September 2016 we received the verdict. It was damning for Uber and I thought the judge really believed our side. It was then I started to feel hopeful again. We immediately called a meeting with drivers who were all proud to have taken on Uber.

Even though we won the first tribunal, Uber appealed the decision. James and I fought both Uber, and increasingly found ourselves fighting GMB too. In 2017 I no longer wanted to be part of the union. We built up UPHD as an independent organization while we were in GMB, which was free for drivers to join. In 2017, we voted to become an autonomous branch of the IWGB union—a small alternative union that "is a non-bureaucratic, grassroots, 'bottom-up' organisation" (Roberts 2018). They represent workers like me: Deliveroo drivers, cleaners, foster care workers, and couriers. This meant we left GMB to become members of another union, but this time we had control over our own struggle. Three days after we joined the IWGB I received an email from the lawyers stating that GMB would no longer be funding the case. This meant James and I became personally liable to costs from Uber—something we definitely could not afford. The IWGB stepped in and secured us new counsel. As Jason Moyer-Lee (2018), the general secretary, has argued, there is no need for confusion in the gig economy: "We say the law is pretty clear and the companies are clearly on the wrong side of it." The IWGB was therefore keen to support our legal case.

Uber's legal appeal succeeded, meaning we are now seeking to overturn the decision. We have targeted Uber directly in the courts, as well as holding demonstrations and strikes. We first went on strike in October 2014 while we were organized with LPHADA. This was coordinated with drivers in San Francisco, Los Angeles, Chicago, and New York (Leroux 2014) and was the first app-based workers strike. While we were members of GMB we managed to vote for a protest outside the Uber headquarters in London (Hellier 2015). However, GMB did little to help organize the protest—even trying to overturn the decision—with James and me left to rally drivers. This changed when we joined the IWGB. On October 9, 2018, the IWGB called a strike of Uber drivers, demanding an increase of fares to £2 per mile, commission reduced to fifteen percent, an end to unfair deactivations and bullying, and worker rights protection. As James Farrar argued: "We ask the public to please support drivers by not crossing the digital picket line by not using the app during strike time" (IWGB 2018). In 2019, we held protests in the run up to Uber's IPO, as well as demonstrations and flash occupations of their headquarters in London. This brought us into contact with drivers across the world, starting an international network against Uber. Throughout all of this, we have found the space within the IWGB to debate and decide on our tactics and strategy, pushing the campaign forward ourselves.

In addition to targeting Uber, we have also confronted the regulator TfL and the Mayor of London. The Mayor announced that private hire drivers—but not Black cabs—would have to pay a congestion charge of £11.50 per day to drive in central London. In addition to Uber's commission, paying for a vehicle, insurance, and so on, this would represent a significant cut to driver's income that many cannot afford. At the start of 2019, we called demonstrations every Monday for twelve weeks, targeting the busy London Bridge and Parliament Square, shutting down the road with our cars. After the mayor refused to repeal the charge, we launched a legal challenge that minicab drivers were facing indirect discrimination under the Equality Act. The "charge is being imposed on a workforce that is mainly BAME [Black, Asian, and Minority Ethnic] (94 percent of London's 107,000 minicab drivers are BAME according to TFL), while black cab drivers, who are mostly white, continue to be exempt" (UPHD 2019). In our struggle for respect and workers' rights we have taken on more than just Uber.

Learning from the Struggle Today

As drivers, our campaign has gone through different organizational forms, each with strengths and weaknesses from which we have learned. We have built up organizations and then had to restart them. Although our experience with GMB was negative, it was a personal turning point for me. It made me question whether the campaign was possible—especially if this large union would not help. However, leaving GMB and coming out the other side gave me the confidence to carry on. James and I rebuilt UPHD from scratch, meeting members, doing the administration, arguing with drivers, speaking to the media, self-funding the project, fighting, and protesting.

Throughout all of this I have learnt many lessons. When we first started organizing people said we would never succeed—included trade unionists, academics, and journalists that we thought would be on our side. Few people believed in us or gave us the support we needed at the time. Instead people talked to us, got what they wanted, and left. We never heard from most of them again. However, I knew that what happens at Uber matters for workers in other industries too. Platforms like Uber are "laboratories of class struggle" (Cant, forthcoming) used by management to test new strategies. If these work, they will be used against more workers. Our fight at Uber is therefore part of a much larger fight.

It is the journey since 2013 that has made us who we are today. Like driving in central London, our journey has taken many turns. At each stage, we have kept trying to move forward, experimenting with new ways to organize. These bring us together as workers in new ways—new moments of "political recomposition" (Notes from Below 2018)—as we find successful forms of organizing in these new kinds of work. We have built these from the way drivers are organized by Uber at work, as well as the social factors beyond work like community and migration.

When people look in from the outside, they often think that worker-organizers must have some sort of special characteristics—but this is not true: organizers are made. Our organizing at Uber has, to say the least, been a very bumpy ride. We have had to suffer physically, mentally, financially, and our families have suffered too. That is the commitment that it has taken for us to organize at Uber. We have taken on a multi-billion-dollar company, confronted regulators, but also won many small victories like helping a driver keep their license and livelihood. While we may lose a battle here and there, we have our sights on the larger war. Our journey continues.

References

Alquati, Romano. 2013. "The Struggle at FIAT (1964)." *Viewpoint Magazine*, September 26. viewpointmag.com/2013/09/26/struggle-at-fiat-1964.

Cant, Callum. Forthcoming. *Riding for Deliveroo: Resistance in the New Economy.* Cambridge: Polity.

Hellier, David. 2015. "Uber drivers protest over fee rise in first London demo." *Guardian*, November 12. theguardian.com/business/2015/nov/12/uber-drivers-protest-at-fee-hike-in-first-london-demo.

IWGB. 2018. "Uber Drivers to Strike for 24 Hours in London, Birmingham, and Nottingham." *IWGB*, October 8. iwgb.org.uk/post/5bbb3ff1bf94a/uber-drivers-to-strike-for.

Leroux, Marcus. 2014. "Uber Faces Driver Mutiny Over Pay." *Times*, November 8. www.the times.co.uk/article/uber-faces-driver-mutiny-over-pay-09l6z6c7nbf.

Moyer-Lee, Jason. 2018. "When Will 'Gig Economy Companies Admit That Their Workers Have Rights?" *Guardian*, June 14. theguardian.com/commentisfree/2018/jun/14/gig-economy-workers-pimlico-plumbers-employment-rights.

Notes from Below. 2018. "The Workers' Inquiry and Social Composition." *Notes from Below*, January 29. notesfrombelow.org/article/workers-inquiry-and-social-composition.

Roberts, Yvonne. 2018. "The Tiny Union Beating the Gig Economy Giants." *Guardian*, July 1. theguardian.com/politics/2018/jul/01/union-beating-gig-economy-giants-iwgb-zero-hours-workers.

Rosenblat, Alex, and Luke Stark. 2016. "Algorithmic Labor and Information Asymmetries: A Case Study of Uber's Drivers." *International Journal of Communication* 10: 3758–84.

Scholz, Trebor. 2017. *Uberworked and Underpaid: How Workers Are Disrupting the Digital Economy.* Cambridge: Polity.

Slee, Tom. 2015. *What's Yours Is Mine: Against the Sharing Economy.* London: OR Books.

Srnicek, Nick. 2017. *Platform Capitalism.* Cambridge: Polity.

Temperton, James. 2018. "The Biggest Legal Crisis Facing Uber Started with a Pile of Vomit." *Wired*, June 13. wired.co.uk/article/uber-employment-lawsuit-gig-economy-leigh-day.

UPHD. 2019. "IWGB Launches Legal Challenge of Minicab Congestion Charge on Discrimination and Human Rights Grounds." *UPHD*, March 1. uphd.org/iwgb-launches-legal-challenge-of-minicab-congestion-charge-on-discrimination-and-human-rights-grounds.

Waters, Facility, and Jamie Woodcock. 2017. "Far From Seamless: a Workers' Inquiry at Deliveroo." *Viewpoint*, September 20. www.viewpointmag.com/2017/09/20/far-seamless-workers-inquiry-deliveroo.

Woodcock, Jamie. 2014. "The Workers' Inquiry from Trotskyism to Operaismo: A Political Methodology for Investigating the Workplace." *Ephemera* 14, no. 3: 493–513.

Biju Mathew

Magic Wands and Monkey Brains:
Is Labor Ready to Lead Society in
the New Struggle Over Data?

On June 12, 2019, Dara Khusroshahi, the CEO of Uber, and two of his counterparts from Lyft wrote an op-ed in the *San Francisco Chronicle* in which they argued that Uber, Lyft, and other gig companies were being forced to work within an outmoded "century old" labor regime. Apart from the banal fact that current labor law is nowhere near a century old—maybe it is time to call Khusroshahi's bluff. If we accept Khusroshahi's premise, labor law is outmoded, but not his argument, labor law imposes too many requirements on business, it offers a different question: what additional requirements need to be considered given the fundamental changes that are underway in the production and distribution (the labor process) of service commodities? But, before we engage this question, we need to first take several steps back.

It is no surprise that the employer/employee relationship and worker misclassification remain some of the most important arenas of struggle today. The two categories, employee and employer, emerged through countless struggles over the last two centuries—struggles around one of the central contradictions of capitalism—the question of appropriation of surplus value. Labor law, at any point in time during these two centuries, can be understood as an approximate and particular manifestation of the temporary resolution of this contradiction based on the relative strengths of the two forces involved—capital and labor.

I do not intend to elaborate the story of struggle over the last two centuries in this paper. Instead, with singular attention to the contemporary moment, my effort here is to underscore and make visible the need to artic-

The South Atlantic Quarterly 119:2, April 2020
DOI 10.1215/00382876-8177995 © 2020 Duke University Press

ulate the two realms identified above — the theory that seeks to understand how value is appropriated by capital against the ways in which workers and unions struggle through categories such as employee/employer to resolve the contradiction produced by appropriation of surplus in their favor. I undertake this in three parts. First, a very brief intervention into how contemporary capital, technology, and labor are structured in this late neoliberal moment. This part is a brief commentary on why we must move away from treating neoliberalism as unchanging and monolithic. Next, I point to the rapidity with which workers in the gig economy, such as Uber drivers, are able to point to the precise ways in which capital seeks to appropriate surplus through data. And finally, from such a standpoint I try and theorize some new aspects of the processes unleashed by contemporary capital towards appropriating surplus and how such theory may be of value in order to articulate a contemporary strategy for labor.

Capital, Technology, and Labor Over Fifty Years of Neoliberalism

The conventional telling of the story over the last fifty years, even from within the labor movement, is that of an unbridled rise in the power of capital, specially finance capital, that has worked systematically to destroy the cornerstones of the Keynesian compact, including the labor-capital compromise that was framed around a logic of joint growth (Harvey 2005). In this telling of the story of the neoliberal period, labor is largely a victim, as capital enlisted the state to break the back of the labor movement (Reagan's breaking of the air traffic controllers' strike and Margaret Thatcher's assault on the coal miner's strike are the iconic tales of this narrative). While there is nothing fundamentally incorrect about this rendering of the story it is important to point out that there are many nuances and inconsistencies that we must account for. Such an accounting of the divergences and inconsistencies is necessary as it sets up the frame, at least partially, for thinking about the future. Here I mark three key aspects.

First, neoliberalism has long ceased to be a monolithic unchanging regime of capital. Over the last half century significant new institutional formations have emerged even within finance capital, such as private equity/ venture capital. If the origin of neoliberalism was a crisis of profitability experienced by capital, then the first two decades of the period saw capital regain much of the ground it had conceded during the period of the Keynesian compact and move into a period of super-profits. Thus by the late 90's / early 2000's a new crisis began to take shape for capital—unprecedented availability of capital that needed new spaces of investment—in short a crisis of over accumulation. In other words, for much of the last two / three decades what we have is a situation where there is a giant pool of capital sloshing around the globe seeking spaces of investment.

At the same time, technologically, the opening decade of neoliberalism and the current decade could not be more different. The 1970s had not seen the personal computer. What capital has been able to do with technological mediation to the labor process over the last two decades needs to be independently assessed and understood. In several tracts through the nineties David Harvey outlined the specific mode of a spatiotemporal fix that produced the twin phenomena of globalization and flexible specialization (Harvey 2001). Harvey's theorization is specific and insightful. However, what should be clear is that beginning in the late 1990s early 2000s capital undertook a second spatiotemporal fix. This second spatiotemporal fix was based on further advancements in digital technology that fundamentally reorganized both physical and cognitive space through a dense embedding of networked sensors in physical space and wireless technologies. Together this has meant the potential for further radical transformation of the labor processes.

The unity between the spatiotemporal fix that Harvey identifies, and the one I seek to outline in this paper, lies in the fact that the control of data is the central mode through which such a reorganization of the labor process is engineered. It is fundamentally the centrality of data that leads other theorists to talk about such concepts as surveillance capitalism (Zuboff 2019). Surveillance in this case has little to do with the narrow concept of privacy but much more fundamentally to do with control over the labor process. I will return to this theme later in the paper, especially because it should be of no surprise to us that workers—and in this specific case—app-based drivers—articulate this tension around the labor process in illuminating terms.

Finally, to focus on the neoliberal period does not mean that our attention must be entirely occupied by shifts in capital and technology. It is critical to understand the shifts in labor as well. While it is true that the labor movement has been in retreat during this period, it is important to note that the same period has seen the rise of a range of militant grassroots movements especially among immigrant, black, and women workers. The hegemonic control of business unionism that has at its disposal no analytical frame except narrow pragmatism has essentially meant not only a deep chasm between the traditional older business unionists and new social movement immigrant unions, but under conditions of venture capital's aggressive break all rules approach, has meant the development of the worst forms of business unionism as represented by yellow dog company unions such as IDG in NYC and the efforts of IBT Joint Council and other powerful locals in California. The inability of the labor leadership to resolve this internal division has meant that the militant new unions such as the Taxi Workers Alliance in New York, the IWGB in London, or Ride Share Drivers United in Los Angeles have no choice but to invest resources into their own defense against such business unionism but beyond that it has meant that such unions are unable to put the time and resources required to amplify a new imaginary of the twenty-first-century labor movement.

We will return to these issues of a new hegemony of venture capital, the new arcs in technological development and the inability of labor to dissolve its internal crisis in a later section but as suggested above I now wish to move to documenting in brief some of the ways in which workers—in this case app based drivers—talk about the current experience of work. A new kind of attentiveness to how they talk about themselves and the language that they use is needed.

"We Are All Just Monkeys"

I was with Rahmat Ali on the terrace of a cultural center in Hyderabad, India, poring over some of his Ola statements, screenshots, and bills. Two other Uber drivers, Vasu Kumar and Mahesh Yadav, were also there with their Uber statements and bills. As we went through the details of each transaction it became increasingly frustrating for all of us, in terms of building an understanding as to how Uber and Ola were doing all the calculations, till Rahmat suddenly exploded:

> You know it's impossible to understand these accounts because if we look into accounts over just 1 month or 2 months there's nothing common to it. You are a worker, you are driving and you are sitting behind that steering wheel and you are dealing with an app and so everything seems to be constant on a daily basis, but really if you look at these numbers that's not true. Uber or Ola they have a magic wand—their jaadu ki chhadi and everything changes instantaneously. What is happening inside the App is no longer what was happening yesterday. If I did not drive for 5 days at a stretch on the 6th day when I switch my App on what I experience is very different from what I had experienced the previous week when I was driving, or if I have driven 16 hours a day for the last 5 days then when I open up my App on the 6th day what I experience is very different from what I had experienced on the first of those five 16 hour days. So we don't see it, but they are waving this jaadu ki chhadi and everything changes and what is produces is a situation where I don't know what is coming into it.

He looked around and everyone was silent except for the imperceptible nod.

> I don't know what is going to happen to me in the next hour, the next day, in the next week, in the next month, in the next 2 months, the next 6 months. . . . It's all unknown whereas to anybody standing outside it looks like the same thing there's a car, there's an app, there's a guy driving in it, somebody presses the button and the guy shows up . . . so everything looks the same. But that's hardly the case.

I was struck by Rahmat's assertion and the poetry with which he said it— the jaadu ki chhadi pointing to the ephemeral character of his daily work experience. Rahmat still kidding around waving his hand as if it held the magician's wand. Mahesh laughed and switched to Telugu, another local language.

> Manam chesedanta bangaram. . . . Everything we do is gold. . . . If we run, if we walk, if I take a break, where I take a break, if I cancel a ride, if I don't cancel.

There is nothing fixed about their daily work experience and that lack of fixture is not simply what used to be common in the taxi industry historically. In the taxi industry of the past the uncertainty was that when you drop a passenger off, you don't know who your next passenger is and when you will get one. And neither was determined by the boss. That is not what Rahmat and Mahesh are referring to. What they are talking about is the specific and fundamental way in which literally every ride is tailored and niched either by virtue of who the passenger is or by virtue of who the driver is and their specific history in terms of their patterns of behavior over the last several months or years. It is even possible to argue that every ride is a new product.

This moment in Hyderabad, brings to mind so many conversations I had with drivers in New York and Los Angeles, in London and across India. Something about Rahmat's magic wand reminds me of a conversation with Luis Reyes, a longtime New York City yellow cab driver who switched to Uber in 2017. "I am Uber's river of data," he had once told me when we met accidentally at a street corner in Washington Heights. It also reminds me of a moment in California. I was at an Afghani restaurant drinking sweetened tea with a group of drivers—most of them Afghani but also some Arab drivers and a few Latinx drivers. One of the leaders of that driver group Anwar— an older gentleman with sparkling eyes and a dimpled cheek—leans over across the table and tells me in a tone that would indicate confidentiality: "Biju bhai hum tho bas bandar nai." I look up as to what Anwar means when he says that we are all just monkeys and he continues:

> We are all those monkeys that exist in a lab. You know monkeys that are being used to test various medicines, you know what they do, right, they inject a medicine or they do something else and then they are watching the monkey's brain. They open up the head and they look at the brain . . . that's how I feel. I think UBER is always looking at my brain. When I leave the airport and take a passenger to downtown San Fransisco, everytime I do that trip I know that I am not, let's say, getting the same fare but that's not the end of it. . . . I know that beyond not getting the same fare that Uber is intensely watching my brain, Uber is looking at my brain when I go at 80 mph, Uber is looking at my brain when I slow down or speed up to switch a lane.

Anwar's articulation of who he has become or what he is for Uber is interesting and important because, like Rahmat, he is capturing the relationship between a series of moments and labor process regimes. Through magic wands and monkey brains we are offered a window onto the relationship between the current experience of driving, the past experience, as well as the future of what is to emerge. I have had countless conversations that offer insight, but for now I will just pull out a set of propositions to which such stories point.

Labor Process and Surplus Value in the Gig Economy

What Anwar, Mahesh, Luis, and Rahmat and countless other drivers do on a daily basis is find a way, as they drive through different sets of urban roads, to get behind the app in order to understand how their work lives are being designed and redesigned. If the number of stories I have heard is any indication this points to a workforce that is deeply involved in a collective effort to understand the ways in which capital is reorganizing their work lives. These are efforts to understand the labor process and the ways in which capital organizes the labor process so as to facilitate the extraction of surplus value. My first effort therefore will be to use the narratives of the drivers to think through labor process theory. It is not my intention to explore labor process theory in any great detail here. Instead I will only pull out a few key concepts and present a very brief reading of the taxi and the app-based industry.

In the development of capitalism Marx (1990) identifies two "stages" in capital's subsumption of labor in order to extract surplus value—formal and real. In the formal subsumption of labor, capital does not interfere with the actual labor process itself but controls the input and output markets, the credit markets and all of such infrastructures at the very edges of the labor process and thereby extracts absolute surplus value. While Marx presents formal and real subsumption of labor as successive stages, it would not be incorrect to say that formal subsumption continues to exist in some sectors even today. For instance, small farmers in many parts of the world would still fall within this frame as capital fundamentally operates through the control of input (seeds, pesticides, fertilizers), credit and output markets. In contrast, real subsumption of labor is where capital takes full control of the labor process—organizes and reorganizes every minute aspect of it and enters into a process of extraction of relative surplus value. The iconic image of this of course is the mass production assembly lines. It is important to note that the regime of employee-employer relation as codified in law represents the temporary resolution of the capital/labor contradiction from this period—the resolution that led capital to its crisis of profitability by the 1970s.

Since the 1970s, right from its outset, in the neoliberal period, we began to see several experiments from capital to escape the specifics of the earlier resolution. In the US taxi industry for instance, leasing was first introduced in the late seventies and spread through much of the United States through the 80s. Under leasing a driver paid the boss a fixed lease amount at the top of the shift and worked without any direct control from the boss for his / her entire shift. The boss did not tell the driver where to go to pick up passengers, the boss did not care about how many fares he made in a shift or for that matter whether he drove fast or slow. In every way it resembled formal subsumption and drivers were no longer rated as employees but as independent contractors. The first changes to the story begin to appear in the late 80s with the introduction of the electronic meter. With every new generation of the electronic meter the boss could now have detailed knowledge of the entire shift and was in a position to manipulate the lease based on what was actually happening during a shift. The boss effectively had full knowledge of every single driver in his fleet. So, while the overall structure seemed to remain one of formal subsumption, it is possible to see that elements of real subsumption had begun to appear through the collection of data. I have called this arrangement elsewhere as hybrid subsumption, or nested subsumption (Mathew 2015). By the mid 1990s and early 2000s it was increasingly clear that the data generated by the driver, however insignificant it may seem in comparison to the levels of data collection today, was being used to reorganize the production process, while keeping some of the external appearances of formal subsumption. In the yellow cab industry in New York the electronics within the car was used to disable the meter in the middle of a shift and force the driver to return to the garage or to repossess a car in the middle of the night. Those early days only emerge with clarity when we see the level of data collection and use in app-based services today.

It now becomes clear what Anwar, Luis, Rahmat, and Mahesh are signaling. If we were to break down the narratives, apart from the deep sense of surveillance and control that drivers experience—the magic wand and the monkey brain are metaphors that run the course between the physical and the cognitive. Here we can return to the concept of the second spatiotemporal fix. This fix, which I argue characterizes the current moment, uses the control of data as a central mode through which to reorganize the labor process. To illustrate I want to mark three clear sets of data that form the nexus of the second spatiotemporal fix:

1. CURRENT DATA: This is data about the immediate daily experience. The daily work experience of a driver is produced from within a cage of data the driver is structured into. Apart from the most immediately visible decisions such as where to pick up a passenger, what route to take, what rates apply, there are other decisions that are not so easily visible. These include the allocation of fares, the disciplining of a driver and the targeting of drivers for incentive programs. Building on this, a third set of decisions that also an almost daily logic includes decisions around deactivation of driver permissions and other disciplinary procedures connected to ratings. This data grid seems local—that is most of the above decisions seem to be structured through local data and this data is located entirely within the firm.

2. DATA FOR MEDIUM TERM PRODUCT REORGANIZATION: There is a second data grid that operates locally, regionally and sometimes globally and is connected to product redefinitions or the creation of new products on a medium-term basis. This is data, for instance, that is used to make a decision such as upfront pricing.[1] There is evidence to suggest that some of the initial experiments on Uber's upfront pricing happened in India before being branded in the United States. Similarly, data from the eHail product was Central to the definition of the new Uber Eats product. In other words, data produced (or value created and subsumed) in one labor / production process enters, as if it were capital, in an entirely different production / labor process. The key shift here is to understand data as value / latent capital that can enter any number of product reorganizations or new commodity forms. Thus an infinite cycle of value appropriation that moves spatially and temporally is at play.

3. INTER FIRM DATA: Here we are looking at data collected by a firm such as Uber that may enter any number of Uber subsidiaries or partners. Here driver's data would be used in the Uber autonomous car project or could be used in product design at an auto manufacturers that Uber partners with or for instance, in in road infrastructure development projects or in an auto insurance product. The logic is the same as outlined above—that is, data

as unaccounted value moves across firms being transformed into input-capital in a different firm's production process. Thus value/data produced by workers moves simultaneously spatially and temporally across firms and is arguably part of the calculus of surplus appropriation that private equity/venture capital is making.

The first set of data—what I have called current data—is the data that is central to the classical case of real subsumption of labor. The second (medium term) and the third (inter firm) data sets are part of a form of subsumption in which data is itself part of the surplus drawn from labor subsumed in one location. This data (an unaccounted surplus so) is transferred, as if we're capital, to other production processes and it is used in multiple forms many times over. In other words, labor subsumed by capital in the course of one labor process enters many other labor processes in the form of input-capital and it is part of an ever-expanding spiral of surplus value appropriation moving across time and space. To use language drawn from the world of finance capital, data is a form of labor derivative and has a market of its own and enters as capital into other production processes. It is this use of data that marks this moment of capital's development and can be signified as a second spatiotemporal fix.

These massive transformations in the labor process return us to Khusroshahi's gauntlet that we are operating under an outdated labor regime. The proposition, from labor's vantage point, should be very obvious by now. The category of employee rights/demands must include an aggressive effort on the question of data. If the traditional category of employee rights includes fair wages and benefits, it must now also seek an ever-expanding compensation for the labor derivative that is the workers' data for every production process it may enter. Contemporary battles against Uberization and yellow dog business unionism such as the one over vehicle caps and minimum pay for app drivers in NYC led by NYTWA or the battle over AB5 in California led by RDU are almost entirely around data category one (current data). As of now Labor has no clear understanding nor a strategy on how to draw categories two and three (medium term and inter-firm data) into the ambit of struggle or how to yield leadership to these new unions of our times. Labor must invest resources in building the infrastructure required to make such a demand politically viable rather than at such a crucial moment sell out the working people across the world through the worst forms of business unionism.

What is more, this is the kind of struggle that could rekindle the relationship between the labor movement / working classes and the broader middle class that is approaching the same issue of data from the consumer end. The middle class will remain broadly unable to articulate its' demands as consumers because of the lack of any collective consciousness. If labor takes the leadership in the articulation of this struggle, it could at the minimum build a new conversation with the middle class and if all goes well produce the next moment of labor's hegemony over society as a whole. This must not be left to accident. Labor must plan and execute a strategic battle where it takes a new emergent working class struggle over value and use it to transform the current middle class concern over data as "privacy" into a new one of data as "value" and wealth.

Notes

This essay owes much to the hundreds of discussions that I have been part of at the Taxi Workers Alliance, most especially the ones with Bhairavi Desai who has led the drivers movement for over two decades.

1   Under upfront pricing what a passenger pays for a ride and what the driver makes for the same ride are completely disconnected. When a passenger books a ride he/she is quoted a fare (say $12 for a three-mile/ten-minute ride). This quoted fare is ONLY for that ride and is not calculated on the same rate at which the driver is being paid. For the above $12 ride the driver is, say, being paid at $.99/mile and $.25/min with a $1.50 drop—or a total of $7. Thus with the passenger paying $12 and driver making $7, the effective rate of commission the driver is being charged is forty-one percent, counter to what is popularly believed, namely, that drivers pay a twenty-percent commission.

References

Harvey, David. 2001. *Spaces of Capital: Towards a Critical Geography*. New York: Taylor and Francis.

Harvey, David. 2005. *A Brief History of Neoliberalism*. Oxford: Oxford University Press.

Marx, Karl. 1990. *Capital Volume 1*. London: Penguin.

Mathew, Biju. 2015. "The Neoliberal Firm and Nested Subsumption: Labour Process Transformations in the NYC Taxi Industry." *Urban Studies* 52, no. 11: 2051–71.

Zuboff, Shoshana. 2019. *The Age of Surveillance Capitalism: The Fight for a Human Future at the New Frontier of Power*. New York: Public Affairs.

Notes on Contributors

Yaseen Aslam is the National General Secretary of UPHD (United Private Hire Drivers), a branch of the IWGB (Independent Workers Union of Great Britain). He is a co-claimant, with James Farrar, in the employment rights court cases against Uber in the UK.

Callum Cant is a doctoral student at the University of West London. He is the author of *Riding for Deliveroo* (2019).

Irina Ceric is currently based in Vancouver, BC, where she teaches in the Criminology Department of Kwantlen Polytechnic University. A longtime activist, legal support organizer, and radical lawyer, she researches and writes about the intersections between law and social movements.

D. T. Cochrane is an economist. He works with the Indigenous Network on Economies and Trade, as well as the Blackwood Art Gallery. His research focuses on finance, governance, and corporate power.

Kylie Benton-Connell is a doctoral candidate at the New School for Social Research and a contributing editor at the *New Inquiry*. She has worked in research and organizing roles in Australia, Bolivia, and the US.

Deborah Cowen is a geographer at the University of Toronto, a settler on the lands subject to the Dish with One Spoon Wampum, and deeply committed to the transformative potential of infrastructure.

Deborah Curran is an associate professor in the Faculty of Law and School of Environmental Studies and Executive Director of the Environmental Law Centre at the University of Victoria.

Eugene Kung is a staff lawyer at West Coast Environmental Law Association.

Winona LaDuke, Anishinaabe writer and economist, loves and works on the White Earth reservation, and is the executive director for Honor the Earth.

Biju Mathew is the Secretary of the National Taxi Workers Alliance (AFL-CIO) and Associate Professor of Information Systems and American Studies at Rider University in New Jersey, USA.

Clara Mogno received her PhD in political philosophy from l'Università degli Studi di Padova and Université Paris Nanterre. She is currently working on a book on gamification and platform work.

Shiri Pasternak is Assistant Professor of Criminology at Ryerson University in Toronto, Ontario, and author of *Grounded Authority: The Algonquins of*

Barriere Lake against the State. She is also the Research Director of the Yellowhead Institute and a consultant with the Indigenous Network on Economies of Trade.

Dr. Sherry Pictou is a Mi'kmaw woman from L'sitkuk (water cuts through high rocks) known as Bear River First Nation, Nova Scotia, and an Assistant Professor in the Women's Studies Department at Mount Saint Vincent University with a focus on Indigenous Feminism. She is also a former Chief for her community and the former Co-Chair of the World Forum of Fisher Peoples. Her research interests include decolonizing Treaty relations, Social Justice for Indigenous Women, Indigenous women's role in food and lifeways, and Indigenous knowledge and food systems.

Dayna Nadine Scott is a socio-legal scholar and settler on lands subject to the Dish with One Spoon Treaty. She holds a research chair in Environmental Law and Justice in the Green Economy at York University, and is currently completing a project on extraction in the "Ring of Fire" area of Ontario's Far North in partnership with Indigenous communities in the region.

Ǧáǧvi Marilyn Slett is Chief Councillor for the Heiltsuk Tribal Council and in that role is a spokesperson for the Heiltsuk Nation.

Todd Wolfson is Associate Professor of Journalism and Media Studies and Co-director of the Mic Center at Rutgers University. An anthropologist by training, his research focuses on the intersection of new media and contemporary social movements. Wolfson is author of *Digital Rebellion: The Birth of the Cyber Left* (2014) and co-editor of *The Great Refusal: Herbert Marcuse and Contemporary Social Movements* (2016).

Jamie Woodcock is a senior lecturer at the Open University in London. He is the author of *The Gig Economy* (2019), *Marx at the Arcade* (2019), and *Working the Phones* (2017). His research is inspired by the workers' inquiry. His research focuses on labor, work, the gig economy, platforms, resistance, organizing, and videogames. He is on the editorial board of *Notes from Below* and *Historical Materialism*.

DOI 10.1215/00382876-8178079

Keep up to date on new scholarship

Issue alerts are a great way to stay current on all the cutting-edge scholarship from your favorite Duke University Press journals. This free service delivers tables of contents directly to your inbox, informing you of the latest groundbreaking work as soon as it is published.

To sign up for issue alerts:

1. Visit **dukeu.press/register** and register for an account. You do not need to provide a customer number.

2. After registering, visit **dukeu.press/alerts**.

3. Go to "Latest Issue Alerts" and click on "Add Alerts."

4. Select as many publications as you would like from the pop-up window and click "Add Alerts."

read.dukeupress.edu/journals

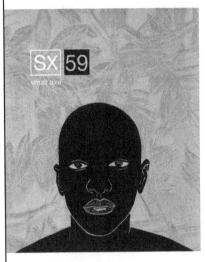